# THE PSYCHIC SASQUATCH

## and their UFO Connection

By Jack "Kewaunee" Lapseritis, M.S.

The result of 40 years of documented research.
A factual account of a scientist's astounding
journey, finally revealing answers to the most
perplexing unsolved mystery in modern times.

Copyright © 1998 by Jack Lapseritis

All rights reserved. No part of this book may be reproduced in any form or by any electronic or mechanical means including information and retrieval systems without prior permission from the author in writing.

Library of Congress Cataloging-in-Publication Data
Lapseritis, Jack, 1943 –
The Psychic Sasquatch and Their UFO Connection
by Jack "Kewaunee" Lapseritis
p. cm
Includes bibliographical references (p. 214) and index.
ISBN 1-495316-30-0
1. Human-alien encounters.
2. Parapsychology.
3. Sasquatch.
I. Title.
BF2050.L36 1998
001.944-dc21
98-13417
CIP

Volume IV
The New Millennium Library

Cover Artwork: Corey Wolfe
Manuscript editors: Terese Sayers, Brian Crissey, Julie Sherar

Printed in the United States of America

Address all inquiries to:

Comanche Spirit Publishing
c/o Kewaunee Lapseritis
P.O. Box 1062
Duvall, WA 98019
U.S.A.

## DEDICATION

This book is dedicated to all anomaly researchers who are genuinely seeking God's truth.

# The Psychic Sasquatch

*Preface* **vii**
*Foreword* **xvii**
*Why Me?* **xxi**

## PART ONE: FIELD DATA
Athropology or Zoology?  **1**
Mrs. Jones' New Friend  **9**
The Mt. Hood Experiment  **15**
Sasquatch And The CIA  **27**
The White Sasquatch  **37**
Terror In The Midlands  **51**
Sasquatch In The Pickle Patch  **59**
Bigfoot In North Carolina  **65**
Legend Of Medicine Mountain  **67**
Bigfoot In Ohio  **79**
Communicating With Bigfoot  **85**
Bigfoot In New England  **101**
Spiritual Keepers  **111**

## PART TWO: ANALYSIS & IMPLICATIONS
The Bigfoot/UFO Connection  **133**
ETs, Sasquatch and Psychic Healing  **147**
The Interdimensional Bigfoot  **161**
A Genetic Experiment?  **175**
Universal Reality  **193**

## PART THREE: SUPPORTING MATERIALS
*Wisdom from Sasquatch* **209**
*How to Contact a Sasquatch* **211**
*Bibliography* **214**
*Jack "Kewaunee" Lapseritis* **218**
*Acknowledgments* **220**
*Index* **221**

# Preface

## by R. Leo Sprinkle, Ph.D.

As a counseling psychologist, I have heard many tales of human experiences. For more than 42 years, working with thousands of clients at five different colleges and universities, and in private practice, I have listened to tales of achievement, anger, doubt, failure, fear, guilt, incest, joy, love, passion, rape, suicide, violence, etc. All of these stories can be compelling; however, I am most intrigued by the statements of persons who are experiencing "spiritual" emergence.

Our current philosophy of science and our current psychology of science do not permit an adequate theory of spiritual development. Perhaps our society is not yet ready for an adult science of consciousness. However, a Canadian psychiatrist, R.M. Bucke (1901), has provided us with a model of "cosmic consciousness," in case we become interested!

Perhaps our emphasis upon youth, at least in the USA, keeps us "down to Earth," with a focus on "younger" sciences of biology, geology, and physics, rather than the "older" sciences of communing with the Cosmos and God. But now, once again, we are looking at the stars and wondering if they were once our "home" and wondering when we shall return.

The current surge of interest in space travel and space communication is "new" to some of us, but "old" according to the historical records of earlier civilizations. For example, Argüelles (1987) interprets the Mayan calendar as demonstrating that August 16-17, 1987, is the end of a 5125-year cycle, which began in 3113 B.C.; and, by 2012 A.D., a new age will be emplaced on Planet Earth. (It's about time!)

The urge for space travel and intergalactic communication is denied by some persons, but the urge is experienced by most persons, at least as shown by commercial messages on television programs. And the burning question is: Are there extraterrestrial (ET) who are ready and willing to communicate?

According to a few scientific authorities, we are alone in the universe; however, the majority of astronomers (Swords, 1986) and other scientists assume that intelligent life abounds throughout the universe. But, if so, who and where are they? How, and why (!), would ETs make contact with us? Would they use slow rocket ships, or would they use space/time propulsion systems?

Deardorff (1986) has provided a model of ET strategy for Earth, which includes a "leaky" embargo on communications: The alien message is received by the general public (in the form of science fiction) and then, gradually, the message is received in the form that is acceptable to the empirical scientist, and the governmental official: physical evidence.

The controversy over reports of Unidentified Flying Objects (UFOs) is continuing, with various shades of believers on both sides of the skeptical middle ground (Saunders, 1968). Some scoffers, e.g., Klass (1983), would have us believe that there are only two categories: sane skeptics and silly believers. However, there are "believers" who know that UFOs are real, and there are "believers" who know that UFOs do not exist! And the true few skeptics, in the middle, often are those who are forced to search for evidence (e.g., Rutledge, 1981).

I know of what I speak, because I once was a "scoffer" before I experienced a UFO sighting, with a buddy, in 1949-50, at the University of Colorado, Boulder. After that sighting of a "flying saucer," I became a "skeptic": I was aware that flying saucers were being observed, but doubtful that they were piloted or controlled by ET intelligence. I thought to myself: Surely, this craft must be a secret device of the U.S. Army or U.S. Air Force!

Then, in 1956, my wife, Marilyn, and I had a sighting over Boulder of a strange, silent, hovering object or light. After that experience, I became an "unhappy believer." Then, in 1980, during a hypnosis session with another psychologist, I explored a memory (or fantasy or daydream?) of a childhood event, when I was 10 years old. My impression was as follows: I am standing in front of a large window, looking at stars which seem to be moving toward me. I am standing next to a tall man who is dressed in a one-piece suit, which tapered down to his boots. He has his right arm around me, touching my right shoulder with his hand; he says, "Leo, learn to read and write well; when you grow up, you can help other people learn more about their purpose in life."

*Preface*

Did that event actually happen? Perhaps I imagined it; perhaps I created the memory from some 1940 movie; perhaps I fabricated that impression in order to ease my fears about a recurring dream of a "man" who came upstairs when I was asleep; perhaps the image sprang from my fear of a loving, but strict, father who used a razor strap as punishment for misdeeds or failure to finish the chores of feeding the cow, pigs, and chickens, cutting the weeds, cleaning the cow shed, etc. Perhaps the memory was a fantasy for me to explain why I woke some mornings with blood on my pillow, a nose that was sore, and a feeling that, somehow, I had been visited by that strange "man" in my "dreams." Perhaps the event happened! I believe it did.

So, let the reader beware! I am biased! And my bias will show in my writing: Not only do I claim to be a counseling psychologist, a UFO investigator, and a UFO researcher, but I also claim to be a "repeater" UFO witness, a UFO abductee, and a UFO contactee. I can offer written documentation to support the earlier claims, but I can only offer sincere speculations as support for the latter claims. So, the reader is cautioned in regard to an acceptance of my comments and conclusions.

In the following section, I describe my discussions with persons who claim encounters with Bigfoot (BF) and UFO entities, or who have examined evidence of these reported Sasquatch encounters.

I have talked with several persons who have claimed BF/UFO encounters, including persons in Colorado, Utah, and Washington. I shall provide a brief summary of these discussions.

*A Colorado Case:*

In the late 1960s, I accompanied other UFO researchers on several weekend trips to Alamosa, Colorado. We were interested in the reports of UFO sightings and in the mutilation report of Snippy (actually, Lady), the horse owned by Nellie and Beryl Lewis. During one of our overnight sessions at their mountain cabin, one of the investigators described his sighting of a huge humanoid, covered with thick hair or fur. I was impressed by the emotional reaction of the man, although previously I had been unimpressed by his actions (he insisted on carrying a sidearm and he seemed more fearful and hostile than curious and cautious about his approach to UFO phenomena).

However, I listened as he described his reactions to the appearance and antics of the Bigfoot (BF), and I puzzled over several questions: What if the man is reliable and accurate in his claim? What if BF is alive and well? What if BF, animal mutilations, and UFO activity are related?

*A Utah Case:*

I have provided hypnosis sessions for approximately 500 persons, so that they might explore their memories of UFO abductions/contact encounters. A doctoral study of 225 persons was completed by Parnell (1987) in order to compare the personality characteristics of persons who claim UFO experiences with "normal" USA adults. Her analysis showed that group profiles of scores are in the average range of scores of USA adults, regardless of whether the participants claimed "lights", "objects", crafts", or "on board" experiences. However, those persons who claimed communication with UFO entities (approximately 2/3 of all participants) scored somewhat higher on some scales than did the participants who did not claim UFO communications.

A couple from Utah, MK and CK, talked with me in 1981 about their strange experiences (Sprinkle, 1982, p. 241). The husband, MK, described his experience as follows: he had been driving at night along an eastern Utah highway toward a Colorado town; he heard his full name spoken over the car radio; after a 10-second interval, he heard it again. Puzzled, he felt as if he should stop the car, so he drove up onto a viaduct and parked. He waited a few minutes, then began driving again, but he was surprised to note that his car was on the other side of the viaduct. He finally arrived at his destination at 3:00 A.M., but he had expected to arrive around 1:00 A.M. During the hypnosis session, he recalled the "loss of time" events as follows: he feels sleepy, and he drives onto the viaduct over the highway to an isolated field and waits. A flying saucer approaches and hovers. He gets out of the car, with the motor running, and walks toward the UFO. He steps onto a platform, which lifts into the craft. Six aliens, who are four-and-one-half feet tall, communicate telepathically. He returns to the car, then he drives to his destination.

In a hypnosis session, the wife explored two conscious memories: A sound over the house when she awoke one night; and a "bar of light," which she and her husband saw from their car one night. Then, she recalled a 14-year-old experience when she and a girlfriend, camping out in the yard, saw a glowing light which descended. Frightened, the girls went into the house, closed the drapes, and locked the door. They saw nothing outside their window, but heard a "humming sound."

Later, the husband wrote to me of the results of his investigation of his own experience. He stated that he had driven his car back over the same route that he had travelled earlier. He drove over the viaduct, toward the isolated field. He got out of the car, with the motor running. He stepped over the ditch, and barbed wire fence, that he had recalled during the hypnosis session. He waited during the same time period that he had estimated for the "on board" experience; then, he re-entered his car. He was pleased, and bothered, that the fuel gauge showed a similar drop in gasoline! He was pleased at his detective work, but bothered by the result! Now, he was faced with the possibility that the hypnosis session had obtained impressions that were "true" rather than "fantasy."

Did these procedures prove that the impressions in the hypnosis session were a direct result of what physically occurred? That depends on one's definition of proof. MK did not know, and I did not know, whether those impressions were memories of a physical encounter with UFO entities. However, the results of his investigation were significant to him; and, apparently, the results provided him and his wife the courage to write about another unusual event: their observation (and photographs) of some Bigfoot tracks in the snow. They indicated that they had been reluctant to tell me about the Bigfoot tracks because they thought it would be too weird for me and I would not believe them!

I continued to learn from this case, as with others, that the attitude of the UFO investigator is as important as the attitude of the UFO witness. If we inform the witness that we are interested in only one level of evidence, or one topic of observation, then we may be neglecting important information, as well as teaching UFO witnesses to ignore the holistic aspects of their UFO experiences.

*Wyoming Studies:*

In my efforts to understand the complexities of Bigfoot/UFO encounters, I have talked with many persons, including two "real" scientists: R. Lynn Kirlin, Ph.D., and George W. Gill, Ph.D. Dr. Kirlin is a Professor of Electrical Engineering, and Dr. Gill is Professor of Anthropology. Both are respected faculty members of the University of Wyoming, Laramie. Although each is reluctant to speculate on the "reality" of Sasquatch, each has conducted empirical and theoretical studies of evidence of encounters.

Dr. Kirlin has analyzed an audiotape recording of sounds, which are assumed to be those of the Bigfoot creatures. His analysis, using sophisticated electronic equipment, indicates that the sounds do not show readings like those of humans or of gorillas. He is puzzled about the sources of the sounds.

Dr. Gill, a well known physical anthropologist, has studied the Sasquatch phenomenon for years. Gill (1980) has provided a review of the anthropological evidence, including support for Bergmann's Rule, or the hypothesis that vertebrates whose populations are closer to the equator will tend to have smaller body size than those toward the poles at cooler latitudes.

These two men are among the many scientists who, using their own time and expertise, are attempting to shed more light on the Bigfoot puzzle. Perhaps someday, there may be more support and encouragement for studies of psychic Sasquatch and the connection with UFO activity.

*A Washington Case:*

In 1979, I worked with a man who was so anxious that he refused to tell me his name and address. Indeed, he initially called from a public telephone, in case his telephone was being "tapped!" (Sprinkle, 1982.)

Over the course of many weekend sessions, he gradually began to ease his distrust of me; however, he asked me to use initials (not his true initials, I learned later) to identify him in my notes. He was a lonely but intelligent and articulate man. The reader may choose to regard this case as the fantasies of a neurotic or psychotic person, but the haunting question is this: What if some, or all, of his claims are true?

The man who appeared before me, at our first meeting, was tall, with rumpled clothes, and a very nervous manner. He spoke in a hesitant voice, apparently in conflict between his distrust of a psychologist on the one hand, and, on the other hand, his need to talk about his experiences.

He spoke of his interest in hypnotic procedures to learn more about his childhood experiences. As we gradually became acquainted with one another, he seemed to ease some of his doubts about me, but he continued to be plagued with doubts about the reality of his conscious memories and subconscious impressions of Bigfoot and UFO encounters.

During our many hours of meetings, he unfolded a tale of many Bigfoot encounters as a child, including huge creatures which suddenly materialized and dematerialized in his bedroom. He claimed that FBI agents had visited his elementary school teacher and then talked with him about his story of seeing a huge apelike skull by the side of the road on which he walked to school.

Later, as we explored more childhood memories, he gasped as he seemed to relive the frightening experience of being abducted by a group of Bigfoot creatures. His emotional reactions, as well as his verbal comments, indicated that he accepted these impressions as memories of real events.

What he found difficult to accept was the apparent memory of little men, in space suits, who were standing beside a landed "flying saucer." His fear was great when he became aware that the Bigfoot creatures were being monitored and/or controlled by the UFO entities. He gasped and writhed in

## Preface

the chair as he apparently relived those traumatic childhood experiences. Later, he tried to learn from me whether I viewed him as "crazy," and whether I believed that he was "fantasizing" these events.

I attempted to be honest with him. I told him of my concerns about his distrust of me and others, his appearance, his speech patterns, his emotional reactions to the strange claim of childhood experiences, including the purported visit by FBI agents, etc. However, I also told him of my work with other UFO abductees and contactees, who described childhood visitations, and adulthood visitations, by men who claimed to be FBI or CIA agents, etc. He did not wish to think of himself as a UFO contactee (he thought of them as being weird!), yet he could not rid himself of the troublesome memory of those little men standing beside the landed spacecraft, who were mentally communicating with the group of Bigfoot creatures and guiding their behavior.

Furthermore, it was difficult for him to think of himself as "insane" (he did not view himself as posing a threat to himself or others) or "incompetent," (he showed me a ledger which indicated that his investments had yielded him a much greater yearly income than that of a university professor!).

I was fascinated not only by his apparent Bigfoot/UFO memories, but also by his introduction to my research. He claimed that he had been driving his truck one night and he heard a radio program in which I was interviewed about my UFO investigations. He said that he heard my voice talking about UFO abductions, and Bigfoot abductions, and the procedures by which persons could be helped to recall their Bigfoot experiences.

As far as I could recall, I had not mentioned Bigfoot abductions in connection with UFO investigations! However, I did not doubt that he had "heard" those comments. I know from past experiences that UFO contactees and UFO researchers are "connected" in strange ways. I decided, when I heard his introductory comments, that it was appropriate for me to listen and to learn!

I cannot claim that I know whether those strange and puzzling events occurred or whether a psychic Bigfoot (BF) and Spacebeings (SBs) revealed themselves to this man. Yet, I also cannot claim that these events did not happen to this man. What I can claim is that more and more people are describing these BF and SB encounters (Cooper, 1987). Furthermore, I believe that it is important for us to listen and learn from these persons.

Thus, I am pleased to introduce the reader to Jack Lapseritis, MS, a man of courage and curiosity, who has devoted many years to the study of Bigfoot/Sasquatch.

When Jack, or Kewaunee as he is often called, was first introduced as a speaker, years ago, at the Rocky Mountain Conference on UFO Investigation, there were some persons in the audience who expressed puzzlement about any connection between UFO reports and Sasquatch reports. They soon learned that Jack could provide a fascinating and persuasive response to their questions.

His academic degrees, and professional training, provide an intellectual basis for the evaluation of his personal experiences in the field. Not only has he interviewed many persons about their Bigfoot sightings, but he also has encountered a variety of these huge and hairy humanoids. He has learned what some investigators are reluctant to admit: Sasquatch are psychic! The reader is encouraged to relax, and to enjoy this journey into the realms of mental as well as physical encounters with spiritual as well as empirical implications.

Jack Lapseritis is to be commended for his willingness to describe what he has experienced, and to share what he has learned. He is among those pioneering investigators who recognize that these phenomena provide implications for physical sciences, life sciences, human sciences and transpersonal sciences (Harmen, 1988).

Yes, there is need for skepticism. No, there is no need for scoffing. Yes, there is a need for caution in interpreting reports of encounters with Sasquatch and UFO entities. No, there is no need to reject these reports and ridicule those who describe these experiences.

Psychologists have developed a useful experimental science which is based upon individual differences between persons in regard to their psychophysiological processes of sensation and perception. Behavioral scientists (anthropologists, psychologists, sociologists, etc.) have developed useful empirical methods for the study of various group and social behaviors. However, behavioral scientists now are faced with a delightful dilemma: Do we continue to serve as the "gatekeeper" for the fear of scientists by holding back the merging evidence for ESP (Greely, 1987), or do we undertake the task of evaluating the puzzling deluge of empirical and experimental evidence for PSI? (The Society for Scientific Exploration has been established for the study of anomalous phenomena, such as ESO, UFO, and "Manimals".)

Now, in my opinion, is the time for interested readers to collaborate with various scientists, in order to explore the reports and implications of psychic Sasquatch and ET encounters. Perhaps someday, we shall come to a better understanding of the significance of these phenomena for our stewardship of the planet and our evolutionary development. Perhaps the Bigfoot and ET encounters are helping us to learn about our new age tasks: Awakening to the memories of our heritage and returning to the stars.

# Foreword

## by Dick Robinson

I am a writer, cinematographer, and originator of the Grizzly Adams concept for television. Presently, there is a soon to be released movie entitled, *The Magical Valley of Grizzly Adams*, starring myself in a role with bears and an array of wild animals. Previously I worked as an associate producer for six years with Dr. Marlin Perkins, filming the Wild Kingdom series.

As a seasoned naturalist, I have spent most of my life experiencing and loving nature. I know Jack "Kewaunee" Lapseritis is telling the truth about his anthropological research in this book because, for the last twenty years, I too have had the privilege of receiving telepathic communication with the psychic Sasquatch. In fact, in one situation, they saved my life. So the contact is ongoing, as they occasionally visit at different stages of my life. I am profoundly grateful it occurred and hope people will begin to better understand just how real this paranormal phenomenon is, while dispelling the "monster" myth created by well-intentioned researchers who have not experienced this. Hopefully this documented book will educate science and society by bringing them mentally into a more spiritually-oriented science where there is greater respect for all living things, no matter how unusual or racially diverse they may be.

Once in a while a book comes along of such magnitude that it brings about a new look at what exists out there besides ourselves. People have a tendency to accept only that which they can see and actually feel, yet here is proof that another world exists beside us. It is real! This book is about those beings who cannot be seen except under the circumstances in which they wish to mingle. Paranormal people like Sasquatch and ET-types have social contact with humans in this world when they choose to be seen; otherwise, they go about their business.

Looking at it from a slightly different direction, those rare witnesses who are contacted soon realize that they must speak for this group from the unseen dimension next to us. When I sit to write, there is that something that guides my thoughts which could express views of others who are standing unseen behind me. So my apartment is filled right now with interdimensional entities, standing, watching, and chatting amongst themselves while this is being written. They dictate the lines of my thoughts and have already decided what they want to express to the world at this time. Those of us who are in communication with these beings are producing various books, videos, and well-documented movie programs which will bring some of their thoughts forward so we can understand why they exist as they do.

These interdimensional Sasquatch are here in limited numbers, have set programs under which they operate and oversee many of the programs currently operating in our civilization. This group blends their activities with the beings who pilot UFOs who also actively work observing the human race at a critical time in history.

Many failed civilizations have been left behind and new attempts are constantly being brought forth to examine the possibilities of obtaining better forms of human behavior. *Love* is foremost on the minds of all who work with evolving humans. Universal harmony is being propagated as an objective to be reached by all. But, spiritual love is the active ingredient which can only be mixed into the formula of human behavior when conditions are right. The preparations for this event occur at preset times and then come about. But what about a whole civilization that is waiting for this event?

Seemingly, many organized religious groups are also waiting for one to come along and bring about this event. They are waiting for one special being to appear from the next dimension who will take charge and bring about this change to the planet. But—will it ever happen? Or has it happened already and gone unseen?

This unique book brings forth new ideas and discoveries, expressions of thought, which are now becoming more commonplace. They are here! Other cosmic beings are here! This beautiful planet on which we live, though, is nothing but an experimental farm to those who use it. There is a constant mix of various paraphysical cultures and groups that inhabit this place. They were brought here and planted along with ideas and conditions which change the conceptions of those who are trying to rule through political deception and negativity.

Benign communication is the key. In early times, there were few people and word could spread by social contacts. Now we have great communications and yet few are reached in set proportions. Sasquatch activities are fairly common, yet many are not recognized when they occur and never reach those who have need of them.

Books are steps in the progression of enlightenment. It only takes one with an idea whose time has come to bring about profound changes to the planet. This book will certainly bring forth thought-provoking concepts to help with a new scientific approach that will contribute to a positive human transformation.

*Dick Robinson*
*Salt Lake City*
*January 1998*

# Why Me?

This book is about undiscovered science. It is also about mysticism, intrigue, and psychic phenomena, as well as discovering one's full potential in life. The book is also about truth and honesty—not just being honest with the reader but also about being academically and spiritually honest with myself.

In 1979, when the events in these chapters first began, I promised myself that I would never tell anyone because such surrealistic experiences with elusive beings would be considered by many to be crazy at worst, and pseudoscientific at best! But, when the profoundness of these anomalies triggered in me what one might call a "spiritual transformation," I soon realized it was my duty as a responsible scientist and citizen to share such significant insights with the world at large.

Then I thought: "Why me?" and I became frightened that I would be ridiculed for my veracity. Was the world ready for this? How would people view me? Would it ruin my reputation? Would the government threaten and harass me? All of these concerns flowed through my mind at that time.

Was "non-holistic" Establishment Science ready for my research? Probably not, even though it's exactly the challenge that it presently needs. I soon learned that I was not alone. There were many other academicians who were frustrated with science's defensive attitude toward the unknown as well as its dysfunctional relationship with living nature. One prime example is that people in responsible positions are still in deep denial about the fact that the entire Earth's biosphere is dangerously polluted. As physicist Dr. Brian O'Leary put it:

> History is replete with examples of resistance to fundamental change when a culture is confronted with anomalies. Most of Galileo's contemporaries refused to look through his telescope because they didn't believe—or didn't want to believe—it could make things look bigger. During the 1700s, the French Academy of Sciences refused to believe meteorites existed because rocks couldn't fall out of the sky. [1]

---

1. O'Leary, Brian, 1993, p. 16

These were encouraging words that helped me complete my work in "anomalous" anthropology, which is holistic and all-encompassing. Yet science remains arrogant, "insecure," rigid, and seemingly stuck for many reasons. Dr. O'Leary succinctly says it best:

> It is part of human nature to hang onto older paradigms out of a sense of safety for the ego; funding, power, and prestige generally go to those who work within the boundaries of accepted science. This was certainly true in my case, until I could no longer function honestly within a framework that did not permit the inclusion of anomalous data. [2]

This is exactly how I feel, based on my own research. Presently, the entire world is going through a planetary transformation, instigated by lethal weather patterns, ozone depletion, geological upheaval, unending pollution, deadly untreatable diseases, a continued increase in UFO activity, and political violence that seemingly stem from prophetic Earth Changes, Revelations, and what the American Indians call the Great Purification—all variables that force social and spiritual change. These changes, whether they be positive or negative, are sure to affect us all, especially the way the Establishment practices science as we enter the Twenty-First Century. I am truly happy that perhaps my research, in some way, will give our present "old-world" science a fresh perspective when researching elusive phenomena. The spirit of this book is dedicated to other intrepid scientists pioneering in areas previously unrecognized by mainstream science. As the late Joseph Campbell bravely asserted:

> The mystical theme of the space age is this: the world, as we know it, is coming to an end. The world as the center of the universe, the world divided from the heavens, the world bound by horizons in which love is reserved for members of the in-group; that is the world that is passing away. Apocalypse does not point to a fiery Armageddon, but to the fact that our ignorance and our complacence are coming to an end. [3]

*Jack "Kewaunee" Lapseritis, M.S.*
*April 1997*
*Tuscon, Arizona*

---

2. O'Leary, Brian, 1993, p. 16
3. O'Leary, Brian, 1993, p. 16

# PART ONE

Artist enhancement ©1998 by Suzanne Maksel, from original photograph

# FIELD DATA

# Anthropology or Zoology?

*OVERVIEW*

In the summer of 1977, an elderly woman sat quietly reading a book on the porch of her cottage in a densely wooded area in northern Wisconsin. Suddenly, an invisible force sent the book out of her hands onto the porch floor. Bewildered, the woman looked about for the source of this mysterious happening. She heard someone laughing. At the edge of the forest stood the form of a huge apelike creature with dark auburn hair all over its body.

"I have been standing here for some time. I did not mean to frighten you; just wanted to get your attention," the creature politely said, as it pleasantly laughed again.

In three separate interviews, this elderly woman explained to me that for four consecutive summers she had telepathic conversations with a giant man-creature she came to know as Bigfoot—Sasquatch! The woman also spoke of seeing UFOs hovering above the trees, as well as hearing an eerie generator noise in the night!

*EPISODE*

A prelude to a science-fiction thriller? Not at all! With astounding regularity, this scenario has been experienced by numerous credible witnesses during the last 40 years I have been researching the Bigfoot phenomenon. Most veteran researchers reject the possibility that psychic phenomena and UFOs are an integral part of the Bigfoot mystery and at the core of the problems that have thwarted researchers for years. Instead of objectively investigating unusual reports, they cringe, wishing that these bizarre stories would somehow go away.

But the opposite is happening. The persistence of these hitherto almost unbelievable "tales" has exploded into a whole new awareness. For the open-minded researcher, the paranormal concept of a non-ordinary reality has greatly broadened the scope of knowledge and understanding in the search for answers to this most perplexing enigma. Objective researchers who have taken the initiative to investigate these "weird" reports have been rewarded with a whole new array of inexplicable truths. Still, most aficionados continue to bury their heads in the sand. They refuse to investigate paranormal reports associated with hairy giants because they fear their peers may label them unscientific—if not crazy! Dr. Grover Krantz, physical anthropologist at Washington State University in Pullman, publicly reflects that attitude, when he states:

> There is also much speculation about connections with Unidentified Flying Objects and other paranormal phenomena.... Many scientists who might have studied a wild primate refuse to be associated with these speculations and with the people who make them. I have listened to a few such accounts and am satisfied that each of the witnesses was missing some mental faculties. It does not follow that all such stories are being made up by the lunatic fringe, but I have no intention of finding out. I don't know what the truth is in that area and refuse to investigate it any further. To study the Sasquatch, even on one's own time and money, is to use up all the deviation points the profession permits.[1]

The major problem is that a majority of natural and social scientists do not accept the existence of hairy giants on the North American continent, especially when the story is associated with UFOs and psychic phenomena. Modern science demands indisputable proof in the form of a corpse or skeletal remains. What they do not realize is that a *significant number* of cases, like that of Mrs. Jones, directly imply that these psychic beings are indeed *human!* I have compiled an enormous amount of first-hand oral testimonies from interviewing witnesses in my 26-state search. I have documented 76 witnesses who have not only physically encountered the Sasquatch, but who also cautiously admit to having psychic, UFO, and/or extraterrestrial (ET) manifestations directly associated with their Bigfoot encounters! Enough data has been compiled to pull this subject out of the twilight zone and into the lap of the scientist.

Then which scientist qualifies for the job? Do we need a zoologist? Anthropologist? Or a holistic eclectical?

---

1. Krantz, 1978, lecture

## Anthropology or Zoology?

Zoology is the science that studies creatures of the animal kingdom. "Animals, as defined, do not have culture, do not pray (because they are not aware of a higher spiritual power), do not have a language to pass on survival information to their offspring, and do not make or use tools. Based on my years of Bigfoot research, I discovered, by repeatedly observing patterns objectively and experiencing patterns subjectively over and over again, that this Sasquatch phenomenon is anthropological. Webster defines the discipline of anthropology as "the study of human beings in relation to distribution, origin, classification, and relationship of races, physical character, environmental and social relations, and culture." I know of no anthropologist in the world who feels they must kill the object of their studies—except Dr. Grover Krantz, who may be correct in believing the Bigfoot-people are a living remnant of *Gigantopithecus*, a relic humanoid that some think was more ape than man. Pei Wen-Chung, the Chinese scholar and authority on *Gigantopithecus* believed the giant ape-creature to be about 12 feet tall, which fits the description of Sasquatch.

Gorillas were seen as dangerous until later when they were discovered to be gentle nature animals.

I am one of the 76 percipients who experienced the psychic Sasquatch as well as extraterrestrial (ET) beings associated with them. I am the first scientist to claim to have had numerous close encounters with a psychic Sasquatch—nearly 500 in all over a 19-year period. Further, the experiences are *ongoing*! From this collection of 40 years of research data, the notion that Sasquatch is nonhuman is totally dispelled! All evidence points directly to the fact that the creatures called Bigfoot/Sasquatch are, in reality, giant hairy "*humans*" with an extraterrestrial origin. This conclusion took me years to

3

accept. I was in denial for a long time because my previous reference was empirical. As a scientist, I wanted to make a contribution to science by helping to solve the Sasquatch mystery—nothing more. But immediately after my first telepathic contact, I changed in personality and underwent what Eastern mystics might call a "spiritual transformation" or "awakening." I am not speaking about a type of belief system within a certain religion. Rather I am speaking about a dramatic shift in consciousness from an evolutionary standpoint. It's almost as if God (or a Godlike being) had come and bestowed a spiritual gift on me that instantly changed my life. All I can do is express myself from a heart level, state the "experiential" facts, and reveal the happenings of the 76 witnesses I have documented. These "normal," warm-hearted non-researchers have repeatedly matched up their unique experiences with mine.

In presenting the truth as I experienced it, I keep struggling with a reality that I have found baffling, traumatic, and consuming. Though I present the "experiential" evidence here, I came to realize it was also some bizarre cosmic drama of great meaning and universal purpose in the scheme of human evolution. In short, my anthropological research became a two-sided coin that, incredibly, also became a spiritual odyssey. It is these nonordinary happenings that I am now sharing publicly because I realize we live in a time when modern man has made technology, power, money, and ego their God, rather than genuinely working toward ameliorating the human condition on this planet.

In no way do I expect mainstream science to accept metaphysical "experiential" evidence in place of physical empirical evidence, but my ET/Bigfoot encounters have formed a *universal reality*—the objective truth in living nature—that has led me to firmly believe that a balance of both types of evidence can make present-day science truly *modern*. We cannot have black without white, male without female, yin without yang, or positive without negative. All of these are natural unions right down to an atomic level as part of a "dipoled" universe that creates the dynamics for a true *cosmic balance*. Therefore, physics and metaphysics are really an interwoven discipline. Physics is an extension of a metaphysical process somewhere on a subatomic level called quantum physics. There is no such thing as a one-sided coin. An entirely new paradigm is needed that includes both aspects. Science will remain limited until it recognizes it needs to approach each problem "holistically."

It is unthinkable for a cobbler to mutilate a foot just to make a shoe fit. The shoe is an artificial creation of man, styled to meet his needs. A cobbler constructs a shoe based on what he finds when measuring the natural foot. Therefore, it is unnatural to pervert the empirical model in order to fit the anthropocentric needs of modern science. To dismiss illusive phenomena because of an *incomplete* system of measurement is clearly distorted, subjective, and thus unscientific. This is a *major* point to remember throughout this book. The scientific paradigm is grossly deficient and sorely in need of revamping. I have never seen "gravity", only a demonstration of its effects, yet I am convinced that gravity—and its dipole antigravity—exists.

But *fear* is holding science back: fear of the unknown, fear of being wrong for so many years, fear of upsetting a political and financial apple cart, which has nothing to do with real objective data collecting. *Truth* is the only thing that matters if we are to vividly view the world around us in its purest form. Then we can all feel secure in understanding earlier encountered anomalies, especially UFOs, the PSI realm, and other puzzling phenomena.

And how do I know my perceptions are an integral part of universal reality? Because I and 76 others have been fortunate that our personalities contain a "natural" psychic sensitivity, combined with a deep respect for all living things, that has attracted the Sasquatch into our lives. I have discovered that certain people have a benevolent combination of attributes that the Sasquatch find non-threatening, and which is unconsciously "projected" through their own thinking. When a person has an intelligent, telepathic conversation with a being that demonstrates profound cognitive reasoning, then *clearly* one is not relating to a wild animal!

No academician or veteran Bigfoot researcher has ever claimed to have in-depth encounters with the creatures in order to intelligently understand the true basis of Sasquatch ecology. Most of the researchers have proven to be Bigfoot "hunters" and "historians," who redundantly hash through reports from the past. A few find tracks and produce plaster casts as proof of their efforts. Many aggressive enthusiasts parade around with guns looking for a Bigfoot to shoot. Yet, just how scientists and lay researchers expect to understand and solve the Sasquatch problem without personally experiencing them *on the creature's own turf* is a mystery in itself. "Kill it before understanding what it is" has become the cry. So the "experts" sorely lack *experiential expertise*, which has led them down a blind alley.

Science has not yet shed its superstitions when it comes to discussing, researching, and investigating Bigfoot, UFOs, Starpeople, and psychic phenomena. It is a very sad state of affairs indeed. Science was established to explore, identify, and explain the living world around us, and yet, ironically, a majority of academicians staunchly avoid certain areas of the unknown, as if it were nonintellectual to discuss fringe areas of "contemporary" science because it is too embarrassing to know there is no viable model to adequately measure and explain it. Zoologists and maverick anthropologists have labeled Sasquatch an animal. Many psychologists say that all these fringe phenomena exist only in the mind, that they are not real, that the source of the experience is *not* extrinsic.

They are correct, of course, when stating that a dead specimen would settle the whole issue. Still, it would not answer the question of *who* it is and *what* it is capable of doing as a living entity in nature! So why settle it with violence? Why must we approach the problem in such a primitive fashion? It is precisely this unevolved thinking that has perpetuated the expanding problem that has continuously led to failure.

To emphasize the importance of this statement and how one's *thinking* and *attitude* are key ingredients to successful Sasquatch research, I share a quote from Amerindian attorney Vine Deloria, Jr.:

> Behind the apparent kinship between animals, reptiles, birds, and human beings in the Indian way stands a great conception shared by a great majority of the tribes. Other living things are not regarded as insensitive species. Rather they are "peoples" in the same manner as the various tribes of men are peoples. The reason why the Hopi use live reptiles in their ceremony goes back to one of their folk heroes who lived with the snake people for a while and learned from them the secret of making rain for the crops. It was a ceremony freely given by the snake people to the Hopi. In the same manner the Plains Indians considered the buffalo as a distinct people, the Northwest Coast Indians regarded the salmon as a people. Equality is thus not simply a human attribute but a recognition of the creature-ness of all creation.[2]

Deloria continues by emphasizing the traditional Indian belief that in order to truly understand the world we live in, it is important to have interspecies communication so that we may learn from one another and better coexist with our animal and plant neighbors. I do not view this as folklore. The spiritual-psychic ability of ancient Amerindian shamans included mental

---

2. Deloria, 1973, p. 103.

telepathy, giving an experiential basis for many of their cultural beliefs about animals. Deloria says:

> Some of these tribal ideas have been classified as "witchcraft" by anthropologists, primarily because such phenomena occurring within the Western tradition would naturally be interpreted as evil and satanic. What Western man misses is the rather logical implication of the unity of life. If all living things share a creator and a creation, is it not logical to suppose that all have the ability to relate to every part of the creation? How Western man can believe in evolution and not see the logical consequence of this doctrine in the religious life of people is incomprehensible for many Indians. Recent studies with the dolphin and other animals may indicate that Western man is beginning to shed his superstitions and consider the possibility of having communication with other life forms. [3]

So a humanistic approach that includes an effort to communicate with Sasquatch better reflects the true modern-ness in man. This book, then, is about communication and human spirituality, not about hunting, tracking, or killing in order to taxonomize another human life-form. My personal odyssey spans four decades. Initially, I was looking for a clever man-animal. But, in September 1979, I received the shock of my life when a Sasquatch telepathically communicated with me! The man-creature was kind, actually gentle in nature. From that time on, my life began to change and evolve in a manner that was totally foreign to me. On occasion new awarenesses and realities became confusing, even frustrating, making my scientific background almost obsolete. Contemporary science could not explain it.

Ironically, when I stopped trying to obtain proof of their existence, the Bigfoot "people" visited me more often. In their conversations, they would share and give advice that always proved helpful. An open-mind, a warm heart, and lack of fear are the criteria for communication. My feelings are equally shared by Dr. John C. Lilly when he says:

> One develops a respect for and a sensitivity to the unknown operating in the area of communication. I believe this is an essential characteristic of a proper scientist in this area. A respect for the unknown is needed at every level, of the media and the modes, but at high levels of abstract. In other words, exchanges may be operating between dolphins in known media and known modes, but at levels of abstraction which we have not yet grasped. Such awareness of the ever-

---

3. Deloria, 1973, p. 103.

present and intimate presence of unknowns keeps one's mind open and one's system of reasoning open. Without this openness, discovery is impeded. [4]

The purpose of this book is *not* to offer proof based on empirical science but to present *evidence* based on in-depth interviews documenting percipients who independently claim to have had Bigfoot/UFO and/or Bigfoot/PSI experiences. Each witness *objectified* my own encounters, and made the Bigfoot/UFO connection a genuinely real phenomenon. After examining the testimonies in this book, the reader will find this conclusion inescapable.

Some people's names and geographic places have been deliberately changed in order to protect witnesses that requested anonymity, including the Sasquatch-people who simply wish to be left alone, to live in peace without being hunted and shot. I respect both requests.

Also, I realize that I have set myself up for possible ridicule, and perhaps harm to my professional credibility. But how long must a person wait and painfully hold these realities inside just to please the ignorant? I wish only to share the truth as I have come to understand it after 19 years of contact with paraphysical beings. As a responsible scientist, I desire to merely raise the consciousness of others and to educate all to the fact that other legitimate realms exist in addition to those we can control and empirically measure. It is important to me to convey to all peoples of the world that it is an inexorable fact that other cognitive, living, feeling, compassionate life-forms exist and breathe just as we do—and not very far from our own back doors. Their purpose has now become my purpose, as I speak for them, by simply sharing my life's work as it has unfolded.

---

4. Lilly, 1969, p. 100.

# Mrs. Jones' New Friend

*OVERVIEW*

An elderly, gray-haired woman, whom I shall call Mrs. Jones, spent her summers in the northernmost region of Wisconsin in the family cottage. Mr. Jones was not an outdoors person, but he would make the seven-hour drive from Milwaukee each summer, leave his wife at their summer place, and return in five or six weeks. Mrs. Jones enjoyed the quietude of the country and eagerly looked forward to being alone. The cottage was located at the end of an old dirt road at the edge of a wild, forested region. The following story was related to me by Mrs. Jones after much reluctance on her part to discuss the matter. She was fearful of being ridiculed or becoming a public spectacle. She swears her story is absolutely true.

*EPISODE*

"It all started in 1977 and was something that I did not understand, that was very confusing, something that I have to keep very secret, even from my husband. He's afraid of stuff like that. This has been difficult for me, as I have not been able to share the details with my husband. I hid it from everyone except my best friend.

"As I told you, the first incident occurred while I was reading a book on the front porch of the cottage. Evidently these Bigfoot creatures have the power to levitate objects, as they did with my book, which flew out of my hands. It was scary, very startling at first, but a kind, warm voice spoke to me in my head. You say it is telepathy, but I don't understand these things. I only have a fifth-grade education. But I do know that he talked to me inside of my head and that was a great revelation. He apologized for startling me and laughed frequently. This relaxed me and I came to realize that he meant me no harm. He became my friend.

"He stood at a distance of about 50 feet, so that I could only see his head and down to about his waist. From what I could judge, he was at least ten feet tall, maybe nine. He was huge. I could see that his hair covered his entire body except the face. His head and shoulders were a dark auburn color with the hair becoming a darker shade of brown on the lower part of his body. His face was similar to that of a man, not quite like an ape, more like a man. The things he spoke of were inquisitive and very intelligent, so I knew there was no question that he was a man. His lips of course did not move, as he spoke to me in my mind, and he kept reminding me to think at him. I would think within myself and he would start to answer. Then I knew that, with each thought, he knew what I was thinking. And, in such a way then, we began to communicate. It was a whole new experience for me. The creature smiled frequently but I was not sure who or what he was, so it took some time for me to put into perspective that I was actually speaking to a creature that many would call Sasquatch or Bigfoot.

"I know that the average person would not understand this, and I'm sure our government would want to know of these things. But I'm more afraid of them than I am of this man you call Bigfoot. In fact, he was a friend. He told me that he had watched me many times over the previous summers and that he enjoyed listening to my thoughts. Thus I came to trust him and to know him some, though there were many things that he would not tell me and hid from me.

"At our very first meeting, out on the porch, I had my pet cat in a small cage on the table beside me. The previous summers I had let my cat loose, but there are many wild animals in the area. Last summer I turned her loose and she did not return for several days. It worried me sick. She kept me company during the time I lived there alone. My cat had the run of the house inside, but when she was outside with me I would place her in this small cage. She understood because she purred and seemed content. The cage was used to transport her up from Milwaukee. So there she was in the cage beside me, keeping me company on the porch, when my friend, the Bigfoot man, began to speak about my cat."

BIGFOOT (BF): What is the animal that you have in that cage?
MRS. JONES (MJ): It is my pet cat.
BF: What is a pet?
MJ: It is an animal that keeps people company. It is something to love and take care of.
BF: If you love it, why is it in that cage?

MJ: I fear it will get lost in the forest or that it will be eaten by a fox or some other wild animal—I only want to protect it.
BF: But your pet must be unhappy in that cage.
MJ: No, she is on her back purring, and to me that means she is very content. She is happy because I am here beside her.
BF: Oh, that pleases me. I did not know that. It is good to be happy.
(Mrs. Jones stands up on her porch to get a better view of her new friend. She walks to the side of the porch and stares while she begins speaking again.)
MJ: Will you please step out from behind those pine trees so I can see you better?
BF: No, I won't.
MJ: Won't you step out? I won't hurt you. I merely want a better look at you so I know with whom I am speaking.
BF: No, I will not step out.
MJ: Why not? You can see me. Here I am—short, fat, and wrinkled up—you can see me in plain sight. You can see my whole body. Won't you show yourself too?
(Mrs. Jones hears a hearty laugh inside her head, not verbally.)
BF: That's a good one. (More laughter.) You said that well about yourself. That's a good one. I must go now, but I will be back another time.
MJ: You will be back?
BF: Yes, I am here frequently but you cannot see me. I am around and always will be around, especially if you need me. I have been watching you for many years. I am always around and know what you are doing. I will talk with you another time.

"It came to pass that a neighbor woman from a few miles away stopped to ask if I needed anything, because I had no car. She would stop to check on me periodically. I told her I needed some fresh milk and several other items, plus the local newspaper. Later she returned and brought me the items I had requested. In the newspaper it told of several remote houses and cottages in the area being broken into. I didn't think much of it until a few nights later. I couldn't sleep, so I got up and went out and sat down on the steps outside by the back door. I sat, smoking a cigarette and looking at the stars, when I noticed what looked like the glow of a cigarette behind the woodshed a short distance away. Then I saw the silhouette of a man, and then the silhouette of a second man pulling the first man back behind the woodshed. Now this was late at night, about 2:00 as I recall, and I was very frightened. I quickly got up, ran inside, locked the door, and shut off the lights. I went into the bedroom and lifted up a floorboard where my husband kept a

**11**

loaded .22 pistol and a small baseball bat for protection. I grabbed these and walked through the darkness to the living room. By that time, the two men were already on the front porch. One was looking in the window and the other was trying to open the door. I was panicky but kept my cool. I went over and got down behind the couch in the corner and crouched there, pistol in one hand, baseball bat in the other. I just didn't know what to do, but I wasn't going to let anyone hurt me. I could hear the men talking and trying desperately to get in the front door.

"All of a sudden there was a scream. 'God, what is that? Let's get out of here!' At this time the two men fled the porch. One moved so quickly that he fell down the porch steps. I stood and walked to the front door. Through the window I could see the two men running across the field toward an old wood road, where perhaps they had hidden their vehicle.

"I unlocked the front door and poked my head out. There was a terrible stench that was a cross somewhere between rotten eggs and a skunk. The smell was overpowering. When I looked to my left, I got a glimpse of a giant figure walking into the forest.

"The next morning I was sitting on the front porch reading the Bible when Bigfoot arrived and began talking to me."

BF: I was here last night. I told you I would be here whenever you needed me. I could feel fear at a distance. I came immediately. Those men were bad. As I said, I am always here, always around. I always know your thoughts. God bless you.

MJ: Thank you, I am grateful. I was very frightened of those men.

"The following year I began hearing strange noises in the forest. Something like a generator sound. It was real strange. It was like a generator winding up and then immediately winding down again, as if it had a broken part in it. I would sit out on the porch and listen to it winding through the night. Then some nights I would see strange lights above the trees, perhaps what other people would call UFOs. It lit up the entire woods. I had seen them go back and forth over the trees and then leave.

"Later I asked a neighbor friend who hiked up to see me (she had a cottage not far from mine) if she had seen the lights over the trees. She gave me a horrified look, saying that she and her husband observed the lights and heard a frightening howl, so he decided to take a flashlight and investigate. His wife waited on the porch. Minutes later he came running back with a look of terror on his face. When I asked her what he saw, she immediately withdrew and refused to discuss it further. She did not come back to visit me for the rest of the summer.

"A few days later I was again sitting on the front porch when my big friend came to visit me. The creature stood in his usual place where I could see only his torso with his usual wide grin."

MJ: Hello. I have not seen you for a while.
BF: Yes, I know.
MJ: Where have you been?
BF: I cannot tell you.
MJ: What were the lights I saw over the trees the other night?
BF: It is none of your business. (He said this in a kindly tone.)
MJ: I won't tell anyone about the lights, but I am real curious. Was it a space ship? And what was the strange howling when it came over? Was that you?
BF: It is none of your business. It is not for you to know.

"We spoke of many things that day, but he would not tell me about the eerie generator noise, nor about the strange lights in the woods.

"We spoke several other times over the summer. He came two days before my husband was to pick me up, and I told him that I would be going back to the city soon."

MJ: I will miss you, dear friend, for I will have to go soon. My husband will be picking me up in a couple of days.
BF: What is a husband?
MJ: He is the man who brought me here. He's the one I'm married to who cares for me.
BF: Oh, you mean your mate. Yes, that man. I know of him.
MJ: I will be back again, perhaps in the spring.
BF: What is spring? I do not know that word.
MJ: Spring is the season right after winter.
BF: I do not understand your words.
MJ: It is the season right after the snow melts.
BF: What is the word snow?
MJ: It is when the ground becomes white all over and is cold.
BF: Yes, I understand. But what is spring?
MJ: Spring is when the water has the ability to flow again. When the water is free to move and the weather gets warm.
BF: Oh, now I understand spring. Now I understand (gives a hearty laugh). That is a good one. I like how you explain that. Yes, that is a good one.

"Later, when my husband picked me up, I told him I must say good-bye to my friend in the forest. I told him I was going to walk down a small trail not far from the lake. My husband understood but he did not want to discuss it. These things frightened him. He couldn't discuss it. He sat quietly in the car reading a newspaper while I walked into the woods to look for Bigfoot. I walked some distance and then sat down under a tree for a short spell. In my mind I began telling him I was leaving now and wanted to say good-bye, hoping that we would talk again next year. He answered me immediately, though I could not see him. He said he had enjoyed talking with me and would indeed see me the following year. I was so happy. There was something beautiful about his words that gave me a warm feeling about this man. There was a true sense of love. I really did not want to go back to Milwaukee, to the city, to all the people.

"I turned to walk back toward the cottage but, after only a few steps, I heard a noise behind me. When I turned around Bigfoot was just 10 or 12 feet from me, walking back into the forest. Now I don't know why, but I didn't see him there all the time I was sitting talking to him. I don't know where he came from. He was just there very suddenly. I don't understand why I didn't see him before then. He just appeared out of nowhere.

"It came to pass that these summers meant a lot to me. I always looked forward to going back to speak with my friend again. In 1980, when I returned, we arrived late at the cottage and it was dark. While getting out of the car, I saw a huge shadowy figure standing in the trees. My husband and I went in the house in order not to disturb the creature. We were busy arranging our groceries and clothing. Suddenly, we heard a heavy thump against the side of the building. I was not frightened because I knew it was my friend letting us know that he was there. However, my husband became quite upset. I told him not to worry, that Bigfoot was a friend, and, as usual, my husband said: 'I don't want to talk about it.' I spoke to Bigfoot only one time that summer and I was very disappointed. In fact, that was the last time we talked. He said they were leaving and would go to a different area now. He said there were too many people, too much activity in the area, and he had to leave, as it was no longer safe for him. My friend promised that, if he was in the area again, he would visit me.

"I have not told others of this experience because I feared people would not believe me. I don't want anyone making fun of me. This was an experience that I'll never forget and in many ways has changed my life."

# The Mt. Hood Experiment

*OVERVIEW*

Extreme terror, confusion, and shock were the results of a dramatic incident that happened in 1979 while I was conducting a scientific experiment deep in the Oregon Cascades. The astonishing event traumatized me so, that when it happened it was the nearest I ever came to suffering heart failure! Yet, the experiment itself proved to be a major turning point in my own Sasquatch research.

Previously, I had pondered how I would locate a Sasquatch out of thousands of square miles of woodland and wilderness nationwide. Since most Bigfoot research had been conducted in the Pacific Northwest, I chose that part of the country for the study, using a proliferation of demographic data available in the historic literature. After studying maps constructed by researcher John Green, that indicate clusters of Bigfoot sightings over the years throughout the Pacific Northwest, the northern Oregon Cascades became the target area for the field work.[1] Over the years, dogs, traps, electronic equipment, helicopters, and computers had been used in attempting to locate an active Bigfoot area. All approaches had ended in failure. Thus, my idea was to use an unorthodox procedure by conducting a scientific experiment using psychics as a "research tool." I am aware that I may be criticized for dabbling in what some may label the "occult." I assure the reader, this is not the case. It was actually an experiment using established principles of parapsychology that I have applied here. After all, no other previous field method has proved successful. Therefore I had nothing to lose and everything to gain if it worked. My main objective was to capture on

---

1. Green, 1978, p. 93

movie film photographic evidence to compare with the controversial Patterson-Gimlin movie film taken on October 20, 1967.

Four psychically sensitive people were used in the experiment: three map dowsers and one clairvoyant. My hypothesis was that if each person claiming psychic sensitivity could pinpoint an area on the map independently of each other, tuning into key zones of Bigfoot activity, then I would compare one "reading" against the other with hopes of producing a cluster representing a legitimate target area. In theory then, the results of the experiment would produce statistical percentages based on mathematics, the purest of measurable science. Those psychics who pinpointed activity outside the cluster were assumed to be less accurate than the others. I knew of no other way to set up the experimental design.

There were three phases of the experiment: Phases I and II consisted of the use of maps; Phase III tested the validity of the results of the map readings by actual field work to acquire evidence of Bigfoot activity in the designated area. The map work was conducted in Milwaukee, Wisconsin, some 2,000 miles from the target.

For Phase I, a map of 2,705 square miles was used. Later, with Phase II, a more detailed topographic (quadrant) map was procured from the U.S. Geological Survey. Each dowser independently used a pendulum over the maps, which was done on separate days so each psychic did not know the results of the other. I was awed by the fact that *all* three pinpointed almost exactly the same area. Statistically this is highly improbable! In parapsychological experiments it is virtually unheard of under controlled conditions! Yet that is precisely what happened. Two of the dowsers were 50 feet apart, the third 100 feet from the others, forming an elongated triangle in relation to each other. This was far too "coincidental" for one not to suspect that some inexplicable metaphysical process had occurred. The proof (or disproof) would be produced by the field work.

The fourth psychic, a clairvoyant, preferred not to use a map. This disappointed me. Instead, she merely presented information in trance which I considered totally worthless at the time. It should be noted that both the clairvoyant and one of the psychic map dowsers independently indicated that a "home-cave" was present on the mountain targeted as the area for Bigfoot activity.

Based on information from these map "readings", I prepared to fly 2,000 miles to the Mount Hood Wilderness Area in order to test the validity of the experiment.

## The Mt. Hood Experiment

*EPISODE*

After taking leave from the American Indian agency, where I worked in applied anthropology as Assistant Director, I flew to Portland, Oregon, to begin Phase III. Greg, my wilderness guide, picked me up at the airport and we drove eastward toward the Cascades, discussing my plans enroute. Greg was a woodcutter who spent his free time backpacking and mountain climbing throughout the Cascade Mountains. He impressed me as a highly experienced woodsman. His job was to aid me in obtaining and transporting food supplies for my two-week stay. He was familiar with the target area and could read maps accurately; and since I had only two weeks leave from the agency, his help saved me valuable time.

The rugged mountain terrain was far different from the Green and Berkshire Mountains I had known as a boy. The gigantic trees of the Cascade Mountains created an environment uniquely different from my previous treks in the Himalayas, Andes, Alps, and Guyana Highlands. Upon entering the vastness of the northwest forest, I became a dwarfed figure among wooded giants. The long hike through the five-and six-thousand-foot mountains was exhausting. Greg and I trudged from one stand of timber to another, over mountain passes that led into some of the most splendid wilderness scenery Mother Earth ever created.

As we came closer to our destination, we left the trail to climb a steep butte. By now the slope of the land was so angular and rugged that it became necessary to stop and rest every few minutes. The combination of high altitude, brush, boulders and heavy backpacks, made for a very difficult climb. Nevertheless, before long we arrived at the designated location that had been dowsed on the map some two months before back in Milwaukee.

A general survey of the forest revealed that only a tiny, level shelf was available on which to pitch my tent. Judging from the map, the alleged cave was approximately 150 to 200 feet around the back side of the butte.

The first task was to hang my food supply high between two trees to avoid animal theft. Then Greg and I walked down the slope to look for a daily source of drinking water. The ridge was steep and treacherous. Several times I stopped to examine animal spoor as deer runways were fairly numerous crisscrossing the dense stands of timber.

Then we noticed something peculiar. The ground was hard-packed, well-used, yet unlike all the other trails, was void of indentations of deer hooves. Our first thought was that it was being used by a bear. We looked for more spoor. Ten feet from where we were standing we were astonished to discover a distinct human-like footprint in dry, hardened earth, obviously made after a heavy rain. It was a left foot. The print measured twelve inches long by six inches wide, sporting five clearly indented toes. No claw marks extended beyond the toes as would appear in a bear track. The well-worn trail traversed the steep ridge leading high into rock ledges and to the area designated by the psychics as a Bigfoot cave!

It had been less than one hour since arriving at the target area and one hundred yards from my campsite was the first sign of the man-creature.

Greg's face looked uneasy. With a serious tone of voice he said: "Don't know if I ever told you this Jack, but it's similar to the tracks I ran across last winter ten or fifteen miles from here. I was cutting wood and there was a fair bit of fresh snow. I spotted these tracks that easily measured 14 to 16 inches long. It had human toes just like this one. While examining them, I had a feeling I was being watched. The feeling was strong, kind of creepy, and wouldn't go away. Made the hair on the back of my neck stand up. I got the hell out of there fast."

After telling me the story, Greg looked embarrassed. He was an experienced woodsman showing signs of fear. Previous to this incident he told me he did not believe in the existence of Bigfoot.

By mid-afternoon we found a cold bubbling spring. After the water jugs were filled, Greg and I set a date when he would return, we shook hands and said "Good-bye." Without delay I headed up the ridge back to camp.

After an hour of exhaustive climbing, I reached a rock slide some 75 feet or more below the shelf from where I was camped. Looking up I could see my sack of food supplies hanging on a rope high between two trees and felt content knowing I was finally "home." After a short rest to catch my breath, I moved across the rocks and back into the forest cover once again. Upon entering the timber I stepped on dry twigs that made a loud crunch. Then without warning, a gigantic and unexpected "crash, crash" startled me! My heart began to pound. The sound came from my campsite. I tip-toed the rest of the distance to my tent only to find things quiet and undisturbed. I began inspecting the ground. There were no deer tracks nor any other signs of a large animal. I was perplexed. Yet *something* was definitely there to have made the loud, heavy crash.

Moments later, I crawled into my tent and began arranging my sleeping gear and organizing the equipment. Almost at once I became aware of footsteps outside. Each crunching step told me that a "person" was sneaking up on me. *Distinctly* I could hear bushes moving and twigs snapping. Slowly I unzipped my tent flap and poked my head outside. Nothing! Everything appeared normal or at least near "normal" because the birds were no longer chirping nor the ground squirrels chattering. I carefully scanned the immediate vicinity. Still there was nothing in sight.

Withdrawing into the tent, I continued to unpack. Then I began to feel uncomfortable. I had an uncanny feeling that I was being watched. There was an oppressive "vibration" in the air, an unmistakable feeling of a presence. Suddenly there was a deep-sounding growl. Then a crunching sound of human-like footsteps coming closer, almost to my tent. Reaching for my camera, I slowly unzipped the tent-flap and leaped to my feet. Nothing! Not a creature in sight. I was deeply puzzled. I distinctly heard a bipedal walk. But nothing was visually there, just an eerie silence. How could someone or something walk up to my tent yet not be there? Impossible! Previously, I had heard weird reports about Bigfoot dematerializing, but it made no sense to me at the time. I attributed the stories to someone's overactive imagination. But now I was giving it serious thought. I knew what I *unmistakably* heard and felt, yet saw nothing. It was very confusing.

Crawling back into my tent, I then became impressed with the fact that something with two legs just walked from behind my tent back into the forest. What a startling revelation...it was not my imagination! I decided to grab my camera and make a more thorough investigation well beyond the confines of my campsite.

I heard a single "snorting" sound similar to that of a pig. But there are no wild pigs in that region. (I later checked with Greg, as he is knowledgeable about the fauna in Oregon). Cautiously I tiptoed into the forest, straining to get a glimpse of any movement. Still I saw nothing. Then there was another snorting "grunt." As I moved in the direction of the sound, I could hear the twigs cracking ahead of me. The sounds of quick long steps of a man-like creature became apparent. It seemed to be heading over the mountain toward the area on the map marked as a cave. A drawn-out, high-pitched whistle was sounded by the creature as it headed towards the other side of the ridge.

Every day thereafter, strange noises became commonplace. Frequently distinct twig-snapping, rustling and shuffling in the brush, deep growls, from low pitched "oinking" sounds to high-pitched whistles, and bipedal walking all became an everyday occurrence. The most common sound was the odd "oink" or "grunt" which occurred about five times daily. Also there was the uneasy oppressive feeling that I was being watched. Whenever I investigated the origin of the noises, I would inevitably hear heavy, manlike footsteps in retreat. This happened frequently during the two-week period. I could not mistake the sounds of long-strided walking for anything else. After all this was the wilderness, not a camping area in a public park. Each time I investigated the growls, grunts, or walking sounds, it became apparent that I was always driving the creature away from me. I decided to remain nonthreatening and passive to the frequently occurring noises, with hopes that it would increase my chances of catching a glimpse of the creature. I kept my zoom-lens movie camera with me at all times.

In the solitude of the mountains, I spent my days reading, writing, going on casual hikes looking for spoor, deliberately putting myself into a nonaggressive role. Again, I carried no gun and I did not try to track the creature to its lair or to harass it in any way. Stalking had never proved successful with other Bigfoot investigators, but had only driven it further away. On the contrary, luring the shy man-animal into camera range was the purpose. I wanted my friendly approach to be the object of curiosity. A year later I read a superb, award-winning book called *The Snow Leopard*. The author and world traveler-naturalist Peter Matthiessen says:

> Perhaps the best way to find Bigfoot is to set up camp in a likely region and live there until this creature, in its primate curiosity makes a few investigations of its own.[2]

During this period I refrained from exploring the area near the "alleged" cave. I was advised by two of the psychics who aided me with the experiment that I would be in extreme danger if I approached the cave. Though I could not verify this, I used great caution and respected their words. No creature wants its home to be invaded by strangers—especially a reclusive Sasquatch. To enter the den of any wild or unknown creature where it is residing is inviting serious trouble.

The morning of the eleventh day was thick with fog. I emerged from my tent to have breakfast. There was an incredible air of silence. Barely 50 feet of visibility existed through the dense cloud-covered landscape. The sensation was eerie. Staring into the foggy grayness, I felt helpless and small. Giant firs surrounded me, each limb whiskered with ghostly green moss that hung like webs from every tree. As I puttered around the campsite, my eyes strained to make out the silhouette of the forest growth around me. I felt as if the entire forest had engulfed my very being. Anything could have been lurking out

---

2. Matthiessen, 1978, p. 130

there. Thick fog drifted about me, adding a certain mystery and romance to the Sasquatch search.

As the day faded into evening, I became restless. The off-and-on drizzle kept me in my tent. Time was valuable, and after nearly two weeks the lack of an encounter made me feel discouraged. If I had not needed to return to work I would have stayed several months.

In the early evening hours, it started to drizzle once again. The soft-falling rain was damp and cold. I retreated to my tent to stay warm. Sliding into my sleeping bag I decided to read a book. Later, as twilight drew near, I made plans for the following day. I felt it was time to locate the "alleged" cave. All the while I was on the butte, I wondered with great apprehension if the cave actually existed. I wanted to verify that before leaving the area. Against the advice of the psychics, I decided to approach the cave the following morning. While planning my move I fantasized, visualizing myself near the cave with a surprised Bigfoot creature looking into the lens of my 8mm movie camera.

*Crash!* As I lay there, my heart jumped abruptly at the sound of a falling tree just outside my tent! Then there was a heavy *stomping*-walk. My heart was beating frantically as *loud*, elephantine footsteps approached my tent. The last two steps struck the ground with such force that the earth beneath me trembled!

Sitting up, I held my hands to my chest in an effort to relieve the sudden pressure of a pounding heartbeat. I became so unnerved that my hands were shaking uncontrollably. Here was a chance for a possible photograph, yet I could hardly hold the camera. My mind was overcome with fear. For the first time in my life I knew the real meaning of *terror*!

I slid to the front of the tent and quickly slipped on my boots. Approximately 15 seconds had passed. I reached to unzip my tent-fly, when suddenly a huge gush of rain hit without warning, blowing violently against the canvas. It was accompanied by roaring explosions of thunder. The tent shook as it was hit with a tremendous blast of sweeping wind and rain. Even when the roar of the thunder went into a temporary lull, the intensity of the downpour against the tent became almost deafening. The sudden "freak" torrent was timely, and it heightened my innermost fears. Lying there, huddled in my sleeping bag I kept thinking: "What the hell is going on out there?"

Almost simultaneously, out of the silence of a previously *windless* evening, a tree had come crashing down, I heard manlike steps of a frightening magnitude approaching my tent, then a violent storm appeared out of nowhere just as I was about to investigate the source of the disturbance. It was very alarming, and I was scared!

With the storm in full force nothing else could be heard. I wondered if the creature would crash through my tent any second. For two consecutive hours the rain and wind shook and beat at my tent as thunder boomed clamorously all around me.

When the storm had finally passed, a growing silence fell over the forest. I felt relaxed for the first time. As I lay there, it seemed almost as if the whole incident had never happened. It was like waking up after a nightmare and realizing everything was all right. And since everything seemed all right, there was nothing I could do but try to sleep.

"Errr-rump, errr-rump, errrrrr-rump," an eerie mechanical sound had begun. I became tense again and was thinking: "What now?" The noise was like that of a pumping action with a generator slipping its gears. But what was it? The muffled grinding of gears seemed to be coming from within the earth! Listening intently, I came to realize the source of the "generator" came from the direction of the "alleged" cave. It was 10:08 P.M. I listened for a long time while studying the pattern of the strange chugging sound.

As the winding "generator" chugged away, the rest of the forest remained silent. Temptation struck; I really wanted to investigate. I was curious as to what type of a mechanical device could be out there in the middle of the wilderness. And also, who was running it? But I had no courage left. To me, the creature's earlier display of heavy foot stomping was a stern and deliberate message to "stay away." Eventually I dozed lightly, catching a few winks off and on during the night. When morning arrived, the generator sound was still "errr-rumping." It stopped at precisely 6:25 A.M.

During the pre-dawn hours, while lying awake in my tent, I wanted desperately to understand what had happened the night before. But it was not easy to fit together the pieces of the puzzle. In doing so I had a flash-back. In March, 1979, five months before my trip, the clairvoyant (the fourth psychic I recruited for the experiment and whose material I initially rejected and labeled a fantasy) told me I would successfully locate a Bigfoot cave.

"Do not get near the cave under any circumstances," she warned.

When I asked why, she said, "They will not be as receptive as you think. Just stay away."

When I persisted, pressing for more information, she continued.

"Jack, if you get near the cave you are going to meet another being that you are now not ready to deal with."

Annoyed at the implication that some sort of aliens were associated with Sasquatch, I further challenged the psychic for additional information that might make more sense to me. The clairvoyant sternly shot back, "I distinctly mean an alien being from another planet is involved!"

She then went on to say that Bigfoot was an extraterrestrial creature and some are subservient to other more advanced beings and that the creatures do reconnaissance work for them. Because of their great bodily strength, extreme agility, and psychic powers in eluding Earth people, these giants aid the Starpeople in their work. One of the tasks of Bigfoot is to protect the territory around the cave so that no one goes near it. The clairvoyant emphasized that the alien was using the cave to conduct research and did not want any interference.

The mere fact that a psychic makes such a statement, however, does not necessarily mean that it is true. With my academic background, I found the entire story was too fantastic to believe. I merely placed the recorded interview in my file and forgot about it. It seemed too absurd to evaluate. It is thought-provoking, however, that since then nine other psychics have told me exactly the same thing when shown a photograph of Roger Patterson's purported Sasquatch. Each sensitive told of an "outer space" origin! While conducting the Mt. Hood wilderness experiment, I had to grapple with the problem of what sounded like a subterranean machine in the night, and this inadvertently forced me to think deeper about what I was *really* experiencing. Further, I recalled a statement in the book *Bigfoot* by Alan Berry and Ann Slate, wherein they relate an incident in the Sierra Nevada Mountains of California. The authors were fortunate to record an unusual generator sound in an active Sasquatch area. They reported:

...when the tape was replayed, sounds of machinery were distinctly heard those resembling a generator or hydroelectric plant in operation, but coming from beneath their feet. The sounds do not remain consistent but subtly change, as if new gears are set in motion. [3]

All of these things were running through my mind the morning after the bizarre incident.

Shortly after dawn, I examined the camp area for evidence of the intruder and discovered a downed tree measuring 40 feet long, four and a half inches in diameter at breast height, with its crown lying some 25 feet from my tent. The tree was not rotten, nor was it forced down by the ele-

---

3. Berry, 1976, p. 82.

ments in the windless evening before the storm. It was clearly uprooted from solid ground. Three feet from the tree was a manlike footprint of a left foot measuring five and a half inches wide by eleven and one-half inches long. Five toes were prominently displayed. Though it had rained fiercely during the night, the weight of the creature had pressed its foot deep into the earth. The creature had jumped from a five-foot embankment, placing its left foot on the decline, bracing itself, resulting in a clear, deep footprint. A careful search revealed no hair or other spoor, though I did discover a narrow trail traversing the ridge well above my tent that directly lead toward the area of the "alleged" cave.

While I was examining the footprint, I heard heavy walking sounds from a biped with a long stride immediately in the timber above me. The creature could be heard heading over the mountain. The walking was casual and inconspicuous. This was followed by a blaring, high-pitched whistle that turned into a hideous "laugh." The creature seemed amused. There was no more fear; I was merely dazed, even numbed, by what I experienced. Also there was a noticeable air of lightness and relaxation coming from the creature, as if the Bigfoot was "projecting" a feeling of relief knowing I now would not invade the territory of his cave.

This lighthearted feeling continued until the day I left. The creature made no effort to walk quietly, as if he knew it made little difference that I knew he was there. The previous tree-felling and foot-stomping episode was a harmless warning for me to keep my distance. The creature communicated well; rather than being physically violent and "animalistic," the Sasquatch chose to play on my fears instead. Touché!

Let me mention one more bizarre event. During my stay on the butte, though it took a few days before a noticeable pattern emerged, I began to be aware that whenever there was a temporary lull in the "grunting" and walking sounds at the perimeter of my camp, a hawk would inevitably appear. Instead of fleeing from my presence, it would carefully watch me and often fly closer. Not only did it gawk at me with investigating eyes but it followed me *everywhere*! If I hiked to a side of the mountain with less ground cover, the hawk would frequently glide over me. It was so systematic in its "surveillance" that I became suspicious. So I decided to try to elude the bird. Whenever I thought I had succeeded in losing it, the bird would be waiting on a limb ahead of me in the forest. If I tried to dodge it in the thick brush, the persistent bird would fly from tree to tree always keeping within a range of 50 to 100 feet from me. Once it landed on a tiny shrub some ten feet away glaring at me intensely

One day while eating lunch, overlooking a cliff a few short feet from my tent, I became aware of a distinct feeling that I was being watched. Looking around I saw nothing. I glanced over the cliff and then behind me. Still nothing in sight. Then a voice penetrated my mind saying: "Up here!" Looking directly above my head, I saw the hawk which was balancing itself motionless in the air. Approximately 20 feet from the ground, the bird was stationary with wings outstretched and its head extended downward with piercing eyes. I was stunned! Did the hawk really communicate? Some ten or fifteen seconds passed before it gracefully soared off into the cover of the forest. Though I had *unmistakably heard* its "telepathic" words, I immediately discounted it as a product of my imagination. Yet the hawk incident was obviously an integral part of the Sasquatch phenomenon. The bird's investigative behavior repeated itself day after day for the entire two-week period. Why would a wild hawk that would normally flee from man spend so much time following me? The real shocker was experiencing genuine telepathy from it.

A year later I spoke to a man outside of Spokane, Washington, who told me that whenever he entered a certain valley where he encountered the Sasquatch on several occasions, a raven would periodically *follow* him. In the beginning he thought he was imagining things. But the usual cautious raven showed no fear. The bird was too deliberate in its behavior, making every effort to spy on him, the witness insisted. Whenever the man looked for Sasquatch spoor, the bird would follow him everywhere. After sharing his experience with an Indian friend, he was told the Sasquatch mind is psychically powerful and the creatures recruit these birds to observe intruders when they—the Sasquatch—are busy doing important tasks. Just what these tasks are was not mentioned. Some researchers believe the Sasquatch, at times, work as miners, collecting valuable minerals vital to the mission of the Star-people.

Five years later in 1984, while exploring the Rogue-Umpqua Divide, a pristine wilderness area in the Oregon Cascades, I entered an active Bigfoot area revealed to me by an Indian acquaintance. While looking for tracks by a beaver pond in a remote meadow, I sensed that a Sasquatch was observing me from a wooded area at the base of an enormous cliff approximately 200 yards away. Its "vibrations" overwhelmed me, as if it were standing only a few feet in front of me. By 1984, I had experienced the strong vibrations of the psychic Sasquatch close to 200 times. I almost always know when one is in the immediate vicinity. Albeit, I could not see it from where I stood at the edge of the beaver pond.

Suddenly a hawk flew from the top of a tree next to where the creature was hiding. The bird flew in a straight line toward me, non-stop. When the bird was directly overhead, it briefly scrutinized me, made a 180-degree change in direction, returning once again to the Sasquatch-in-hiding.

On the other side of the creature was a small flock of ravens. As soon as the hawk returned to the base of the cliff, a raven repeated exactly the same behavior as the hawk. It did a U-turn above my head, returning to the tree beside where the creature was lurking. This was no coincidence. As in other little-understood phenomena, one looks for "patterns," whether there is any initial logic to it or not. What usually follows is that a researcher attempts to superimpose a theoretical model onto the phenomenon that is not adequately explicable by present-day standards. When this does not work, he/she proclaims that the phenomenon does not exist or was misperceived by the witness. The observable relationship between certain birds and the Sasquatch may be viewed as absurd by some, but telepathy was an accepted practice among Indians, and it was known among aborigines living close to nature all over the world. The American Indians called it communing with the Oneness of Nature—an interconnectedness with all living things.

# Sasquatch And The CIA

*OVERVIEW*

This story was related to me over a six-year period through a series of letters, numerous telephone calls, and personal interviews. The account took place west of the Rocky Mountains; the names and places are changed to protect the family involved. These events occurred in the latter part of the 1970s and throughout the 1980s. Mr. Jeffery and family are well established members of their community. They are religious, conservative, and moderately well-to-do. Although they have seen Bigfoot on several occasions, they were somewhat reluctant to tell their story. So they had absolutely nothing to gain by sharing their experiences with me. It took time to build a trust, but eventually I received the following story after much assurance that I would not make their names and address public. Like other witnesses I interviewed, the Jeffery family seemed very sincere but extremely troubled about the experiences they had with the psychic Sasquatch. In this case, they became more fearful of the government than the beings they encountered in the deep forest.

*EPISODE*

Mr. Jeffery took his family on a fishing trip to an isolated region deep in the mountains. The family trailer was parked in a remote camping area that was rarely crowded except occasionally in midsummer. On that particular weekend, there were numerous campers and trailers in the campground. By late Sunday afternoon, there were no other vehicles left in the area. That evening they decided to have a cookout. While his oldest of two daughters was gathering firewood, the teenager straightened up with an armful of sticks only to discover that she was staring up into the face of a giant Bigfoot. This abrupt and startling introduction caused her immediately to faint! The event caused a tremendous commotion among the family members. But after the initial shock, they realized that no one was injured and the creature had not attacked them in any way. People commonly do not know how the Bigfoot will act. They usually judge them by their monstrous appearance. By sundown they heard thumping noises from something huge walking in the forest. They expected at any moment to see one of the creatures step out and walk up to them, but there was nothing in sight but a placid coniferous forest.

After retiring to their trailer for the night, the family decided to play cards. Suddenly there was a tremendous "thump" made by something huge and strong against the side of the trailer. For a moment they became frightened. They immediately shut off the lights and peeked out of the windows. There, by the picnic table, stood an enormous apelike creature that Mr. Jeffery thought was looking for morsels. Within seconds it disappeared into the forest. Though they returned to their card playing, the discussion was clearly centered around this rare encounter with the legendary Bigfoot. No one could stop talking about it.

An hour passed, when someone noticed the knob on the trailer door was slowly turning. The family waited in anticipation, wondering fearfully just what they would do when confronted with a real-life giant. They waited in vain; Bigfoot did not open the door. After this, they decided if the creature had wanted to harm them, it had ample opportunity to do so. The family continued to bubble with excitement and soon overcame some of their initial fears.

The following morning everyone went fishing. As they worked their way around the lake to find a new fishing area, Mr. Jeffery noticed a neat pile of trout lined up side-by-side on the beach and giant manlike tracks were seen in the mud leading from the water. The tracks measured 20 inches long, he reported. The eyes of the fish were bulged out with large finger marks around each one, as if the life had been squeezed out of them. How a Sasquatch could catch a fish swimming in the water was a puzzling question. There was no normal way in which this could occur. Yet Mr. Jeffery swore this is what they observed, and the tracks leading from the water spoke for themselves.

By nightfall, fresh trout were laid on the picnic table to entice a hungry Sasquatch to return. The lights in the trailer remained dim as each member of the family occupied a window waiting for the creature to appear. As expected, an eight- to nine-foot behemoth emerged from the nocturnal forest, quickly took the fish and left.

When Friday came, weekend trailers and campers arrived in the campground once again. The creature did not return, seemingly due to the increased number of people in the area.

During that weekend Mr. Jeffery and his wife decided to go for a walk down one of the many trails. To their surprise they reached a "zone" where they could *feel* something invisible surrounding them less than 100 feet away. They could actually hear footsteps walking around them but saw nothing. The couple claim they felt an *energy* projected to them that was clearly from intelligent beings signalling them to "stay out" of that section of the forest. Though no harm came to them, they were terrified at the time. They distinctly felt an *oppressive* energy, as if a group of "invisible" beings were communicating on a level they did not understand. At the time, they did not know how to interpret these arcane "feelings"—only that its energy was powerful and real, coming from real interdimensional beings! It was only in the future, when stranger incidents occurred, that they began to understand the complexity of the Bigfoot phenomenon. Previously, none of them believed in Bigfoot nor had the slightest interest in pursuing the subject.

Two weeks later they returned for a three-day weekend. This time they brought cameras and king-sized chocolate bars to entice the creatures to come closer to them. Though cautious, the family was no longer scared but looked at the whole episode as a new adventure. Fortunately there was only one other trailer in the campground.

On the first night, they decided to walk along the lake after dark thinking they might see a Bigfoot further away from their trailer. After a while, they heard a banging of sticks on a hollow tree. Then loud thumping noises at a distance, as if something with huge feet was carelessly stomping the ground as it ran. The banging on trees seemed to be coming from different directions, evidently by two separate individuals. The noise was heard repeatedly, which greatly perplexed them.

Interestingly, the Great Lakes Indians speak of "the breaking of sticks" when referring to Sasquatch territorial behavior. The Indians say that when you hear the pounding of sticks against hollow trees, it is a signal the creatures give to let intruders know that they are entering Sasquatch territory. The Indians also say that when they find tops of saplings broken and twisted off when entering a region, this is a sign that marks Sasquatch feeding grounds. They never enter that territory and consider it very dangerous.

The Jeffery family decided to hide in the brush in an effort to catch a glimpse of a Bigfoot. Before long, they were astounded by an ungodly cry unlike anything they had ever heard before. What they observed in the moments that followed was beyond their wildest imaginations. They reported that the Sasquatch stepped out of the forest holding a flashlight device, and directed the beam up in the air while howling upwardly. During this time, other unseen creatures hit their sticks against hollow logs making a loud drum-like thud. There were three bangs, then a pause; three bangs, then a pause—always three. Within minutes, a round, saucer-shaped, glowing object appeared on the horizon and hovered over the trees directly above the Sasquatch. The frightened family huddled in the bushes, observing the peculiar ritual.

The following year they returned, bringing a trusted friend. They carefully explored the edge of the lake in search of spoor to see if the Bigfoot creatures were still in the general vicinity. No sign of the creatures was found.

However, that night they noticed a glowing light hovering over the trees at a distance. They grabbed their flashlights and began walking through the dark toward the light. They came to an area deep in the forest and decided to hide and wait. As in the previous summer, soon they saw a Bigfoot creature once again holding a flashlight device, beaming it in the air and howling up into the heavens. This continued until a spaceship appeared. It hovered above the trees over the creature. In a short while, the craft glided off and the Sasquatch disappeared into the forest.

Next morning it was foggy, gray, and overcast. The three returned to the same area to look for footprints. After searching, they decided to hide in the brush once again to see if a Bigfoot would return. They noticed that off to the side a huge log had fallen down. Some two hours passed. Soon, to their surprise, a three-and-a-half to four-foot-tall being, resembling a tiny man, walked mechanically down the log. He wore a type of space-suit. The odd-looking hairless being jumped off the end of the log and began digging in the earth. He wore no helmet or any visible breathing device.

Mr. Jeffery decided to give a yell to get the being's attention. When he did, it did not look up and was not distracted in any way. The three of them began to shout and wave their hands, but still they could not attract the spaceman's attention. When the tiny man finished digging in the earth, apparently collecting a soil sample, he climbed back up on the log, walked somewhat stiffly down its length which led into thick brush, and slowly disappeared into the forest cover.

The next year more incidents followed. This time another friend asked to join them. It took a whole month before anything happened. After returning from a long hike, the group was stunned when a nine-to-ten foot Sasquatch stepped out in front of them a short distance away. Then, in the twinkling of an eye, the Bigfoot *completely disappeared in front of the witnesses!* The witnesses insisted that it literally dematerialized! Mrs. Jeffery reported that she was so awed at what she saw, that when they returned home, she did not leave the house for two weeks. The woman was in such a total state of shock that she did not return to the area for some time.

During this period the family noticed a car watching their house. Whenever Mr. Jeffery left to go anywhere the vehicle would follow him. This began to unnerve them. When he contacted the local police, they could not locate the mysterious car that was watching their home.

Also, the family noticed that on occasion when they used their telephone there was a clicking noise on the line, as if their phone was being tapped. At one point they received an ominous call. The voice said: "Do not return to the campground to look for the Sasquatch unless you want your head blown off." Whoever it was immediately hung up. The family became panic stricken and Mr. Jeffery immediately called the police. In spite of an investigation, the identity of the caller remained a mystery.

One day two men knocked on the front door and began asking questions. They avoided telling Mrs. Jeffery who they were. Mrs. Jeffery started closing the door because the men refused to identify themselves. Reluctantly, they showed their identification as agents from the Central Intelligence Agency. They showed a distinct interest in the Bigfoot and UFO sightings that occurred near the campground. Surprisingly, they knew all about their encounters. When Mr. Jeffery came home from work, he reluctantly took them to the campground and into the forest where the encounters had taken place. Before leaving, he stipulated they were not to bring any firearms. They emphatically agreed that no guns would be brought.

While sitting at a picnic table, the two members of the CIA talked and questioned Mr. and Mrs. Jeffery at great length, showing an intense interest in every detail. At one point in their conversation, one of the men turned around to look behind him. When his coat swung open, the butt of a pistol could be seen strapped to his body. This infuriated Mr. Jeffery, who stormed off in his car and drove home. He refused to help them any further. A few days later they again knocked on his door asking for more information. He told them he would not help them anymore because they had violated his trust. Also he told them that the creatures were psychic and knew when anyone had a gun or camera in their presence. Since the Sasquatch had never hurt anyone he would not bring a gun, or any person who carried one, into the forest with him.

The agents left his house but continued their surveillance. Still, the family experienced a "clicking" sound on their telephone. In time, both the surveillance and telephone tapping stopped.

The following summer the Jeffery family returned to the same campground once again. This time they claimed to have taken several pictures of the creatures. Mr. Jeffery stated that he approached a Sasquatch while it was examining some stones, as the creature was holding them in its hand up close to its face. Because the Sasquatch was intensely preoccupied, it allowed him to sneak up on the creature and take a picture. (As proof of his success I asked to examine the photograph. He refused to show me the picture he had purportedly taken.)

A few days later he received a second threatening phone call from an unidentified caller telling him to stop going up to the campground to look for Bigfoot or they would blow his head off. Being frightened, he did not do any more field research for some time.

Mr. Jeffery reported to me that over the winter he went into that region to look for tracks in the snow and hoped to find a cave or some type of shelter used by the creatures. He and two friends found tracks leading to the base of an escarpment where the tracks disappeared going up the side of a steep bluff. The cliff was so steep that they were not able to climb it. He returned the following spring with ropes and one companion. They climbed the side of the cliff and located a large cave. Just inside the mouth of the cave, Mr. Jeffery claimed he found a crudely-built pyramid some four feet high made out of a green, quartz-like rock. He took a photograph with a Polaroid camera of the three-sided pyramid and later showed it to me for study. The pyramid could have been built anywhere, in any cave, by anyone. Whether it actually was built by a Bigfoot is total conjecture. However, it is a very interesting story and I found the photograph fascinating. At no time was I able to persuade Mr. Jeffery to show me either his alleged photographs or movie film of the Sasquatch.

That same summer, Mr. Jeffery returned to the campground and caught a glimpse of a Sasquatch at some distance. As he sat reading a book at the picnic table he heard a thumping noise that sounded like one of the creatures walking toward him. When he looked up there was nothing there. Nevertheless, he continued to hear the footsteps coming closer to him. He could feel the creature's "vibrations," its presence, as he has done numerous times before. Then Mr. Jeffery claimed the Sasquatch telepathically spoke to him. The actual nature of the conversation was never revealed to me. He was very much afraid of the CIA and did not want information leaked out to others. He once said:

"I shouldn't worry so much about someone killing one of the creatures; they are profoundly psychic and difficult to catch off guard. They can easily read your mind and know your every intent. Yet I have discovered, if they are concentrating on something else, if their mind is diverted, they will drop their guard and you can get close to them. This happened on two occasions and that's how I got the pictures."

Mr. Jeffery also told me of the time he was in the field and saw a Bigfoot hiding behind some trees. He waited and in a short time it stepped out into the open. The creature appeared unusually nervous and guarded, even though there was no sign of anyone else in the area. Soon it disappeared back into the security of the forest. Although he remained sitting patiently for some time, the creature did not return and so Mr. Jeffery walked back to his car and drove home.

When he returned home, his wife made coffee and they sat chatting on their back patio. They live at the edge of town in a residential area. After an hour and a half had passed, Mrs. Jeffery went into the house to check on the dinner. Soon, Mr. Jeffery felt a familiar "vibration" and he instantly recognized it was that of a Sasquatch! His first reaction was: "Impossible!" Then he heard quiet footfalls, as if an *invisible entity* was approaching. In fear the man bolted for the back door, then stopped by the entrance-way thinking how foolish he was acting—that he was probably imagining things.

Then, all of a sudden, he was startled when a giant invisible hand reached out and gently grabbed his arm. He quickly retreated into the house, mind-staggered and disquieted at what he had experienced. He later told me he did not believe that the Bigfoot would have hurt him in any way, but nevertheless, he became frightened over the whole matter since it had occurred at his home. The family did not understand how the creature traveled that distance and accurately located them, and for what purpose, except to possibly demonstrate to the Jefferys their psychic and interdimensional abilities.

A few weeks later, when the Jeffery family was entertaining friends in their home, the subject of Bigfoot dominated the conversation. All at once the group felt an oppressive presence. Looking out the window they saw, at the edge of the roof, something sticking out that was silvery and round in shape.

When the people stepped out into the yard, they were awed to see hovering about five feet above the roof, a motionless "flying saucer." It was approximately 35 feet in diameter and was close enough that Mr. Jeffery said he could have climbed up on the roof, swung out and grabbed the side of it.

As they stood there, it casually lifted off and floated away. It made no effort to conceal itself, making a slow departure. He noticed that several of the neighbors from the surrounding houses had come out to observe the craft as well. The next day they looked at the newspaper, listened to the radio and watched on television to see if anyone had reported the incident. There was no mention of the sighting in the media.

During the same summer, their teenage daughter was on a hike through the forest in "their" Bigfoot area. Suddenly she was jolted! There, only 20 feet from her in a stooped-over position was a man-creature, busily rubbing two rocks together in its hands. The giant appeared to be in deep concentration and did not notice the girl. In a few minutes it stood up and walked away without showing any recognition of the teenager's presence. They insist the creature becomes almost mesmerized at times because of its intense power of concentration. When a Bigfoot becomes absorbed in a project, a person can walk up on the creature and catch it off guard. The family members also claim that the daughter snapped a quick photograph of it on one such occasion before fleeing back to camp and the safety of her parents.

For a while the family became busy with domestic matters and there was a lull in their visits to the campground. Once again, the family became unnerved by the presence of someone sitting in a car watching their home. Whenever Mr. Jeffery left the house, he was followed. The local police never arrived in time to catch the snooper.

Finally the family returned to the campground and spent much of their time exploring the many trails, looking for Bigfoot spoor. On one of the trails, Mrs. Jeffery noticed high in a tree, a sophisticated-looking camera focused on the pathway below. Later, they discovered still another.

Though they never saw the person(s) who discreetly placed these partially-hidden cameras in their Bigfoot area, the family strongly feels it was the CIA. Apparently, since the Jefferys' refusal to aid the CIA in locating a Sasquatch, the agents took it upon themselves to obtain their own field data.

In David Michael Jacobs' book, *The UFO Controversy in America* (1975), he states that a CIA-sponsored panel was organized in 1953 because, along with the Air Force, they thought the increasing UFO reports might constitute a possible threat to national security. The government was gravely concerned that the American public would lose confidence in them if logical answers were not presented to explain these unidentified craft. It was important to the government and military agencies to be able to show the public that they had everything under control. Consequently, the government expended a lot of energy in their Blue Book program, which many people felt was a clear "cover-up."

After giving a lecture in Los Angeles in 1994, a well-educated man cautiously approached me, carefully waiting until every person who came up to make additional inquiries was gone. He began by saying,"Are you aware that everything you stated in your lecture about a Bigfoot/UFO connection is true and that the CIA knows all about it?" The gentleman said that a very close friend of his, who could locate people and animals psychically on a map, was recruited by the CIA to find a Bigfoot! With the use of advanced technology, the man claimed the agency captured two of the creatures and later released them. He said one was captured when an Army jeep hit a Sasquatch and knocked it down, rendering it immobile. The jeep was totally demolished, but the Bigfoot was only slightly injured. His psychic friend, who worked for the government, insisted that the giants are a type of ETs because there really is a UFO connection.

It is the job of the CIA to investigate any unusual activity going on in this country where national security is involved. The Sasquatch and space beings come under the heading of "Unknowns"; therefore, the continuing reports about both are enough to keep agency officials wondering. My own research shows that there are plenty of reports to be gleaned from the public if investigators would only take the time to locate them. Undoubtedly, this is why the CIA came to visit the Jeffery family. They heard enough stories and became aware that a Bigfoot/UFO connection appeared to exist on a level that is not yet understood. The more witnesses who experience this unusual association, the more of an interest the CIA would have with this subject—always in the name of national security.

# The White Sasquatch

*OVERVIEW*

This exceptional first-hand report was contributed by White Song Eagle from Indiana. Her in-depth encounters with Teluke occurred between 1973 and 1974. She is one of several fortunate persons to have had the privilege of being approached telepathically by a Sasquatch. The documentation in this chapter has been analyzed, and the majority of Sasquatch behaviors described by White Song Eagle is congruent with previously established behavioral patterns based on research data on psychic Sasquatch ecology. Such accounts, though rare, are being reported more and have great anthropological significance when attempting to understand just who the Bigfoot-people are rather than concentrating on the "what." The time has come to reveal more of these psychic Sasquatch happenings so that the world may begin to understand intelligent telepathic beings who have inhabited alternate forms of reality all along. White Song describes her contact with Sasquatch by the following account in her own words.

*EPISODE*

"My experience with the Sasquatch named Teluke and his family, although unique in content, is not as uncommon as one may believe. I believe the reason is that people who have had ongoing encounters with Sasquatch, in order to avoid ridicule and maintain privacy, have no reason or desire to report it. The Bigfoot reports one hears on television and in the newspapers are always from people who don't understand what's going on and/or are afraid for their safety. Most of these people have not experienced this type of reality and view it solely as a spectator having an accidental meeting. Others, because of their rigid beliefs in the reality they live in, are intimidated by a phenomenon they are unable to understand. They believe the Sasquatch is a monster or a wild animal at best. They are wrong.

"I believe there are many people such as myself who are not threatened by the unknown, and that makes them prime candidates to be of assistance to these Sasquatch "people." Before I met Teluke, some of my friends and I stopped by a house in Beech Grove, Indiana, where they were building a housing addition. I had never been to this house before, but had ridden my horse by, coming through the wood lot at the end of the dead-end street. My friends said that the people living there were somewhat weird and should be avoided, but at the time they had business there, so it was necessary to stop. As it turned out, the teenage boy was helping a Sasquatch man that lived in the wood lot. As we talked out in the driveway, the boy commented that he couldn't have us inside because he was taking care of some special people who would be afraid if we saw them.

"Being curious, I inquired about these people, and he told us they were Sasquatch. It caused a stir among us and we asked to meet them. When the boy called one out and he stepped around the corner of the house, it was immediately apparent that he was a human being, yet one could see right through him. I am not sure if we saw him with psychic ability through our third eye or whether he was an 'astral' ghost kind of apparition, but it was obvious to all of us that he didn't appear to be a dense flesh form like we were.

"I realized that this was the same 'man' who had ordered me and my horse out of the woods one day. When he stepped out for us all to see him, my friends got panicky and immediately wanted to leave. I didn't want to, but because I'd come with them, I had to either leave or walk home.

"As in my case, the Sasquatch this boy was helping was occupying a small wood lot—the remnant of what was at one time a forest—in which the plant life is reduced to such a degree that he didn't have the food or true shelter he once had. Earth people who are capable of dealing with this reality are then located by the occupants of UFOs to assist the Sasquatch as they need. This is my own first-hand experience, so I know it's true. But since that time, I have found there are a small percentage of people assisting the Sasquatch this way. These people are able to work with the Sasquatch because they recognize them to be a psychic people and not some monster. You don't hear about it because it necessitates privacy. If a person in a rural town was hand-feeding deer in his backyard, you wouldn't expect him to advertise it, either, for fear of hunters or public disturbance to them. It is counter-productive to interaction with the Sasquatch.

"I suppose it is my Native American background that allows me to view this parallel world as normal. Yet, because it is generally viewed as abnormal, it is further reason for silence. My people have always related to the "sky-beings" in UFOs and accepted non-ordinary realities as valid, and so things like shape-shifting and supernatural powers are just second nature to us. To tell people I have taken care of a Sasquatch family is hard enough to accept, but when you go telling them that you have been taken care of yourself by the Starpeople, well, who is going to believe you?

"Talking about this with close friends never really bothered me, but now that I have a few seasons behind me, I see that the truth doesn't depend on whether people believe you. That doesn't change the truth.

"I guess it is time that I related this publicly because times are changing and things are different now. More people are having these experiences, and they need a healthy reference to support this new reality with which they are dealing, in order to assist the Sasquatch with their needs for food and shelter. There are less wooded areas and plant life diversity these days in the mid-west, and our assistance in these areas as well as our understanding is important for the Sasquatch to be able to survive.

"My association with Teluke and his family has made me hold to my priorities, to see what is truly important in life. It helped me to evaluate how we live and to choose a better path for myself. We have much to gain from sharing our Earth with the Sasquatch and learning to coexist with all our other-worldly neighbors.

"It was essential that I keep the Sasquatch family a secret to protect them. Though I know many good people, everyone has fear to some degree, and you get surprising results from even your most trusted friends when they are confronted with an unknown. I tried to keep my mouth shut, but it didn't work. I found myself still interacting with Teluke while others were around, which drew questions. Or I would have the explanations on hand relating to Teluke for the little mysteries that cropped up from time to time. So when Teluke asked me why I wouldn't talk to him in the barn one night, I explained: 'These people have two ways of seeing. One way, the way they generally live each day, is just about completely blind and deaf to your psychic world. They don't see or hear anything. Just once in a while they may get a glimpse into your world, and it scares them. There are a few of us who can and willingly do see into your world with little or no fear. I am one of them. But I am supposed to keep you a secret. It is too easy to make a mistake when others are around and reveal your presence. So when anybody else is around, I purposely let myself be blind and deaf, like they are, to protect you. I simply didn't allow myself to acknowledge that I saw your world last night. I wasn't aware of you.'

"When people physically see a material Sasquatch, it is indeed a rare and honored incident. I was only allowed a few brief glimpses of Teluke and his family in his physically visible form. For most of the year I viewed him using my "second attention," through what most people refer to as psychic abilities. We all have access to this second attention, but few people allow themselves to translate it down into the conscious mind. It was basically a matter of believing myself that what I was seeing was real. When we said good-bye at the end of the year, he was fully material in this dimension, standing before me. I shook hands with him, and we both cried. It was worth believing myself that he was not of my imagination. I had a privilege few people on Earth have ever had. I'm not out to prove anything to anyone, and, though some people would like to ridicule me for stating my experience, all I can tell them is they can find out for themselves by not dismissing everything as imagination and give believing themselves a good chance to pan out. The Sasquatch are interdimensional people and can be interacted with if you open up a little and let go of fear. Simply allow yourselves to play around with this psychic stuff that is so easily dismissed as imagination. I'm *not* fabricating anything.

"Many of the same problems come up for Bigfoot researchers as those experienced by UFO investigators. This parallel world will fool the senses if one operates on this (everyday) awareness alone. But we all have a second attention, or subconscious awareness, that processes information into the conscious mind. It is always up to the individual whether this information is accepted or not. It is based on one's level of fear and love. It's kind of like whether your right hand wants to know what your left hand is doing, but in this instance it's your mind.

"In my case, I lived with four other people at the time who wouldn't allow themselves to know about the Sasquatch. So I frequently 'short-circuited' this second attention that saw and understood the complete picture, thus remaining as consciously ignorant as everybody else in order to keep my Sasquatch family a secret. With this second attention short-circuited, I had no awareness at all of the Sasquatch because very little had been validated with my physical senses. All of our conversations were telepathic, that is, going directly into each other's heads, bypassing the organs of the ear altogether. So I could somewhat hide the information from myself simply by not acknowledging it as real—a trick everyone does without realizing it.

"My father-in-law and husband were too frightened to consciously deal with this nonordinary reality. One day Pop was renovating the barn and Teluke came in to be with me for awhile. As Teluke and I talked, Pop's second attention picked up our telepathic conversation. He was relaxed and that's when it's easily picked up. Pop asked me what I was saying and stuck his head out of the stall. What his second attention saw shocked him and he telepathed, 'Oh, it's him! I don't want anything to do with it,' while he nervously laughed and said, 'Oh, I thought you said something,' then made himself scarce to our presence while Teluke and I conversed. He wouldn't acknowledge the information on the conscious level that was translated from his second attention.

"My husband loved the movies about Sasquatch and was interested in it, but he was much too frightened on a deep level to be able to handle anything consciously. So when I needed his ignorant cooperation in order to taxi the Sasquatch in the pickup truck once, I had to prepare him for it by speaking to him telepathically on this second attention level.

"'You know how you have always loved Bigfoot?' I asked him through this psychic mind transference. 'Well, I have been keeping a secret, and I need your help. I am taking care of a Sasquatch family and they want to go swimming with us.'

"'What? You know I can't be part of anything like that! I'm too scared!' he replied telepathically with great anxiety.

"But I explained that he didn't have to let himself know about it and, in this way, he could be a part of it too! Taking stock of himself, he realized this conversation was taking place without his conscious knowledge of it, so he was delighted. I had succeeded in gaining his ignorant cooperation through the unconscious mind.

"When Teluke and his wife and child came up to the truck, my husband awakened. Teluke only had three toes and my husband couldn't handle this. His body showed extreme signs of stress, so I broke his awareness by speaking verbally to him about needing to 'do something first.' I went over to put the tailgate down for them to get in. In a normal state of consciousness there seemed no reason to do this; however, this act drew his attention back into the physical realm. Because his second attention understood, he didn't question me and said, 'Oh yeah,' and got into the truck and ignored us totally.

"On the way to the lake, my husband's body was fretful, and he kept wanting to look into the rearview mirror. He didn't consciously know why, but it was causing him great physical anxiety. So I telepathically told him, 'Here, I'll help you forget about them,' and I took the rearview mirror and twisted it so that he couldn't see into it. Again, this would have normally been questioned, but his second attention understood. He telepathically thanked me for taking care of him. His conscious ignorance was very important to his mental stability and well being.

"This same attention that is separated by a kind of blindness and deafness is why UFO abductees feel their mind has been erased. It hasn't been. It is a built-in safety valve to protect our fragile minds. Once the unknown has been accepted on some important level of our psyche, we allow ourselves to remember. This is what is meant when the ETs tell us we will die if we don't forget the encounter. It is too great a shock for us to handle because of our rigid belief systems at that time. Our reality is only held together by a thin fabric of beliefs.

"If a person is traumatized by the memory of an encounter, he is still within his own safety limits. He simply swallowed a larger piece of information than was comfortable. Only time allows for the proper digestion in the psyche needed to make the information palatable to the individual's own makeup or belief system.

"This nonordinary reality can be shut off to the senses from internal or external sources. Thus, it is a fact that UFOs are sometimes seen by some witnesses and not by others, yet they are visibly present to all. Still, they, like the Sasquatch, can be fully viewed by the senses when they are within our realm of this physical world, and that is up to them.

"Teluke explained to me that he goes into another world or dimension when he is invisible, but they cannot stay for long periods of time. Ultimately they belong to this world, our three-dimensional world. The Starpeople also share this other dimension with the Sasquatch. Teluke told me the Starpeople would come for him if he called for them. I didn't believe this until it happened and I saw it for myself. This same telepathic communication that existed between the ETs and Teluke also existed between myself and the UFO occupants, but it was more difficult for me to be aware of them until recently.

"One must realize that telepathing is the transference of information, and it is not limited to conversation. It includes feeling along with hearing and seeing. Through this, Teluke and I often shared one another's eyes. If he wished to show me something that I could not see for myself, he would look at it for me, then project the image, and I would view it from his eyes telepathically. Likewise, when he wanted to know how we get hot water but it was questionable as to whether the basement stairs would hold him, I went down and looked at it for him and asked if he could see it, which he acknowledged. We did the same thing a few times when he felt a new sensation. I too experienced the newness he felt in his body, even though my senses had learned to take it for granted. I reexperienced things for the first time in this way with him.

"This wonderful quality is part of the reason they are successful in evading the Bigfoot hunter. There is nothing mysterious to me when you (the author of this book) reported that the Sasquatch use hawks and crows as sentinels. They are simply taking a bird's-eye view of a situation they do not wish to get too close to...quite a good reason why so few are encountered by the Bigfoot enthusiasts who refuse to open up to the psychic side of these phenomena.

"This way of sharing allows them all to partake in the knowledge of one individual. A code of ethics is present, though, that unless you are being spoken to, you generally are not to listen. It is merely impolite to invade this code, but it happens. So by keeping one's thoughts to oneself, provided others are respecting the code, your private thoughts remain your own. I found this proved Teluke to be polite. At the lake he was so polite that he could shut out verbal conversation as well, thus he remained ignorant of the dangers that were mounting. He wasn't paying attention to the words of panic that he could have been aware of. He was minding his own business. On the conscious level, the public at the lake could only acknowledge them as bears and when it was announced over the loudspeakers for the management to bring a gun down there, Teluke never heard it. I had to tell him what was going on because of his politeness in minding his own business.

"If he spoke to his mate, I may or may not be included to listen to it. But he, being more adept with it, was better at shutting others out of conversations than I was. If he experienced something new, his mate could share the feelings right along with him without having the actual experience herself. Thus a mass knowledge can be shared by the Sasquatch people by opening this telepathic channel, which to them is a way of life.

"I found this way of interacting a joyous blessing to be exposed to. It was so useful and thrilling, giving one a whole new range of opportunities while sharing this way. It created a bond between the three of us that secures a person in a way that our naive society doesn't know of.

"Regarding the general safety of people being around Sasquatch, what I found was this: Like anyone having been harassed and chased from the safety of their home, it is hard not to be protective. We don't like it when the city forces us to move from our homes because they want to put a freeway there. Imagine having this done constantly and for all generations of your people to the point of having little food or shelter, when you once had everything at your disposal. There is a certain kind of greed that makes some people feel they can displace others, even if means genocide.

"American capitalism has given us a poor reputation by our using up valuable resources throughout the entire planet. The Sasquatch don't trust us or care to be around us any more than they have to. Trust is hard won by them, especially if the particular Sasquatch in question has been previously harassed.

"If one would notice, the reports show that Bigfoot may scream around a house, kill some livestock or dogs (which likely harassed them) leave something dead in the yard, throw rocks, or tear stuff up, but they are smart enough and positively strong enough that if they were going to do a body harm, they would! But the creatures don't. They prefer to be intimidating rather than violent to get their point across, even when shot at.

"In my encounters with Teluke, he quite often tried to bully me at the beginning of our association and often threatened to kill me. I guess because of some natural innocence in me, I trusted in the goodness I saw in him to believe that as long as *I* didn't threaten him, he would have no reason to follow through with his threat. I never received more than a snarling reprimand.

"He was generally very reasonable socially, and the times he was not, I was allowed to press the issue. For instance, when he was disgusted with me at first, he moved the force field barrier from one-third of the pasture (which the horses wouldn't graze in and the birds in the woods didn't frequent anymore) to include not just the whole pasture, but the whole farm. Then he demanded that I get off *his* land. He was being unreasonable and we both knew it, so I stayed put and even backtracked to resume the space in which I had originally placed myself within the edge of his reasonable barrier. But I didn't have to cross the line to know when not to push him either. Common sense determined for me if he had reason to carry out his threat. Making him mad wasn't enough, I found out.

"He claimed the small wood lot as his, and I was not allowed in it. It was the only wooded area in the vicinity. I respected him this way. When I needed firewood, he would get it for me and dump it over the back fence to keep me from intruding. There was one time when I was forced to press him when he insisted he would kill me. It took a great deal for him to reach the point of actual contact, and obviously he still didn't kill me.

"In spite of his snarling attacks and threats, he was a good person, and I knew it instinctively. He was merely just leery of people, and I couldn't blame him. I could see in his actions that it wasn't in him to hold on to malice or anger as we do. When an upset was over, it was as though it never happened to him. He kept his heart clean this way. Teluke once told me, 'I am just a human being like you are who wants to be left alone and take care of my family!' He was 99% bluff, but I weathered some pretty rough gales to discover this. But it takes common sense and respect to maintain this safety margin. Any fool can go get themselves killed, though Sasquatch are not killers. They are rational people and only want us to be as well.

"I was often attacked in the beginning with a roaring snarl when I broke our code of ethics by looking him in the eye. Anyone can expect to be swiftly reproached if they threaten their safety. The only reason to run away is in respect to their wishes. They run like the wind, so if it is their desire to harm, running is no guarantee of safety.

"Teluke threatened to kill me many times, but it was always when the attention was on them personally. Otherwise, we interacted together peacefully. I finally asked him if he had ever killed anyone and he said no, but he was willing to change that if it had to be. He remained extremely protective of his wife and child.

"They enjoyed humor. Laughter in the barn always brought them up. We were their source of entertainment. Any sound of merriment attracted them, yet he said they do not like our social parties because of the stuff we drink that makes us crazy.

"He loved children and babies of any kind. He showed a feminine kind of gentleness and empathy toward them that was heartwarming to watch. I do not feel people should worry about harm coming to their children from a Sasquatch. They appreciate the innocence of children; I guess because they share that innocence. They likely wouldn't bother stealing one because they generally don't like our people, yet they would still show kindness to a child. That's just the kind of beautiful people they are.

"Anatomically, Teluke was the most beautiful creation I had ever seen. I even told him that God had really made something when He made him! Though it doesn't do him justice at all to say it like this, he was a man in a gorilla's body. Looking into his gorilla-like face, I was always struck with genuine awe to see a human man looking out through his eyes. There was a human being hidden inside a gorilla's vessel that was wholly revealed in his eyes. His mouth hinted at his humanness and his nose was clearly a mixture of the two. He was gorgeous! To this day I am left in awe of the beauty of his creation.

"He seemed top heavy because of a muscular hump on his shoulders where a neck would normally be. He had hackles down his back that looked like a mane when it stood up. He only had three toes that were pretty much of equal size, and he was not a large man for a Sasquatch. He stood just a little over six feet tall. My husband was exactly six feet tall, and Teluke wasn't much taller than my husband.

"His torso was muscular and plump like a gorilla's, yet not overly so as to distract from his humanness. His arms and legs were bulging with muscles and were well proportioned like that of a human being. His wrists and ankles were large, giving him a stocky appearance. He was bipedal like us.

"His eyes were blue and his hair was white, except for around the knees where it was yellowed from use. His hair was roughly three inches long in most places and felt like an Irish Setter's silky coat. The hair on his face was shorter and pretty much covered the same areas as a normal man who didn't have much of a beard. It came to the sides of his face and not so much to the front. His head was somewhat pointed on top, giving him an odd appearance from the front where his humanness seemed most apparent. From the sides he also looked human, but there was an angle from the waist up when you were standing close to him that could look extremely gorilla-like. He had no neck, which added to his uniqueness. His teeth were like human teeth and proportionately larger and very white. His canine teeth were slightly larger also. His ears were small and gorilla-like and fuzzy, as I recall.

"As we came to enjoy each other's company, he seemed like a best friend and a beloved pet all in one. He was a joy for me to be around on every level. As Teluke came to enjoy my company, it was extremely rewarding to me. The treasure I gained in the association was a wonderful reward for the small price of believing that I wasn't imagining him. But I was never beyond reproach. When he snarled and growled, it came with the authenticity of a savage animal. He was quite impressive, and he got the point across perfectly.

"Interestingly, he and his mate could run on all fours like a dog. I'm not sure, but sometimes I would think I saw a tail when they did this. Possibly this was part of the shape-shifting ability when will and intent are powerfully enacted by their imagination. His legs seemed to somehow disappear

The White Sasquatch

*Teluke, a white Sasquatch, as sketched by White Song Eagle.*
*©1998, White Song Eagle*

from the knee to the hips when he ran on all fours. I asked him to show me what he did with his legs. He bent down to demonstrate it and his knee to hips seemed to run parallel to his body, while his body rested between his thighs. He explained that, "you put your leg in that place," assuming I knew what he was talking about. I asked him if he meant that it locks into some place and he acknowledged this. I told him we can't do that as our bodies are built differently.

"Therefore, I assume they use only the knee down for this way of travel. It looked wonderfully exciting to be able to do. They bounded through the pasture like huge bears or playful dogs. Also, their feet seemed to transform when doing this. I could never tell for sure, but instead of seeing long appendages at the end of each limb, there seemed to be a shorter, round kind of paw. Once he playfully bounded up to me by surprise and knocked me backward accidentally when he put his rough pads of these 'paws' on my face. It happened so quickly that I didn't have time to be afraid. But seeing them run on all fours was probably the most frightening of anything to me. It was just so alien that I wasn't sure what I was seeing. It appeared bruin-like, yet doglike. Other times he almost resembled a lion to some degree when he ran on all fours. I did get used to it eventually, as trust was gained between us.

"They were semi-nocturnal, and when it got dark outside they were always disappointed to see me go inside. We stood outside talking one evening as it got dark and he asked me why I was hitting myself. I told him the bugs were eating me alive and I had to go in. I asked him if they didn't bother him and he said no. A can of repellent remedied the situation, the smell of which neither of us like, but it allowed me to stay out longer, which we both appreciated. They stay up quite late and sleep in until mid-morning. Once I rose early and telepathed to the back lot, asking if I could come up to his place for a visit. He told me to go away because they were still sleeping and he would come up to the barn later.

"Though I desperately wanted to interact with his mate, Teleel, and their baby, he caused her to feel I might steal their child, so she was easily frightened of me then. But off and on we were able to speak to each other, and Teleel and I understood each other wonderfully on a respectful women's level. It may be difficult to believe, but his mate was not the gorilla type, but looked like a beautiful woman with a shaggy hair cut wearing a fur coat. She was as tall as Teluke, had dimples, brown eyes, a clean feminine nose, and gorgeous lips. She had a round tummy and the average 'saddlebags' that most women have.

"They explained that there are two types of their people, meaning a gorilla type and a more human type. Sometimes they take mates with each other. Teluke had a clean skunk odor to him most of the time, which was not strong when he was invisible. When he had strong emotions, whether anger, love or fear, it smelled like strong garbage. He said he didn't know why, but "all the men smell like this." I asked him if the women smell that way also and he said no, just the men. And, indeed, when I was able to get real close to Teleel, she had a fresh, clean smell to her—a sweetness something above a clean house pet. They said that all of their women are beautiful like she was.

"Their baby was probably the most gorgeous child I had ever seen. She had huge brown eyes and was beautiful by any standards. She had brown fuzzy hair on her ears and silky hair all over her. She was, as her mother was, the human type of Sasquatch rather than a gorilla type as her father was. At the age of one year, she was the size of a two- or three-year- old human child. And since they communicate by telepathy, they 'speak' earlier than human children.

"They are capable of verbal speech but do not practice it. Teluke wanted me to teach him this 'talking with the mouth,' as it intrigued him. So, as I stood out in the pasture, it was only my belief that someone was there that caused me to interact with him. To my senses, I was verbally talking to thin air. I just didn't let my senses fool me. I had him watch my mouth as I said the word 'mother,' and had him try it. Because my eyes saw no one there, when my ears heard his verbal attempt to pronounce his first word, it was so absurd to my ears and such a shock that I broke out laughing, not at him but at the situation. It embarrassed him and he would not try it again in front of me. But he reported later to me that he and his mate have a lot of fun learning to speak with the mouth back at their place. I asked him what words they were saying and he said 'shit' and 'God damn it,' etc. I was appalled that he chose the barn language first. He asked what it meant. I told him that if he didn't know what it was, then he shouldn't say it. I suggested they practice saying, 'I love you,' or 'may I help you' to each other instead.

"During the course of the year, we did many things together. Though they were invisible to the eye, there is a method of seeing that does allow us to view them if we are able to accept it when it is translated into the conscious mind. They retain weight and mass while invisible. When we went swimming, his invisible body created a hole in the water that was a perfect mold of his anatomy. He still left footprints while unseen, and I could feel him with my hands as well as feel him touch me in his concealed state, just as I would anyone else who was physically visible.

"There is a great deal about these people to be shared. I have written as much as is reasonable about this entire year of close interaction with Teluke and his family in my forthcoming book. Most of it I am sure few people know. If it is nonsense to some people, it is balanced by one incident that will strike truth into the hearts of some Native Americans who know. The Sasquatch are in constant communion with the Creator. We shared this spiritual subject on a deep level.

"I realize it sounds absurd to think a Sasquatch can be living in a rural setting, but it's true. It happened to me, and it happened to that boy I met briefly with my friends, and I'm sure with many others around the country as well. I have had other such encounters with these people and in some of the most unexpected places. I'm not out to prove anything to anyone. All I can say is that if you want to know and are serious, you can encounter these people just by putting yourself right, in heart and mind, and explore the outdoors more. If they weren't in your wood lot before, it can pay to go check again, because they can be dropped off by the ETs from their spacecraft anywhere for brief periods of time. I feel if your heart is right and strong, that's all it takes to be included in the lives of the elusive Sasquatch."

# Terror In The Midlands

*OVERVIEW*

In the early 1980s, a tiny rural community in Michigan was besieged by Bigfoot and UFO sightings with several close encounters, and paranormal incidents. The uniqueness of their presence was viewed with fear because the Sasquatch that plagued these farm families, seemingly without reason, became belligerent and destructive. However, no human was attacked or harmed in any way during this time.

Because of occasional reports about Bigfoot killing livestock and domestic animals, and periodic threatening behavior without apparent provocation, I am including this chapter to cover the negative aspects experienced by some witnesses and the events that possibly precipitated the hostile action. Here, we must also look for potential reasons from the creature's standpoint, not ours. In addition, it is important to know that not all Sasquatch "instinctively" act the same way in every situation or encounter. There are deranged, misguided, and hostile people living among the "norms" in our society. So too, we must expect an occasional maverick among the Sasquatch people, especially given that they are surrounded by human beings who are ostentatiously aggressive toward the unknown.

Throughout this book I seek to diminish Bigfoot's stereotypical image, while at the same time presenting what I believe to be the truth. At times Bigfoot behavior resembles that of a brutish animal—for that capacity is surely there with some creatures, no less than the good, bad, and indifferent that characterize all world societies from New York City to the Amazon rainforest.

*EPISODE*

It was in the fall of 1981 that I began interviewing the family. Their story started with a series of disturbing events that completely disrupted their lives. The domestic cows and horses became uneasy and nervous. For a time, no one knew why the animals were so skittish. During the day and early evening, the ducks and geese were also restless and noisy. The family felt as if they were being watched by an unseen presence that left a certain eeriness over the farm.

Then the family noticed that the apples in the tree in the front yard were beginning to dwindle. Within a week every apple had disappeared, even the ones on the ground. They immediately suspected a bear, but no claw marks were found on the tree.

Soon a metal pole that was firmly implanted in the ground near the barn was completely twisted off at the base. A thorough inspection of the ground for clues proved fruitless. No sign of the vandal could be found. They wondered who had the strength to do such a thing. There was no indication that a hacksaw was used.

The mystery continued. A week later they awoke to discover their wire fence mangled and several fence posts pulled neatly out of the earth. This time the culprit left a clue. Fourteen-inch, human-like footprints were found in the soil. The Department of Natural Resources (DNR) was immediately contacted, and an official was sent out to investigate. After talking with the owners, who presented the evidence and described the inexplicable happenings, the official announced that the culprit was "a bear." This finding startled the people, because no bear tracks had ever been found. Still the DNR representative insisted it was a bear, dismissing all the evidence. Yet it was impossible for such a bear to vandalize the property in the manner in which it had been done. No explanation was given as to how a bear could "twist off" a metal pole, pull out fence posts, or climb a tree without leaving claw marks. This very point was adamantly argued, and, after a souring debate, the official left.

The following night, the lock on the grain bin cover in the barn was twisted off. The lock had been broken, the grain had been sampled, and some of the meal had been spilled on the floor. Nothing else was touched, and no animals were harmed. That same night the woman who lived at the farm and two of the children heard an unusual growling sound just outside the house but were afraid to go out to investigate.

Then one day they saw it! The intruder was six-and-a-half feet tall, 250 to 300 pounds, standing at the edge of the barn. The family was terrified! Now they knew what was at the crux of the mysterious happenings. But the whole matter was perplexing. What was such a creature doing on an American Midwest farm land?

The scary growling sounds continued intermittently at night, close to the house. At times the farm animals were spooked without apparent reason and became difficult to handle. The mother of the family told me that the children began having nightmares about a big hairy "monster" attacking and kidnapping them. Heavy stress, worry, and fear began plaguing everyone. A constant uneasiness hung over the entire household.

In time, relatives, close friends, and neighbors of the family became aware of what was going on and some became instant skeptics. The experiences did not sound logical or real, and some people laughed at the whole matter. An 18-year-old nephew was one of the skeptics who quickly altered his way of thinking when he personally encountered the Sasquatch for himself. One of his cousins saw it standing in the field during the day—bold behavior indeed for an elusive Sasquatch in rural America. The teenager grabbed a shotgun and ran to the edge of the barn. Before that time, he had rationalized the phenomenon with excuses that it was simply a troublesome bear. There, in the middle of the field, between the barn and woods, was a strange being that resembled both ape and man. Its head was raised skyward, seemingly preoccupied with its thoughts and unaware that it was being observed. (Paradoxically, in spite of their keen elusiveness, on rare occasions the Sasquatch apparently lets down its guard and briefly reveals itself at a time one least expects.) The startled young man was impressed with its bulk and musculature. Fearful that he was slightly out of range and might wound the man-creature, the youth fired a round up in the air to scare it away. Instead, the surprised Bigfoot was so startled that both feet left the ground. In apparent anger at being caught off guard with a loud bang disrupting its tranquility, the Sasquatch turned, and with great speed and agility, ran at the daring young man. The perpetrator became unnerved by what appeared to be an attack and bolted for the house as fast as he could run. Once on the porch, he turned with gun in hand to face his adversary, but there was nothing in sight. The creature lurked somewhere between the barn and the woods, out of view of the young antagonist.

After this episode the press somehow discovered the story. Insensitive reporters called, pretending to understand the problem, promising not to divulge the name of the family, but instead made them look like fools by sensationalizing the bizarre happenings in the newspaper. They were furious! To make matters worse, because their name had been made public, vehicles of armed men began driving up and down their long driveway. A "private property" sign was erected warning intruders to keep out, but it was completely ignored and numerous pick-up trucks carrying gun-toting hunters using spotlights continued to boldly invade their privacy. Everyone wanted to bag a Sasquatch. The place became a carnival of activity because of the press and consequent public reaction to these reports. The family agonized while sharing this story with me.

To add to the intensity and weirdness, other inexplicable happenings exacerbated their frazzled emotions. At night the four-year-old son would wake his mother, saying he had just spoken with a man in his room. When the mother would investigate, finding no one in the child's room, she would put him back to bed and check the rest of the house. Each time this happened, she was panic-stricken to discover a glowing white basketball-sized sphere floating around the living room.

"It appeared to be a controlled intelligence recognizing me as I entered the room. Other times, the sphere would not be present, but instead a brilliant blinding light would be coming from immediately outside the house. This frightened me, and I ran in the bedroom and attempted to wake my husband, but he always sleeps so hard that he only mumbled and stayed asleep. He's always been that way. I'd jump into bed, throw the covers over me, and say the 'Our Father' over and over again until I fell asleep. It was terrifying!" the witness reported. I asked her if she tried to communicate with the spherical object, but she said she was too panic stricken.

She also added that on some nights, though no sphere was observed, after her son was awakened by a mysterious man—one must consider the possibility that the boy could have been dreaming—an unexplained breeze would blow into the room, disrupting the curtains and clothes hanging about, as if someone had just opened the front door. Later, she would sneak around the house and check the front door, only to discover that it was firmly locked from the inside. This frightened her even more and her husband began accusing her of hallucinating due to stress and fear. By then the entire household was in a quandary. Everyone was in a dreadful state of panic, and no one knew what to do about it. With all of these anomalous events occurring, they never knew what would happen next.

When I spoke to the teenage daughter, she said she had seen the Sasquatch on several occasions, once within 50 feet. Her first "impression" was that it was a young creature that was lonely and needed companionship. She was convinced it could intelligently communicate with her. But the hairiness and appearance of the creature scared her to a degree that these feelings repelled her effort. She was so appalled that she usually turned away, not wanting to look at its face.

The family's religious beliefs accentuated their anguish, and the problem soon became even more out of hand than it was in the beginning. They no longer saw it as an invasion by a hairy giant. In an effort to explain why they were chosen as the object of harassment, they sought counsel from their church. No one could give them an adequate solution to the social malady that had raised so much havoc in their lives. Therefore, they began to examine the spirit realm for their much-needed answer.

Their well meaning priest tried to convince them that they had somehow sinned deeply and were being visited by Satan in the form of a hairy "devil" that would harass them until the family repented. Soon after, a man telephoned them, fanatically bellowing with religious fervor that they indeed were in the midst of the devil himself! This phone call sent the woman over the edge. She began having bouts of depression and feelings of doom so intense that she told me she feared a total breakdown. I requested a visit with the family immediately so that I could put the matter in a perspective void of unnecessary fear, letting them know that the creature was not a harmful being from the Nether World, but an innocuous creature with as much curiosity about them as they had toward it. Yet I could not explain its occasional destructive nature around the property or the intimidating manner in which it presented itself.

The woman of the house gave me the fire-and-brimstone man's telephone number to call, saying she knew he was correct in his evaluation and wanted to prove to me that he was right. She insisted I should hear his opinion. When the man answered the phone and began talking in a masterfully "controlled" voice using fear in a sensational religious vernacular, I was immediately overwhelmed with the feeling that I was speaking to a potentially dangerous person. He was an extremist! His emphasis about what he believed in relation to Bigfoot was almost "militant" and full of hate. The man's projected negativity literally sent chills up my spine. Now I could fathom why this emotionally vulnerable woman was so injected with the fear of Satan after listening to this negative proselytizer. I did not believe a word he said because of the numerous pleasant and loving experiences I have had with the Sasquatch people. It is really these close encounters with the fanatics that are dangerous and confusing to percipients who are trying to sort out what is real and what is not so they can make some kind of sense out of all this.

Finally the ultimate intimidation occurred. A teenage daughter went out one night to feed the goats. While feeling around for the light switch in the barn, she laid her hand on something furry and matted. Heavy breathing could be heard and a strange moldy stench overwhelmed her nostrils. When the lights went on, she stood face to face with the giant apelike creature that had been stalking the house. It was Bigfoot—Sasquatch! The terror-stricken girl ran to the house, screaming wildly, and immediately went into shock!

Shortly after the incident, the woman of the house reported that an inexperienced Michigan Bigfoot "hunter" arrived, advocating violence. He announced that he would rid her of the problem by lying in wait and shooting the man-creature with a silver bullet he had fashioned. (Sadly, the delusional hunter fallaciously equated Bigfoot with a fictional werewolf. Apparently, he had watched too many monster movies.) This proposal further confused the housewife as to the true nature of the being. She speculated to me: Was it a man-beast with a soul, or a supernatural entity from hell? Though the family could not decide, they did not want murder on their conscience, she said. The husband ordered the Bigfoot hunter to leave. Not long after, all anomalous activity abruptly stopped. All that was left were emotional scares and nightmares with the fear that it might start up again at any time.

There is another case involving aggression in the upper midwest. Patty and Kim Brehm and their cousin Dave of Racine, Wisconsin, visited the family cabin for a weekend. It was located in a remote region of north-central Wisconsin. While on a walk by a pond, they encountered a white Sasquatch which growled and grunted from the forest and ran with incredible speed from tree to tree. It was estimated to be approximately seven feet tall, weighing at least 300 to 400 pounds. The two young women became emotionally upset and frightened by this encounter and ran to the cabin. The creature pounded on the door and walls of the cabin intermittently for two days and even shattered a window but never followed through by breaking in. Yet the three were terrified, convinced it wanted to kill them.

When interviewing Dave, I asked him if he initially threatened the creature in any way by throwing rocks at it or attempting to shoot at it with a gun. He said: "No, that's just it, we never did anything to the creature to hurt it." I asked him what his first thoughts were upon seeing the Bigfoot. He replied "Oh, if I'd had a gun I would have shot it."

That probably was the reason for the Sasquatch aggression. I explained to Dave that the creatures are profoundly psychic and can read a person's mind easily. Dave's thinking he wanted to kill it was in reality telling the Sasquatch he wanted to. His negative thoughts were unknowingly projected, and it angered the creature. It is no different from walking up to a huge man hiking in the woods and saying to him: "Your size and looks frighten me; if I had a gun I'd shoot you!" Try it some time. Threaten a large man, and you might well get a punch in the nose. Nobody likes to be threatened, not even a giant Sasquatch. The creature apparently overreacted, but this report should give additional insight into why some Sasquatch react with aggression. Like attracts like. Think kind thoughts when in Bigfoot territory, because they can monitor your mind. To these highly sensitive nature beings, you *are* what you think. Indeed, you represent what your thought vibrations project to *all* living things in your environment.

Another odd and unnerving episode took place in southwest Wyoming in August, 1983. Two young men in their early twenties were motorcycling when a 10-foot-tall Sasquatch "appeared." It approached the two as the driver desperately tried to get the engine started. Once it did, the creature, with startling agility, ran beside them, nearly running in front of the motorcycle. The driver, fearing an accident, quickly stopped. The giant simply stood there looking curious. Twice again it chased them, forcing the driver to stop. The men were upset over the creature's playfulness. Because of its size and speed, they could not predict what it would do next.

In February 1981, I spent two weeks in the Montana Rockies at a wilderness cabin where the residents told me that the Sasquatch frequently visit the area. The first night there, I set up my tent a half mile behind the log cabin, deep in the forest. For the next two nights I heard a loud unidentified howling screech as one creature called to another, which answered from the other ridge. When I mimicked the sounds to the property owners, they insisted it was a Sasquatch. I have heard the Sasquatch make a range of vocal sounds but never this particular one. The people played a tape of growling and grunting sounds recorded from an open window. They insisted there were four creatures that visited periodically and always came when one of the three women in the household had her monthly period. It was then that the muttering growls became louder and the Bigfoot came closer. No threats or harm ever came to the family. They viewed the Sasquatch as people, not as animals, and came to enjoy their visits.

One incident involved their son on horseback chasing a Sasquatch, which eluded the boy when it dematerialized as it started to climb at the base of a cliff. Another encounter they related concerned three young men who purchased an 80-acre lot adjoining theirs. The men had worked in Alaska for years, and they planned to build a large cabin deep in the mountains. Soon after setting up a temporary camp with large tents, they heard sounds like a giant man walking about in the night. Rifles were kept close to their sleeping bags. Then one day two of the men went into town, 45 miles away to buy supplies. The third man, left alone, lounged in his tent, clothed only in his underwear. Suddenly, he heard the thumping of heavy footsteps. Barefoot, the man stepped from his tent and observed a 10- to 12-foot Sasquatch walking toward him. Though a rifle was leaning against the tree beside him, he was so ruffled by the sight of the giant that he merely turned and ran. Later his companions found him waiting for them miles from the encampment on an old dirt road. When they returned to where they were bivouacked, much of their equipment was scattered around. Telltale footprints in the soil showed where a giant "man" had been walking about. One quick arm-load of their belongings was all they grabbed, leaving several hundred dollars worth of sleeping bags, tents and cookware behind. Shortly thereafter, the locals noticed the property was up for sale, and the three men have never been seen again. Three separate neighbors living at the edge of the 80-acre parcel independently related the same story.

The Sasquatch can be territorial, as in this case, perhaps because a mate is nearby raising young, or the area is a major feeding ground, or perhaps an area where they are doing mining work for ETs. From what I learned, they migrate frequently but have one or two home territories where they feel safe enough to raise young and live without intrusion. If a person innocently invades their territory, the Sasquatch will promptly scare the trespasser off without bodily harm.

# Sasquatch In The Pickle Patch

*OVERVIEW*

The following report occurred in Wisconsin at the edge of an Indian reservation, and is actually three separate Bigfoot stories in one. It is about: (1) the Smart brothers, (2) the Polanski family, and (3) my own encounter. All are interrelated.

The first is about Tom Smart and his brother, Ted, who encountered a Sasquatch in 1978 while hunting deer in the wild woodlands of Wisconsin. The day after their experience, the Smart brothers met a family who had a remarkable experience with six Sasquatch in their pickle patch. The creatures visited their home from 1975 to 1978. These stories did not come to light until the summer of 1983 when the Smart brothers and I investigated this region and discovered the Bigfoot activity was still occurring.

*EPISODE*

In the fall of 1978, Tom and Ted were deer hunting in the Wisconsin woodlands, with approximately two inches of snow on the ground. They split up, and Tom began walking through the woods looking for deer spoor. A cold wind was blowing, and a snow flurry began. Tom looked up suddenly and saw a large 10-foot-high tree "stump" about 40 yards away that appeared awkward compared to the rest of the landscape. When Tom saw *hair* on the "stump" blow sideways in the breeze, he quickly realized he was looking at a living creature! As he focused on it, the head and shoulders of something huge became more visible. Just then large snowflakes began to fall during a sudden squall. As Tom squinted, he could see brown shaggy hair hanging over the face, covering all the creature's facial features. He quickly pulled up his gun and aimed at it but could not fire. Strangely, a voice told him, "Don't shoot." This startled him. He became paralyzed, almost frozen in time, gun to shoulder with no urge to pull the trigger. He was face-to-face with a creature he'd once read about known as Bigfoot. The statuesque creature was staring straight at him, never moving a muscle. Tom kept a bead on it with his rifle for a full fifteen minutes. Both remained motionless.

Then out of the corner of his eye, Tom could see something red moving through the trees about a hundred yards behind the creature. He soon realized it was his brother Ted, who, unbeknownst to Tom, had been following the Bigfoot tracks. Beside the tracks, sapling trees had been snapped off seven and eight feet above the ground. Within minutes, Ted saw the creature with Tom pointing his rifle at it. He noticed the broad shoulders of the giant, its back toward him, but he did not attempt to shoot. Because of Ted's concern for his brother's safety, he did not want to take an unnecessary risk. Ted then circled around the creature and joined Tom. Incredibly, the creature never moved!

The brothers' first words upon meeting were: "Let's get the hell out of here!" They quickly walked away, leaving the creature still standing in place. After walking about twenty yards, they became terror stricken by the sight of a dead deer with a stick grotesquely jammed through its neck. The head was twisted back in an unnatural position. There was no sign of a gun shot wound on the corpse.

The following day the Smart brothers visited the Polanski family, who lived on a tiny farm not far from where the incident had occurred. They had never met these people before, but a close friend in Milwaukee had insisted they stop to visit his good friends at the farm. He told the brothers that the family would tell them where the good hunting was in the area.

The people cordially invited the Smart brothers to come in, served them coffee, and began talking about the deer kill in their area that season. Then one of the family members mentioned how wild the virgin forest was at the edge of the Indian reservation. Ted jokingly commented: "Yes, that's real Bigfoot country out there." Instead of laughter, a silence fell over the room. The entire family abruptly stopped talking and began staring at Ted. The brothers were the only ones who chuckled. After the lull, the grandfather began to tell of the Sasquatch in their pickle patch. He said that over the last three years, starting at the end of July every summer until the first of September, a family of six Sasquatch would migrate from the forest of the Indian reservation and invade their garden. The size of these creatures ranged from as large as 11 feet tall down to as small as four feet in height. The only vegetables taken from the garden were cucumbers, which the

Smart family used to make pickles every year. At dusk, the farm folks would gather at the back windows and watch this family of Sasquatch come out of the woods and gather cucumbers. The children were especially thrilled by the sight. The brothers noticed that the old man kept referring to the Sasquatch as their "friends."

Then, to the brothers' amazement, the old man presented pictures of the creatures he had taken with his Instamatic camera. The brothers told me they were not very detailed pictures since they were taken at a distance, but they definitely showed a group of huge, hairy creatures milling around the garden at sundown.

In addition to examining topographical maps, it was important to me that I personally interview the witnesses and study the layout of the farm. The three of us drove northward from Milwaukee to visit the family. Arriving at our destination, we knocked at the door, and a woman answered whom the brothers did not recognize. We were informed that this new family had purchased the farm after the Polanski's grandfather had died. The grandmother had remarried, and the rest of the family had moved to a small town about 25 miles away.

When I cordially asked the woman if anything out of the ordinary had ever occurred on the property, she gave us an evasive glance and abruptly said, "No." I then asked if she or her family had seen any strange animals in the area. The woman appeared to immediately become suspicious of me and, after a cold stare, I received another coy "No."

I walked back to the car and took out a plaster-of-paris cast of a Sasquatch footprint. Presenting the 18-inch cast to her, I asked: "Have you ever seen a footprint like this around here before?" With a slip of the tongue, she blurted: "No, I haven't, but those damn things won't get into our garden anymore because we stopped planting one!" A look of embarrassment came over her and she quickly retreated into the house, slamming the door behind her.

We drove to the small town where the farm family had moved. Their name was not in the phone book. We started to make inquiries and, to our surprise, the first person we spoke with said the Polanski family lived a few doors down from them on the same street. When we knocked on the door, we found the family at home, and the three of us were invited to come in. I told them the reason for our visit was to hear their Sasquatch story firsthand. They immediately responded openly, relating the same details as the Smart brothers had previously given.

Two of the Polanski children were present, one a teenager, the other in his early twenties. The younger one said, "Mom, should we tell them about the two UFOs that landed beside the house the time the Sasquatch were eating in our garden?"

Mrs. Polanski explained that her father had planted extra rows of cucumbers to accommodate the creatures' large appetites. The family did not mind sharing their food and enjoyed having the Sasquatch around. One night, after the creatures finished feeding in the garden, two flying saucers about 35 feet in diameter landed approximately 75 feet from the house. The children were upstairs preparing for bed. Mrs. Polanski and the three children gathered by the bedroom window to view the spectacle. A door on one of the spacecraft opened and an eerie green light glowed from within. They expected a human form to emerge but nothing exciting happened. Moments later, the door closed and the two spacecraft departed. The family thought the occupants of the craft knew they were being observed, therefore did not disembark. I told Mrs. Polanski that I suspected something was still going on at their old farm. I wanted to return to explore the forest area around the farm for any signs of the creatures. Her son knew the area well and volunteered to accompany us.

The next day we drove to the boundary of the Indian reservation. We parked on an old dirt road about a half mile away from the farm, so as not to alert the present owner that I was still in the vicinity. The brothers explored one region while the young man and I explored another. Then we discovered a delapidated building in the forest with a dark gloomy cellar and ten-foot-high ceilings. We were startled by what sounded like deep asthmatic breathing. The "heavy" wheezing seemed to come from someone who took long, deep breaths. The breathing was eerie and unnatural, sounding like it was coming from a very large "person." My companion became frightened. The only way to quiet the young man was to leave. I had heard the sound once before when a Sasquatch walked up to my tent. A dozen other persons have also told me of hearing this type of heavy wheezing when encountering a Sasquatch. I had no doubt what the source of the sound was! I also had the haunting feeling that someone was spying on us.

Then, telepathically, the Sasquatch spoke to me. I could hear the voice in my head saying: "If you come back Tuesday night between eleven and one o'clock, a ship will be dropping off some of my people." I was so startled that I could not respond. I merely kept walking without saying a word to my companion. (Note that the creature knew something about time and trusted me enough to share the schedule information. It knew that I had good intentions and would not disrupt their activities. Such detail of time from a Sasquatch clearly demonstrates its humanness and cognitive abilities as a "human-type." Anthropologists need to redefine their definition of human.)

Because I had to return to my job in Milwaukee, I decided I would return the following weekend. I told the family that I "sensed" that a spaceship would be dropping off a group of Sasquatch on Tuesday night between eleven and one in the morning. I asked Mrs. Polanski not to share this information with anyone, that it should be kept in the strictest confidence. She agreed to this. However, in spite of our agreement she told several friends and neighbors. The Tuesday after I left, two carloads full of people drove the back roads into the early hours of the morning looking for Bigfoot.

While the group was driving in a forested area not far from the old farm house, they rounded a bend in the road and were excited to see what they described as a UFO sitting in the middle of a field. The craft was perfectly round and was emitting a dim, white luminescence. Mrs. Polanski's car was a short distance in front of the second vehicle, and, when she quickly pulled over to the side of the road, the flying saucer lifted off and flew out of sight. When the second car pulled in behind Polanski's, its beam spotlighted the field, revealing an eight- to ten-foot apelike creature running into the woods. There were a total of 11 witnesses in the two cars and everyone testified to the startling event! *There was no mistaking the circumstances. A Sasquatch was observed in direct association with a UFO, and 11 people verbally swore to it!* I spoke with each of the people from both automobiles the following weekend, and each one confirmed that this was absolutely true! Without a doubt, there is a Bigfoot/UFO connection.

The night after the encounter, four of the same witnesses went for a drive near the Indian reservation. They drove down a dead-end road by a stream and stopped the car. When they got out of the vehicle, they heard heavy footsteps at the edge of the woods. The four young men fanned out to look for the source of the footsteps. One of them reported to me that a voice in his head said to him, "I'm over here." When the young man looked across the stream, he saw a "big hairy thing" squatting behind a large bush. He ran back to tell his friends what he had seen, but when they returned the creature was gone.

When I arrived the following day, the witness took me to the place where he had encountered the psychic Sasquatch. In the thicket at the edge of the woods was an impression where something large had flattened the grass. Also in plain view were footprints of flattened grass leading from where the creature had been squatting. My weight and footsteps could not duplicate these footprints—they were large, far beyond my size. My investigation ended when numerous cars began driving through the area day and night hoping to get a glimpse of a Bigfoot. Apparently the news was out, and a monster hunt had begun. The Sheriff began stopping cars to ask what the people were doing, patrolling and parking along the country roads. This ruined the research in that area, and I did not return there that summer because of the increase in police surveillance and reports from local land owners of an influx of unfamiliar cars stopping in front of their property.

# Bigfoot In North Carolina

*OVERVIEW*

This report is another account that reinforces the concept that the Sasquatch interact with UFOs and their occupants. After reading a Bigfoot article in *UFO Report* several years ago, I began contacting some of the witnesses in an attempt to both verify the story and to obtain a more comprehensive picture of what had occurred. After contacting George Farrell (a pseudonym) he told me in confidence about the UFO aspect that was not mentioned in the article. Fear of ridicule in the tiny community where he lived kept him from revealing the entire story. The reported sightings happened not far from Charlotte, North Carolina, and all percipients asked that their names remain anonymous.

*EPISODE*

In the summer of 1978, in the Southern Appalachian Mountains, people began encountering a creature that is normally seen more frequently in the Pacific Northwest. As the sightings increased, a small-town community began to develop a fear of the huge creature because it seemed to arrive out of nowhere. It took a while for people to realize what they were seeing.

Generally, the bipedal entity was described as being hair-covered, black, between six and seven feet in height, and frightening to look at with long dangling arms and no hair on its face. Several witnesses reported mournful screams almost like a woman in distress, except for the high volume at which it was emitted. George Farrell and his wife had one sleepless night, claiming the creature bellowed at least two dozen terrifying screams close to their isolated house. Mr. Farrell did not investigate the matter because the horrifying sounds unnerved him. Usually the appearance of a person causes the Sasquatch to quickly leave. This reaction by the creature was reported several times in the mountain community. Yet, everyone was frightened by its monstrous appearance. "I agree with you, it isn't a threat to man," Mr. Farrell related. He felt it was only curious about people and how they lived.

The area is rural and the houses so closely built near woods that some of the witnesses encountered the Sasquatch less than 50 feet from their homes, observing it while looking out a window in sunny daylight. When a few daring residents in the area openly discussed their sightings with neighbors, other people began admitting that they too had experienced something out of the ordinary. It was also sighted from trucks and automobiles during the day. All who saw it made clear that it was no bear. On one occasion a woman reported that Bigfoot walked over to her car and looked at her through the window. Later she had a difficult time describing what she saw because it scared her to look directly at the creature. It was estimated that close to 15 people had encountered the creature that year.

George Farrell eventually sighted a Sasquatch in his backyard when he was working on the family car. First, ear-splitting high-pitched screams emanated from the nearby woods. When he investigated the source of the sound, he found a huge black creature looking directly at him. Moments later, it turned and walked into the woods and out of sight.

The night before Mr. Farrell's encounter, unbeknownst to him at that time, his wife also had an encounter in the back of the house, one, he says, she will never forget. Mrs. Farrell observed what she described as a "spaceship" with green lights on it. Oddly, there were reddish-orange flames coming out at the back side of the craft. "It was nearly noiseless except for a soft whirling sound," she reported. The object frightened her because it came straight at her as it glided just above tree line. "All at once it turned to the right and was gone," she related. Mrs. Farrell said it just disappeared and she could not figure out what happened to the craft. She decided not to tell anyone about the experience for fear of being ridiculed. Two days after the UFO incident, numerous country folk in the area began encountering Bigfoot where it had never been seen before.

Mr. Farrell explored the woods in his back lot and located a den into which the creature apparently crawled to sleep. Unusual hair about an inch in length and long slender footprints were found at the scene. The footprints were human-like except for their narrowness with an opposable toe almost at right angles to the foot, which is more suggestive of a nonhuman primate like a gorilla than a human one!

# Legend Of Medicine Mountain

*OVERVIEW*

Mark (not his real name), an Indian who lives in the Cascade Mountains of the Pacific Northwest, claims to have had numerous telepathic experiences with the psychic Sasquatch. He contacted me after reading an article I had written, and he wanted to share his story. Like other witnesses who experienced the creatures, this man wants to remain anonymous. The incident occurred in 1983 and 1984. I was fortunate in that I was able to personally verify his claims. Every two to three weeks for a period of five months, I camped on the property and experienced the same phenomena.

*EPISODE*

I visited an Indian family who were very perplexed over the experiences they had with Sasquatch and the Starpeople. When I met them, they were living in a cabin at the end of a dirt road at the edge of a wilderness area. They had been living there for nearly two years. From the very beginning they had heard a strange generator noise that would "churn" all through the night. Whenever Mark walked toward the generator sound, it would stop. He claimed that when he stood over a portion of rock in the forest that led down into a ravine, less than a half mile from his cabin, he would occasionally hear the clanking of machinery coming from *within the Earth!* There did not seem to be any caves or entrances in that area, so this was very confusing to him. During the day, when he put his ear down against one of the rocks, he swears he heard the shuffling of feet and occasional metallic clinking, as if someone were repairing a machine. Initially, this frightened Mark and he had decided not to share this information with anyone...until he read an article I had written.

On numerous occasions when Mark was cutting wood not far from his cabin, he had the distinct feeling that he was being watched, although he never saw anything. Occasionally when his wife was helping him, she would feel the same thing. One day, while he was hunting up in the mountains, he stopped to rest. He sat down on a stump and, holding his rifle, Mark scanned the area far below to see if any deer were in the vicinity. Suddenly, he was deeply startled when a voice in his head said: "Mark, lay the gun on the ground." He looked around but didn't see anyone. A gentle but firm voice requested, "Mark, I said lay the gun on the ground."

Looking high on the hill behind him, he saw what appeared to be a giant hairy man peering from behind some brush. Before he could react, the voice in his head continued: "It's all right, Mark, just lay the gun on the ground." Not knowing what to do, he decided to obey the command and laid his rifle on the ground. Standing, with the rifle at his feet, he looked back up the mountain and observed an eight- to ten-foot bipedal creature stepping out into the open. It stood, gently swaying back and forth from the hips, while looking down at Mark. He estimated the Sasquatch was about 100 to 125 yards away. He stood for some time watching the creature, then picked up his gun and slowly retreated back down the mountain, still in a state of shock. Mark knew that his telepathic experience was very unusual and that he had to keep it a secret.

Later, he and his wife began seeing large cigar-shaped objects hovering high above the forest. They saw smaller, silver objects entering the larger ones, as if the smaller ones had been out scouting. A woman who lived on the same road told him that UFOs occasionally landed behind her house in the forest. Though Mark never mentioned Sasquatch, the neighbor said she had not observed anything else unusual.

On one occasion, his dog went wild barking and running in circles. At the time, Mark was cutting wood by the wood shed. The dog darted for the house, but there was nothing in sight. He noticed a strange beeping noise that seemed to move in a circle around him, yet he could not see anything. This confused him. He decided to go into the house to see if someone were looking for him. When he walked into the cabin and looked around, he saw no one. The dog had followed him in and by that time was scratching frantically at the front door to be let out. He grabbed the dog by the collar to better control him, then opened the door. To his amazement, standing six feet from the front door were four tiny space beings! They were approximately four feet high, with large bulbous heads, no hair, and the biggest blue eyes he had ever seen. He did not notice any ears, but he saw a small slit for a mouth and a tiny nose with two nostrils. Their arms moved gingerly as they stood there otherwise motionless. The being closest to him appeared to be slightly larger than the rest, yet all looked exactly alike. He told me all of them looked as if they had been "cloned."

To his astonishment, the four disappeared in an instant—they seemed to have vanished into thin air. Mark told me he then realized that the beeping noises he had heard were small "invisible" flying saucers! I assured him that he was not having a delusion, and I told him about the interdimensional nature of the phenomenon that I and others had also experienced.

When I arrived at Mark's cabin, I set up my tent about a hundred feet or more from the dwelling. Shortly after dark, I climbed into my sleeping bag. By 11:00, an eerie generator noise could be heard. It was difficult to tell the exact location, but it appeared to emanate from an area about a quarter of a mile away. The sound was slightly "muffled" as if coming from within the Earth. I lay awake for some time, listening to the rhythm. It was very similar, almost identical, to what I had previously heard in the Mount Hood Wilderness in 1979.

Mark's wife told me that the sound had been there since they moved into the cabin a couple of years before. I investigated the next morning. In the general vicinity of the generator noise we located a 16-inch human-like track that was quite clearly imprinted in the ground (there were still patches of snow on a 40-45° sunny day). There were several of them but only one was in good condition.

Mark then accompanied me to an area where the forest became rocky with a few small ledges. When I accidentally kicked a huge chunk of rock that was firmly embedded in the Earth, a muffled echo of "hollowness" rung as if we were standing over a cave. Each time I kicked the rock with my heavy mountaineering boots, the idea became more plausible that a subterranean laboratory or experimental station could possibly exist below us and was the source of the sounds. When Mark took out a stethoscope for me to listen to the clanking of metal objects below us, I quickly became a believer. However, no entrance was visible in a 200-foot radius. It was baffling.

Two weeks later I returned to the area and stayed three to five days. When I sat down to talk with Mark, he admitted for the first time that he had numerous telepathic communications with the Bigfoot and knew far more about them than he previously was willing to tell. He apologized, saying he

**69**

had to know my true intentions and had to learn to trust me. Mark said he had seen the creatures many times.

One time, he and his wife were driving on a dirt road in the rain and saw what appeared to be a different creature than what he had previously encountered. It appeared to be smaller in size and was sitting under a tree about 60 yards away, seemingly enjoying the down-pour. They observed it for several minutes, then turned away for a few seconds. When they looked again, the Sasquatch was gone. It was nowhere in sight. They could not fathom how the creature could vanish so quickly.

Mark asked me numerous questions about evolution and life in the universe. He asked me if I believed that people from another world could possibly look like us. I told him that I believe there are numerous races of Starpeople that have evolved independently of each other in different times and places throughout the vastness of intergalactic space. I told him I also believed that some races have evolved in other dimensions. Within the universe are thousands upon thousands of trillions of stars—some two hundred billion or more in the Milky Way Galaxy alone. Further, it is estimated that at least another ten billion galaxies exist in the universe—to say nothing of the possibility of other universes. The center of our star system, the sun, has nine planets revolving around it. However, other suns may have fifteen, two, or no planets at all around them. The Smithsonian Air and Space Museum hypothesizes that if only ten percent of the stars in the Milky Way Galaxy are like our sun, then there are ten billion sunlike stars. Out of these similar solar systems, potentially five percent could well be inhabitable. If twenty percent of the five percent had evolved civilizations on them, then there could be just in the Milky Way Galaxy alone approximately one hundred million planets, in addition to Earth, that have intelligent life on them. I find it unnecessary to boggle the mind by computing these figures with the other ten billion galaxies. This mathematical perspective is by no means proof, but it is an aspect to consider when attempting to understand the "extraterrestrial hypothesis."

After my technical dissertation on my understanding of cosmic evolution, and my belief in interdimensional space travel, Mark told me a bizarre story that he swears is absolutely true. He said that the strange generator sounds we had been hearing were from a subterranean city, a part of which extends to the edge of his property! He said that a year earlier he had met a Forest Service geologist who was conducting a survey of the area. The geologist told him Medicine Mountain was an extinct volcano and was most probably hollow. Interestingly, Indian legends state that there is a family of Sasquatch that have lived inside the mountain since long before the Indians arrived in that region thousands of years ago. The traditional Indians in the area also say that "the little people" live in and around the mountain and that anyone seeing these little people should quickly leave because to look at them would mean that you would die! This is the Indian legend of Medicine Mountain.

Mark said he had been curious about what the geologist said and decided to climb the mountain and investigate for himself. After a long search for signs of anything unusual, he sat down to rest. He reports that during that time a Sasquatch came and spoke to him. The giant said his name was "Nie-Tie" and that he had been monitoring Mark since he moved into the area. The creature invited Mark to visit with the people who lived inside the mountain. Mark claims he was taken to a cave entrance that was very well camouflaged—in fact, he did not recognize it until they were almost beside the entrance. Another Sasquatch stood inside, guarding the entrance to the cave. Inside the cave Mark could see no visible lights, just a mysterious glow, which provided adequate light for them to see. To his surprise, three six-and-a-half-foot-tall Starpeople walked up to him. Each one of them appeared to be human in every respect, except for their tall stature. Mark said they could easily pass on the street for basketball players. Two were male and one was female. They spoke English and were very polite; however, in the beginning they spoke only telepathically, just like the Sasquatch he reported. At one point, he forgot that every time he had a thought, they could actually read his mind—which means he was "talking" (thinking) to them without his knowing it. Then he began to speak *verbally*, and they answered him in the same manner.

They purportedly told Mark that they had been there for thousands of years and that their subterranean city ran a mile and a half underground, extending to the edge of his property. They gave him a tour of the underground city. Mark said there was a lot of machinery that was being run by hairless beings, three-and-a-half- to four-feet tall, who appeared to be technicians. They reminded Mark of worker bees, each one doing a set task, going about their business without interacting with one another or paying any attention to him. At one point, one of the tiny creatures, dressed in a tight space suit, walked close enough to Mark for him to reach out and gently touch him on the shoulder out of curiosity. When he touched the being, Mark said a strange electrical charge or vibration went through his system, as if he had touched a mild electrical current. This startled him. He felt certain that these little creatures were all clones, produced and trained to do all of the technical work.

The tall, human-like beings took Mark to many different chambers, pointing out equipment that had no meaning to him. At one point, they told him that he was in their library, even though no books could be seen. He sat down, and they showed him how to press buttons that produced "books" upon a screen. Each page of the book was visually produced upon a screen subtitled with an undecipherable language. Mark said he was intrigued by this computerized library with a television screen that also displayed pictures from all over planet Earth. The beings told him they have recorded the history of Earth and how man is evolving. Mark told me he had been in the subterranean city a total of three times and, on one particular visit, he stayed for as long as three and a half hours. The beings told him that some of the time radiation was being used inside the city and he was not allowed to enter during those times. The leader told him that one of the purposes of the underground city was to continue with their experiments in the laboratories, but that they were also preparing for the aftermath of a nuclear war. They told Mark that if they could not stop the oncoming war, specific Earthpeople would be taken by them—those who were spiritually evolved and open-minded enough to accept them. These chosen few would be taken into the subterranean city to be protected from nuclear fallout. Few people would be selected, because most would be afraid of them and would resist. The Starpeople also told him that if the war were too brutal and destructive, they would transport some of the Earth people to their planet in spaceships—away from the dangers of nuclear fallout and death.

On one rare occasion, Mark claims he was invited to the mountain and, when he arrived, a Sasquatch came and escorted him to a clearing. There, the tall Starpeople showed him a landed UFO. He says that they took him through the spaceship, which had three layers, or floors, to it. He was fascinated by what he had experienced, and subsequently walked around in a daze for over a week. He said he did not share this experience with his wife because he was afraid it would upset her. He admitted it was still too much for him to digest at times.

What does a researcher do with a report like this? My immediate thoughts were: "Could Mark be fantasizing?" However, I too had heard the generator noise. It was a replica of the Mount Hood incident. I had located Sasquatch tracks in the area, and I had heard unusual beeping sounds around me when nothing was visibly there. Mark seemed honest and sincere. By the way he expressed himself, I could see he had a cathartic need to release his pent-up emotions by sharing with someone like me who could empathize with him, as I have heard similar reports of this nature in the past. I had no way of knowing if Mark was delusional or had consciously concocted the tale to impress me. If so, why was his "tale" so familiar? I was impressed with his insistence that I not share his story with anyone or reveal his name. As a social scientist, I wanted verification. The only way I knew was to climb the mountain myself, see what was up there and see if I could locate the entrance to the cave.

Preparing for my ascent up the 7,000-foot mountain was not easy. Although the weather was mild at the bottom, I knew it was freezing cold on top. In addition to warm clothes, I needed enough water to last one week as I had no knowledge of a water source in that region. I wanted to avoid using fire to melt snow for drinking water so as not to frighten the Bigfoot. Topographic maps did not show any streams. I brought a few books along, thinking I could read to pass the time. The idea was to take my time, set up a camp in a leisurely manner, and wait for the creatures to come to me. From the time I departed from the base of Medicine Mountain until reaching the place I intended to camp, I planned to telepath to the Sasquatch my intent, asking to be taken by them into the alleged subterranean city. I was asking permission to enter their domain, sending love and respect to them as I hiked. My mission was one of good will and learning from them, if accepted. I purposely took no guns or camera. If they were truly there, I wanted to interact with them, not drive them away.

A rancher friend drove me to the base of the mountain. I started the tedious climb, carrying a 104-pound backpack. The weather was cold, and the climb up the steep mountain was arduous. I rested frequently. Half-way up, I encountered waist-deep snow. It was extremely frustrating getting stuck in snow this deep, struggling and pulling myself out, using low branches from surrounding trees. In addition, the higher I climbed in elevation, the more exhausted I became. When I was one-quarter of the way up the mountain, I began hearing the striking of large sticks against trees. I had heard this many times before, and I had been told by other researchers that the Sasquatch did this. When I lived in the Great Lakes region with traditional Indian people, they told me the Bigfoot would hit large sticks against hollow trees to signal that someone was coming into their territory. The Indians had told me that they would leave out of fear when they heard this noise, as they had been forewarned that they were invading the privacy of the Sasquatch people. However, I continued to climb.

I was three-quarters of the way up the mountain at about an hour-and-a-half before dark, and I was exhausted. Because of the precipitous mountain landscape, there was no place to pitch my tent. Finally, I reached an area where there was a tiny shelf just large enough to put up the tent. It was windy and cold, and the temperature had fallen to 20°F.

Minutes after crawling into my sleeping bag, I heard the thumping of heavy footsteps coming up the mountain. I counted over 40 giant steps before it stopped near my tent at what I estimated to be about 30 feet away. There were patches of bare ground between the snow and rocks. I lay there telepathing to the creature by merely thinking of him in my mind, saying I was a friend, that I wanted to visit them and would welcome a reply. No message was transmitted. Nevertheless, I was thrilled that the creature approached me. I stayed in my tent. On previous occasions, each time I attempted to exit my tent to see the Sasquatch, it would dematerialize. When I re-entered my tent it would usually shuffle about, making guttural sounds, just a few feet away. It became a proverbial game of cat and mouse! To avoid threatening it, I stayed in the tent. I wanted to be accepted on their terms rather than by being sneaky and creating a distrust. There was no communication from the Bigfoot. After a few moments the creature turned and walked away.

The next morning I went out to look for tracks, and, to my surprise, there were none. I knew what I had heard and psychically felt, as I had experienced this many times before, but for some reason there were no tracks in the vicinity. This reminded me of the Deloris Kaplan case (see next chapter) where the invisible Sasquatch did not make tracks on the bog, probably because it had "faded" into the twilight world of another dimension. Perhaps being in this other dimension gave it the ability to stay above our physical Earth, yet touch the ground in that parallel plane. Thus one hears the stomping as if it were in our physical world, halfway between two planes of existence. As I have come to understand it, the seemingly physical Sasquatch are somewhat "holographic," that is, less dense than us and partially etheric. The reality may be that Sasquatch are in our dimensional reality only 50 or 60 percent of the time. From what I have learned through my years of communication with Bigfoot, these sensitive nature beings have access to numerous dimensions besides our own and North America is their favorite dimensional haunt. Other witnesses have related a similar understanding.

In 1985, a report came to me about an incident that took place in Oregon, where a snowmobiler went into the dense forest and was stunned to see three Sasquatch walking through the snow. He was quite close to the creatures—less than 50 feet away. The man became terrified when he realized he could see through them, that their bodies were "transparent." When he looked at their feet, he noticed they were above the snow, making no tracks. Yet they were almost "physical." Did the creatures hear the snowmobiler coming and fade into the protective zone of another dimension? The "interdimensional theory" I propose frequently applies best as a practical solution to why the Sasquatch disappear so mysteriously. They have proven themselves to me with repeated encounters. Six times I saw them physically, and a few hundred times I saw them astrally, while we were conversing telepathically. If I am wrong, then so are the ETs, Sasquatch, and 76 contactees.

I continued up the mountain in heavy snow. I was on the side of the mountain on which the sun did not shine, which made for more difficult climbing. At one point I crossed the side of a palisade where snow had turned to hazardous ice, forming a long slippery chute. If I had fallen, it would have carried me down into the canyon below. Upon reaching the summit, I explored the area to the southwest, looking for a campsite. I decided to camp in an opening in the forest with a panoramic view.

Early that evening, after setting up camp, I retreated into my tent to read in the comfort of a warm sleeping bag. The sun was peeking behind the horizon, and I estimated there were still 45 minutes of good daylight left. As I lay there reading my book, I heard a distinct whirling sound from above, becoming louder as the sound "descended" beside my tent. This puzzled me for a moment, but I continued to read. All of a sudden, strange lights shone onto my tent, and an electrical buzzing sound began to pulsate with the rhythm of the lights. My heart began pounding furiously, and it took me a moment to calm myself down and relax. Through the tent I could see the faint outline of a spacecraft, about six feet in diameter, scanning my tent. It was hovering just inches above the ground about ten feet away. One light was elongated and scanned the entire length of my tent, going back and forth, while other lights pulsated with each flash to the rhythm of an electrically charged buzzing.

I began to telepath to them, saying I was a friend and was there to make contact. I asked if they would please answer. I said things like, "God Bless you. I am a friend, and I wish to learn from you." There was no answer. I continued telepathing for at least five minutes. The lights and the pulsating buzzing sound continued during this time. I then told them that I would come out to talk with them. I slowly unzipped the tent. One second before I slipped out of the tent, the lights and sound instantly ceased, as if a light switch had been turned off. I quickly poked my head out of the tent, and the spacecraft was gone. Perhaps, by pushing a button, they seemed to have disappeared, but in reality they were still there observing me. I found no marks on the ground indicating a landing.

Within ten minutes of the UFO encounter, I heard giant footsteps coming from the forest. I counted 22 elephantine steps. Looking up through the yellow-tan-colored tent, I saw a giant seven- to eight-foot manlike silhouette tiptoeing over the tent strings. It was still daylight. Just why a creature that size would make so much noise attracting my attention, then tiptoe over the tent-strings, was an interesting question. I watched the creature as it puttered around, walking back and forth, and examining a water flask I had left outside under a tree. During this time, I telepathed to the creature asking him if he would take me into the subterranean city. The idea was to remain open to any experience, no matter how bizarre. I had no fear whatsoever. I lay there projecting love and blessing, asking if he would take me with him to meet the others. In the past, I had found that only some groups would speak to me and others would not. I believe a person should spend several weeks in an active area in order for the creatures to monitor your mind. This develops a rapport and trust before they make their initial contact. One researcher told me that she would spend one or two months in the field before the Bigfoot made contact. The shortest contact time she made happened within a two-week period, she reported. So evidently it takes time for them to feel comfortable before communicating in any way.

Once on the summit, I spent six days waiting to be telepathically contacted. Every day and night I would hear the same endless sound of generator churning, similar to what I experienced in the Mount Hood Wilderness and near Mark's cabin. Twice I gravitated toward the sound, hoping it would reveal clues to the entrance of the alleged cave leading to a "legendary" city, but each time the engines stopped. When I hiked back to camp, it would start again. The source of the sound was as elusive as the tiny saucer and hairy giants! Frustration soon turned to depression.

After the second night on the mountain, I awoke at 3:00 and felt an energy around me, but I could not define what it was. I felt as if someone were invading my space. As I rolled over in my sleeping bag to stretch, my arms swung out in front of me. Suddenly, I was alarmed to see my right thumb-nail *glowing a strange emerald green!* For a moment I relaxed and told myself it was a dream. But, upon placing my hand in the same vicinity of the tent a second and third time, my thumbnail again was glowing an eerie green color. The experience was startling, and I began to wonder if it had to do with radiation in the area. I thought perhaps the Starpeople were scanning me with some device that was causing this particular effect. I never did discover the source, but I do know I was not dreaming.

From that time on, every evening before sundown a tiny ship would land beside my tent flashing eerie lights. Each time, within fifteen minutes

*My sketch of the human-type Bigfoot that interacted with me in 1985. in the Siskiyou Mountains of southwest Oregon.*

after it left, I would hear the heavy foot-fall of the Sasquatch approaching my tent. It always occurred while the sun was lying on the horizon and there was still plenty of daylight left to see clearly—enough light for me to read a book inside my tent. Each time the creature would tiptoe over my tent strings. His giant shadowy form was sharp and clear and easy to see (from four to five feet away). There was no mistaking what was occurring, because it repeated itself over and over again.

The night before I was to depart, I placed a half-filled jar of peanut butter in front of my tent. The top of the jar was left off to release the aroma and entice the Bigfoot to come near. My idea was to get fingerprints of the creature in order to have them analyzed as physical evidence. Dermal ridges had been discovered on a footprint in the Blue Mountains of Washington State in 1982, and I thought it would be important to match fingerprints with another independent source. Apparently the creature had read my mind, because neither the ship nor the Sasquatch came around that evening, as if deliberately staying away from my little "trap."

The last two days on the mountain, I searched every rock cliff that jutted out and where brush was growing, trying to locate the entrance to the cave. I found nothing. My systematic searching proved fruitless. It became apparent that not only was I not invited to meet them, but they also had taken evasive measures so as not to be found. If I had two months of field time available to me, I would have remained at my camp during that time in order to build a strong rapport. Two anthropologists in Brazil patiently waited two years for "the tribe who hides from man" to come out of the jungle and meet them—and eventually they were successful.

Later, upon returning to Mark's cabin, I asked him for more information and requested that he take me directly to the entrance of the cave. He said he could not do that because of an agreement with the Starpeople. This was very frustrating. Yet, I too am protective of the witnesses who have shared with me because they do not want their lives disrupted. I feel a special obligation to respect their requests and anonymity at all costs.

# Bigfoot In Ohio

*OVERVIEW*

In the summer of 1981, Mrs. Deloris Kaplan (a pseudonym) and her family in rural Ohio began having a long series of encounters with Bigfoot/Sasquatch involving numerous witnesses, some of whom had repeated sightings. Again we have evidence of an eastern extension of creatures that at times exhibit extraordinary paranormal behavior considerably more exotic than their Pacific Northwest counterparts. Some researchers who have not done their homework deny any reports east of the Rockies. But, as you will see, Bigfoot's interdimensionality allows them to be rural residents without ever being discovered.

*EPISODE*

Mrs. Kaplan's first inkling that Bigfoot existed in their area came when she found a footprint in the woods that measured twenty inches long. This was in 1975. Thereafter, until 1979, she did not hear or see anything. Then one night there was a heavy snow. The next morning, Matt, a close neighbor, sighted one of the creatures going around in circles on the creek bank. The young man was scared, and his dog became terrified. The dog would not go out into the yard again for some time.

The members of the Kaplan family were not the only people to encounter the Ohio Sasquatch. Another girl in the same neighborhood sighted a Bigfoot by a creek between her house and the Kaplans' country home. Another neighbor reported UFOs landing at the edge of a meadow. Mrs. Kaplan reported that she has also sighted UFOs in the area and feels that the creatures are in some way associated with them. She is convinced that the Bigfoot creatures have highly developed extra sensory perception (ESP). Over the summer and fall of 1981 she found sixteen different places in the woods where she claims the giants had been sleeping. This confirmed her belief that more than one creature was in the area. She said that each of the areas where the creatures were bedding down was slightly different in size, and nearly all were large enough to accommodate a large biped lying down.

Mrs. Kaplan spoke to several experienced hunters, one of whom had shot big game in Africa. She wanted to have a better idea of wildlife in relation to the creatures. She said she needed more insight into what her family was experiencing, admitting that the existence of Bigfoot seemed ecologically improbable for the Ohio region.

The witnesses insisted that the Bigfoot were being let off from spaceships. For her, this was the only logical explanation in the light of improbable circumstances—that is, the simultaneous appearance of giant, hairy creatures and UFOs on her property!

One afternoon about 1:00, Mrs. Kaplan and her neighbor were standing on the lower road by the creek, talking. From a distance, she was surprised to see a Bigfoot cross the dirt road that led into the woods. She had been explaining to Matt earlier about hearing noises near her place—footsteps and thumping sounds—but never seeing anything. They walked down the road to where the creature had just crossed to see if it was still in the vicinity. About that time, Matt signaled her to be quiet. Behind them in the grass was the sound of footsteps, though nothing could be seen. When they approached the area from which the sound of the footsteps was coming, the footsteps increased as if whatever was making the sound was running away! They chased the sound into a stand of timber that led into a marshy area. They could see the grass part as they pursued the sound of the footsteps. At one point, the witnesses were startled to see an uprooted sapling, which was lodged between two trees over ten feet in the air, abruptly broken in two as the sound of the footsteps passed through it. They chased the sound to a swamp until it was longer feasible to follow. The sound of the footsteps seemed to enter the muddy marsh, but *did not* make impressions in the quagmire. Max tried to pursue the sounds into the marsh, but immediately sank well above his ankles.

This episode was very startling to the witnesses. Mrs. Kaplan said that it was *obvious* to them that the Bigfoot creature had the ability to make itself "invisible" yet still have a visible effect on the physical environment, except it did not make footprints upon entering the marsh! This greatly perplexed them. Though this is paradoxical, we simply do not know what unusual abilities the Sasquatch have when they visit other dimensions. It is vital to remain open and objective here.

On the evening of a full moon, Mrs. Kaplan and family, along with several people who were also sharing these strange experiences, witnessed at least ten of the creatures in and around her yard outside the house. She said they noticed a pungent smell, like that of a skunk. Mrs. Kaplan says that at other times they have smelled an odor similar to a cesspool when the creatures were around. A third odor has the distinct smell of a very strong mold.

Throughout 1981, there were numerous creature sightings reported all over Ohio, and that area continues to be a hotbed of reported sightings to date. Mrs. Kaplan stated that the Bigfoot activity in her area had been going on for at least six years. She had discreetly talked to people in town about the bizarre events and had found that most people were not aware of what was going on in the outlying rural areas. I found this lack of awareness to be very common.

She told a story of an occurrence that happened to her son when he was 19 years old. While playing basketball in the yard, he had the feeling he was being watched. Although he had never seen one of the creatures before, he had heard their noises many times and seen the footprints they left. He turned around and saw a Bigfoot standing by the barn looking at him. In Mrs. Kaplan's opinion, the creatures were fascinated by humans and enjoyed observing people. She said that they were occasionally seen at night watching people swim or work around their yards.

She never saw a Bigfoot up close, face-to-face. The only times she saw them were on dark nights, in the shadows, usually moving away from her. They were generally at a distance, never close enough for her to discern clear facial features. Since discovering their presence on her property, she has found footprints measuring from seven-and-a-half to twenty-one inches long, and several sizes in between. Mrs. Kaplan also claims to have possible samples of both feces and urine which she preserved in her refrigerator freezer. She intended to take these samples up to the Director of the Columbus Zoo to see if the zoo personnel would analyze them. Mrs. Kaplan said the stool samples came from an inaccessible spot where something huge had bedded down—very possibly a Bigfoot. She also speaks of finding an unusual orange-colored liquid on the ground in the woods behind her house. After digging around to see if it had oozed out of the ground, she decided that it could only have been deposited there. Later Mrs. Kaplan confirmed this by locating a similar orange liquid in a Bigfoot track along a stream bank. She promptly filled a plastic bag with the unidentified liquid and put it in her freezer for later analysis. (I am unaware of any analysis of these samples to date by a qualified laboratory.)

Mrs. Kaplan's general description of the Bigfoot is that it is "incredibly huge." She says she has seen it bent over at the waist, striding away, in a crouched position, and later standing still in an upright position. It appears to have a "knot" of some sort on its head. (Perhaps she is referring to a "sagittal crest," a term used by physical anthropologists to describe a peaked ridge or crest of bone running from the forehead to the back of the skull of the male gorilla.) She described the face of the creature as not having much hair. She is unsure of whether the face had some hair on it or just sort of a beard, for she was not close enough to get a good look. The heights of the giants vary, she says. She saw one standing under a tree branch that barely cleared the top of its head. Later, when measurements were taken, it was determined that the branch was ten feet from the ground. The family claims to have observed one that was even taller, estimating it to be approximately twelve feet in height. They also said that several appear to be only seven or eight feet tall. All walked with a crouched or stooped-over posture.

One morning Mrs. Kaplan spotted one creature that was very black. As she watched, the creature bent over and picked up something from the ground, looking around to see if anyone was watching. It reached down and picked up something else and put it in its mouth. Then it moved down the creek a bit and repeated the same behavior, as if gathering morsels of food from the ground. That gave the Kaplan family an idea, and they began setting out food for the group. They claim to have observed several hand and finger prints on the food containers that were left out overnight, though they were unable to obtain this evidence for analysis. One time when Mrs. Kaplan was planning to be gone for several days, she set out a large quantity of apples. The creatures were not attracted to the apples, but almost ruined a young fruit tree by picking and eating the tender leaf buds on it. Just why some Sasquatch eat apples and others do not may be no different than why some people liking certain fruit and others do not. Or, they might have detected pesticides on the apples—that is a consideration.

One day Mrs. Kaplan and a friend decided to try to communicate with the Bigfoot telepathically. The two women sat on the bank of the stream, and later on the front porch, projecting their thoughts to the creatures, saying they would like to take a picture of them to prove their existence to the world. The women felt that government legislation should be passed to protect the creatures. Another advantage they saw from such proof would be that food could be provided for Bigfoot in hard times, as is done for animals during severe winters. Mrs. Kaplan and her friend apparently had no success in their telepathy, but at least had good intentions. In my own view, it seems probable that the Sasquatch knew their intent (through mind-reading) and did not feel threatened in any way, therefore continued to stay in the area where they felt safe and unmolested. She did not know that the Sasquatch do not want "proof" of their existence—at least right now.

Mrs. Kaplan believes that people will never be able to catch or kill one of the Bigfoot. She feels convinced that the creatures have a direct connection with UFOs and that advanced alien beings will protect them from earthly harm. There have been three UFO sightings over the Kaplan house since the Bigfoot activity started. When the Kaplans first started seeing the creatures, they were always searching for food and generally only came out at night. Since then, the family set out food, and the Bigfoot became less timid and were seen periodically during the day as well. Mrs. Kaplan says, "You must watch them constantly; if you turn your head even for a second they are gone." She is convinced they become *invisible* at will. She believes they might be able to go into another dimension when they are threatened or feel a certain need. She thinks the Sasquatch are brought to Earth by the UFOs for a rest, to gather food, and raise their young. "Perhaps they don't have the beautiful lakes and streams that Earth does, so they come here to rest and relax," she speculated. She thinks the UFOs transport them here and then pick them up after a period of time. Incidentally, Mrs. Kaplan knew nothing of my conclusions about the creatures. She independently arrived at her own conclusions.

One night Mrs. Kaplan and her son were sitting out on the porch with flash camera in hand hoping to get a picture of one of the creatures. She had moved the "feeding station" so a Bigfoot trying to get food would have to cross the driveway and step into the open, thereby enabling her to get a picture of it. Her son had just stepped into the house to get a drink when Mrs. Kaplan was dazzled by an intensely bright light at the far end of her front yard! She quickly called for her son to come and look. Just above the trees, they observed a row of lights about forty feet long—more than the length of her driveway. There was no noise. Her son stepped out of the house in time to see a UFO descend behind a row of trees. They could see lights flashing for about five minutes, then all the lights went out. Mrs. Kaplan decided not to investigate, as she did not know anything about UFOs, and was afraid to approach the craft. The next morning, Mrs. Kaplan's neighbor reported to her that she had also seen a few UFOs. Several other neighbors and people in the surrounding area had also reported a rash of UFO sightings during the same period when the Sasquatch had arrived.

There are several Bigfoot researchers in Ohio state because of ongoing activity there. I have discovered that there are two main vortices there that the creatures use for safety. Possibly they enter them and stay in them in a parallel dimension when the weather becomes brutal over the winter (and a few may choose to stay or only briefly visit a winter wonderland, then return).

The most heavily utilized vortex is in the east-central part of Ohio, immediately west of Bergholz, not far from Leesville Lake. There is also both Bigfoot and UFO activity near Jefferson Lake because of the nearby vortex.

The second major vortex is immediately south of Wellington, between Findley and Spencer. I was told there are usually seven Sasquatch living in Ohio state most of the time and occasionally some will travel to western Pennsylvania's Allegheny National Forest where another vortex exists.

There is a phenomenon that parallels this one which also points directly to interdimensionalism. The books titled *Alien Animals, Creatures of the Outer Edge*, and *Chupacabras and Other Mysteries* document endless cases of black dogs, black panthers, hairy bipeds, giant birds, birdmen with red glowing eyes and Chupacabras. These creatures remain elusive and vanish when pursued. There is little doubt that all are paraphysical "entities" with a special psychic intelligence and the ability to traverse other dimensions, and ours is only one of them that they periodically visit. If we are to succeed in a true scientific spirit in understanding world phenomena in universal nature, then those with academic credentials should apply their knowledge with an open mind and be willing to objectively pursue anomalies regardless of where they lead.

# Communicating With Bigfoot

*OVERVIEW*

This unusual report came to light in June 1985, in the coastal region of northwest Oregon. Although the family involved had not sighted the Bigfoot on the farm for five years, I took the time to enlighten these good people regarding the reality of the paranormal aspects of the psychic Sasquatch. They listened intently and appreciated my sharing of ideas, although it left them with considerable doubt and a certain amount of anxiety. Initially, when I talked about telepathy and the UFO connection, the couple's response was: "Come on, you're kidding me!" But soon their doubt turned to wonderment. I strongly advised them to project love and trust to the Sasquatch in the event that they returned, and this advice paid off for them. I educated Mr. and Mrs. Wilson (pseudonyms) in the dynamics of mental telepathy as I have grown to understand it by my own ongoing contacts with these remarkable beings. The family already had the qualities to attract the Sasquatch, and so I counseled them as I have done with many others who later experienced successful communication.

In June 1986, the Bigfoot returned. Mrs. Wilson and one of her daughters soon became the percipients of telepathic communication, which, as of this writing, still continues. My assurance that they were being visited by people of a benevolent nature replaced their fears and apprehensions with understanding that they were indeed privileged to be visited by the psychic Sasquatch. Like the other percipients who have had in-depth encounters, the Wilsons are warmhearted, spiritual, giving people, with an immense love for nature and its creatures—all factors that predisposed them for psychic contact.

*EPISODE*

In the fall of 1980, Irene Wilson was walking from her farm house to the barn at dusk. To her astonishment, standing by the barn was a giant, hairy manlike creature staring at her. She froze in her tracks and gawked at it with great curiosity. Excited, Mrs. Wilson quickly ran back to the house to fetch her husband. When they returned, no sign of the creature could be found. Mr. Wilson began teasing his wife, saying she had merely seen a bear, but she sternly insisted that what she saw was the legendary Bigfoot. The woman described it to be at least eight feet tall and recalls that its head was where the barn roof began, which seemed to be an accurate way to estimate of its height. Other than the fact that it looked muscular and huge, no other features were distinguishable. The witness said she is not a good judge of weight or distance, so she declined to comment on it.

On the second occasion, a month later in early evening, the creature was not actually seen. Mrs. Wilson was sewing in the bedroom when she heard a noise in the living room. Upon investigating, she discovered that the heavy sliding glass door leading to the porch had been lifted off its runner, pushed forward, and was tightly jammed into the carpet. There was a large gap of space between the bottom of the glass door and the threshold.

As Mrs. Wilson stood wondering who could have possibly done such a thing—was it a joke or was someone trying to break in?— she noticed a giant palm print made of dirt pressed against the glass. Whoever had the strength to lift the bulky door left its calling card on the glass. This episode understandably upset her. She dashed to the barn to seek the security of her husband. When they returned to the house, Mr. Wilson, using his own hand as a measure, reports that the huge palm print was approximately twice the size of his.

On another occasion Mrs. Wilson walked into her bedroom at sundown and noticed that, standing immediately outside the window, was a small hairy being. She slowly opened the window to get a better look. The creature was a juvenile Sasquatch, approximately three-and-a-half to four feet tall. As she moved closer to get a better look, the young Sasquatch slowly backed away. With great care, Mrs. Wilson put both hands through the open window, palms down, extending them in friendship. Cautiously, the youngster moved toward her, slowly placing its hands under hers, palms up. Once their hands touched, the Bigfoot, with childlike curiosity, gently rubbed its skin against hers. It was at this time that the woman noticed a six-and-a-half to seven-foot Sasquatch watching the interaction some 15 to 20 feet away in the dark. She assumed this was the mother of the young creature, as the youngster constantly scanned with its eyes between Mrs. Wilson and the mother, as if to check for approval.

During that time, Mrs. Wilson was harvesting apples and had stored a couple of crates in the bedroom. She grabbed an apple and presented it to the child. As Mrs. Wilson reached out with the fruit in hand, the mother stepped forward in a protective manner. The youngster again sought approval with its eyes shifting back and forth, finally taking the apple from Mrs. Wilson's hand. As the juvenile stood quietly examining the apple, the mother suddenly raised both arms to waist level palms up, and, flexing her wrist, gestured in a movement that the witness interpreted as meaning: "Come, let's go!" With that, the child immediately turned and walked toward its mother and the two creatures, holding hands, disappeared into the darkness of night.

Her husband, when told of the experience, struggled with the reality she shared. While I was interviewing the couple, he commented in a jocular way: "I thought for sure she went plumb crazy! I even checked the jug of wine in the cupboard to see if she was nipping. But things kept happening. The palm print really convinced me."

During the same period that the Sasquatch were being encountered at the ranch, a low-flying UFO came directly over the house one evening. The four children were getting ready for bed on the second floor and heard beautiful, serene music outside. It was described by one of the young witnesses as eerie, yet enchanting. They ran to the open window and were completely surprised at the sight of a round craft that was slow moving over the rooftop of the house. The UFO was larger than the house itself, overshadowing the entire building. Lights brightened the bottom portion of the ship as flowing, melodious music emanated from it. The awe-struck children ran to their parents so they too could view the spectacle. By the time they rallied their parents, the spaceship had moved over the hill and out of sight. All that remained were exuberant children.

After that, six years passed without any subsequent encounters. Then in June 1986, about 10:30 one morning, as Mrs. Wilson was walking around the side of the barn, she noticed a six-and-a-half foot tall female Sasquatch standing, holding an infant to its bosom. At a distance of 100 to 150 feet, the most prominent anatomical feature Mrs. Wilson could make out was her large uplifting breasts—"like a woman who recently gave birth, her breasts appeared full of milk," Mrs. Wilson remarked. She said the female

Sasquatch cradled the tiny infant in her arms in a protective manner, "just like a human." She also noted that: "The infant did not cling like a monkey, but acted human. At that point I knew it was not an animal," the witness continued. She estimated the infant to be two to three weeks old.

Both faces seemingly had *some* hair on them, except around the mouth and eyes, she reported. "They looked like a cross between a human and an ape—but more human in its mannerisms," she insisted.

At one point Mrs. Wilson thought of moving closer to the creatures to get a better look, but immediately after thinking that, the Sasquatch-woman communicated through "feeling telepathy" (not "verbal telepathy") not to come any closer. Within minutes, the being turned and walked away, down a wood road that led into the coastal hills.

About two weeks later, Kathy, the Wilson's nineteen-year-old daughter, was in the upper level of the barn one night pitching hay to the calves below. It was pitch black in Kathy's section because a light bulb had burned out. She felt her way into a dark corner to grab another bale of hay when "all of a sudden something with large hands grasped both of my hands, and instantly my entire body became paralyzed. I mean, some outside power immobilized me so I couldn't move a muscle, and I became very frightened," the girl related. Then a firm voice telepathically asked her: "Who are you?" She answered: "I am Kathy. I live here on the farm with my parents."

"Who is the other girl?" the being asked more politely.

"That's Susan, my sister," Kathy answered.

Kathy said there were two creatures in the loft during the incident. The Sasquatch were napping in the hay when Kathy happened onto them. The "induced paralysis" subsided as she conversed with the Sasquatch, and she then resumed normal movement without fear. These Bigfoot creatures indicated that they had been alert to intruders with guns near the ranch. The Wilsons suspected that what the creatures referred to was either poachers or vandals, since both had been recently reported in the area. During the incident, Kathy's sister was unaware of the two visitors, as she was busy doing her chores downstairs, at the opposite end of the building.

One day, while Mrs. Wilson was working outside, she received a telepathic message. The Sasquatch told her to be at peace, that a group of its people were migrating through and were enjoying the security of the property and meant no harm to anyone. But then, ironically, the dog and cows went berserk for an entire night, keeping everyone awake. In the morning, one of their cows was wandering in a daze with a nasty gash on its face, with a claw-like mark dug into the hide. This was upsetting to the Wilsons. They telephoned to consult me on the matter. I told them perhaps a young rambunctious Sasquatch got playful and the cow charged it, causing it to react defensively. It was only a theory based on the friendly Sasquatch previously assuring her that they meant no harm. There are contradictions in this borderline discipline. I feel that some incidents are misinterpreted, placing the creatures in the category of "monster." Mrs. Wilson telepathed, asking what happened to the cow, but received no answer.

Less than a week later, Mrs. Wilson was at the coast one morning, about three miles from the farm. While glancing westward across the ocean, she commented to herself how odd a certain island looked. It was then she realized there was *never* any island there before. Focusing on the "island," she became alarmed by the fact that what she was viewing was actually a superhuge, saucer-shaped spaceship! She recalls observing the huge Russian cannery ships a good distance away and was stunned that the partly submerged craft was six to seven times the length of one of them. This frightened her. Then, one after another, four smaller flying saucers came straight down from the sky, entering the dome-shaped "mother ship" before it disappeared into the deep. Mrs. Wilson immediately called me to ask if it were possible that there was a Bigfoot/UFO connection.

A few days later, Kathy "felt" the presence of a Sasquatch once again. This time she decided to creatively experiment by telepathing to the creature to see if it would respond. There was no physical creature in sight, yet she asked in her mind, while thinking of the giant, if it would watch over her pregnant sister who was working nights on a lonely farm as a milker. A series of events with vandals in the neighborhood had caused Kathy to worry about her older sister. Because she "felt" kindness and love from the Sasquatch, Kathy asked, not knowing what to expect: "Would you please watch over my sister Sarah for me when she goes to work at night?"

For the next couple of weeks, Kathy continued to feel watched by an invisible "something," always feeling the same "vibrations" she experienced in the barn when the creature grabbed her hands. Somehow, that strange sensation seemed to project love and concern and, in time, she began to feel totally secure and fearless with their presence.

During this time, Sarah continued with her milking job, unaware that Kathy had requested a protective watch over her. One day Sarah reported to the family, in a puzzling way, that nearly every night at work she had been experiencing an unusual presence around her. She said the cows became restless and nearly uncontrollable, and the dog barked wildly. In time, as the nights went on, the cattle slowly calmed, yet the eerie "presence" remained. Kathy then revealed that she had made the request to the Sasquatch and told Sarah that she was being protected. The attitude of the entire family was that of gratitude and love toward the chivalrous visitors that had serendipitously entered their lives. After this acceptance, I encouraged them to project more love and appreciation and told them that they were privileged people to have developed such a special relationship with the Sasquatch, when veteran researchers have been running around for years chasing an illusion—a "monster"—that did not exist, except in the minds of the naive.

In the autumn of that same year, as Kathy was driving Sarah in from town on a foggy night, they encountered a large white Sasquatch standing by the road. Pinkish flesh-colored skin could be clearly seen in the hairless face and through the sparsely-haired chest and stomach. It glanced at them, then slowly walked into the forest.

Soon thereafter, Mr. and Mrs. Wilson were abruptly awakened by a very loud "thud" on the side of the house. After the third thud, Mrs. Wilson investigated. Opening the back door, she felt a presence but saw nothing.

"Danger, Irene, danger. Watch out for danger," a gentle voice telepathed. It was a white Sasquatch.

Irene asked, "What kind of danger?" but received no reply. The following night, rifle shots were heard and poachers were suspected. The poachers had never been that close to the house before and the Wilsons realized that the concerned Sasquatch thought it proper to inform them of possible danger.

During this time, Sarah was having problems with her pregnancy, and the family eagerly gave their support. Sarah began to stay with family more often in case she went into labor or had complications. After seven months of pregnancy, Sarah quit her milking job.

One evening, as Mrs. Wilson was driving home, the kindly eleven- to twelve-foot white Sasquatch was boldly standing beside the road, seemingly waiting for her. Without any fear, she stopped the car to see what would happen. The being bent down, looked directly in the window on the driver's side, just inches away, and telepathically said, "Tell Sarah to be cautious and stay quiet at home. Watch her carefully. She should not go anywhere." Just as Mrs. Wilson was going to ask why, the headlights of another vehicle flashed in the distance, far behind her. In an instant, the wary giant sprinted away, hopping a fence with such remarkable agility that the startled woman just sat for a moment, viewing a blurred white figure disappearing into the night. "I've seen elk dash in fright, but this thing moved like no other creature on Earth could," Mrs. Wilson related with excitement. During the next two days, she saw the same white Sasquatch in the field, standing at the edge of the woods. The sightings were at a 200- and 300-foot distance.

A few days later, Sarah wanted to borrow the family car to drive into town alone. Mrs. Wilson insisted her daughter stay at home. Sarah insisted otherwise, in an argumentative tone. Soon the persistent daughter drove into town. While waiting at a stop sign for the traffic to pass, a careless motorcyclist slammed into the rear of the car, forcing Sarah's pregnant stomach abruptly into the steering-wheel. She was rushed to the hospital in an ambulance. She was having contractions, which ceased shortly after she arrived at the hospital. By that evening, she was home resting. Was this the event the altruistic Sasquatch foresaw? They have demonstrated profound psychic abilities to a multitude of percipients, as documented in my research. Glimpsing the future may easily be a part of their everyday reality and is an aspect to which we must remain open.

Another time after visiting the Wilsons for several days, I told Irene that the Sasquatch told me that the Starpeople would come to her soon. I expected her to be thrilled at such a privilege, but instead her reaction was one of fear. I told her they were friends of the Bigfoot people and that their visit would be exciting. She said she wasn't ready for that kind of experience.

Three weeks later, I received a phone call from Irene. She said that she had a "close encounter" in her home the day before. She had been sipping coffee at about 12:30 in the afternoon when a white ball of light, just a little larger than a basketball, passed right through the wall and hovered in front of her. She was simultaneously filled with both fear and amazement. It soon became apparent to her that the ball of light was being intelligently controlled by an ET.

The intelligence said, "Do not be afraid. We are friends of Jack's. We are very concerned about your planet. Your people still have not grasped the fact that the Earth is truly a living organism. We see pollution and carnage everywhere. It is important for your people to respect all living things, and that includes a living planet and all the creatures upon it."

"Why are you telling me all of this? Why don't you go to the government who makes all the laws and tell them?" Irene asked.

The intelligence replied: "We have tried to share these vital concepts with several people in power, but they had too much fear and were not open to contact. President Jimmy Carter was the only president receptive enough to listen to us, because he is very spiritual. Now he knows the universal truths that we shared."

"What are these truths you told him?" Irene asked.

"It is not for you to know; this is not your business," the intelligence within the ball of light retorted. It then indicated that it would continue to monitor her, floated back through the wall, and disappeared.

The role played by ETs here was to allow Irene to experience the fullness of the Bigfoot-UFO reality. She has had too many experiences that objectify my encounters to have any armchair theorist convince her differently.

During the ten years that I have known the Wilson family, a number of wonderful anomalies have occurred. I made five- to seven-day visits to the Wilson's ranch two to three times a year. Inevitably, I would be contacted during each visit.

In September of 1988, I was invited to the Wilsons' for their daughter's wedding. Kathy had decided to have the ceremony outdoors on the ranch by a small pond in an old Douglas Fir grove. Chairs and tables had been rented, and arrangements had been made with the pastor. All of the plans had been made, including the table cloths, dishes, and food for the outdoor wedding.

The day before the wedding, the temperature dropped to 38°F and a rainy 40- to 50-mile-per-hour wind was blowing. As I drove to the ranch in my Toyota station wagon, the strong winds blew it to and fro on the road. When I arrived at the Wilson home, the entire family was in a state of chaos and frustration, trying to figure out what to do about the wedding. The weather forecasters were predicting that these torrents would continue for three days. It was too late to move the wedding inside a church. The situation looked grim. I stood in the living room, feeling uneasy as the wind intermittently slammed into the window panes. It gave one the impression that the glass would be blown out at any minute.

I told Irene that I had an idea. I remembered a previous incident in which a Sasquatch had manifested a powerful thunderstorm within less than a minute's time. So, I thought, if they create inclement weather, perhaps they can also reverse it and produce sunshine and calm. I felt a little foolish telling Irene that I was going to contact the Bigfoot people to request their help so that the wedding could be performed outdoors as scheduled. I went into a bedroom and lay down on the bed. As soon as I started telepathing, the Bigfoot people appeared. I explained to them the importance of this human ritual and how desperately I needed their assistance. My contact hesitated during our conversation, so he could get support from his group.

In my head, I could hear the entire group unanimously agreeing to help. As the rain pelted the side of the house, I found myself wondering what they could really do to change the situation. When I left the bedroom to announce to the family that the Bigfoot people had agreed to help, I was amazed to see their reaction. The entire family became relaxed and confident that the problem was now solved. They had experienced too many profound incidents in the past to doubt what I had shared.

I awoke the following morning at 7:00. The weather was placid and sunny, with not a cloud in the sky. By 11:00, it was 65°F. As everyone pitched in to set up for the wedding that morning, we found ourselves giggling each time we passed each other, knowing that seemingly magical nature beings had made our day. The wedding was a success. By 1:00, the sky was covered with clouds. By 2:00, the sky was filled with rain clouds, with the sun barely peeking through. At 2:45, while I was helping to fold the tables and chairs, it began to sprinkle. I quickly telepathed: "Dear Bigfoot people, not now—please stop the rain until we're finished." The rain instantly stopped! The Bigfoot told me that the rain was necessary and they needed the weather to go back to its natural state. By 3:30, it was pouring rain.

When I awoke the next day and got ready to leave, the temperature was 40°F, and violent gales were again blowing. These sentient people had proven to me that they can tap into the universal laws of nature and can successfully use these abilities at their discretion.

In the summer of 1987, I presented a lecture at the University of Wyoming-Laramie, at Dr. R. Leo Sprinkle's UFO contactee conference. When I returned to Oregon, I had a message on my answering machine from Irene. She said it was urgent that I contact her immediately. When I returned her call, she told me that a pregnant female Sasquatch had a baby in her hay loft. Five days before, as Irene was playing with her granddaughter in the living room, a female Sasquatch astrally appeared. Because no one was allowed to hunt on the Wilsons' property, in an effort to create a safe haven for the Bigfoot clan, the female Sasquatch asked permission to stay in the safety of the barn. Irene agreed, later telling her children and grandchildren that the barn was "off limits" for the next week.

A few days later, Irene was again psychically contacted. The female Sasquatch was in distress. She was having problems with her delivery. She repeatedly requested that I, a master herbalist, assist her by bringing herbs to her. At that time, I was in Wyoming and therefore missed a very rare opportunity to assist in the birth. Irene explained to her that I was gone, which caused the female Sasquatch to become even more agitated. We never did figure out why one of her own people did not assist her at this critical time. The being said that her family had gone through the vortex to another environmental dimension.

Two days after the birth, Irene was contacted by the new mother in the barn. The Sasquatch woman requested that Irene bring her one-year-old granddaughter into the barn with her. Irene stood in the barn, looking and waiting, but at first saw no one. Then, in an instant, the female materialized from her invisible state, cradling her infant in her arms. The baby was preoccupied, suckling a hairy breast. From the second tier of the loft, the mother looked down, asking Irene to hold up her granddaughter so she could have a better look. Irene immediately complied. The Sasquatch said the baby was beautiful and special, even though it didn't have hair. Then Irene requested that the mother do the same, but she refused. Irene surmised that she did not want to disturb her child during feeding. This indeed is a most exceptional account.

After hanging up the phone following my conversation with Irene, I decided to telepath across the 200 miles that separated us to see if I could connect with the Sasquatch woman in the barn. Within two minutes, I received a reply. She thanked me for being so concerned and let me know that everything was all right. She sent her love, and I said, "I love you too." They function on love, not on hostility and violence. This is the reality of the Bigfoot people.

The Wilsons' family life outwardly appeared normal, but these experiences, which they kept a secret, continued. More of the family members began to have encounters. On one occasion, Irene was in the kitchen preparing dinner while holding her infant grandchild in one arm. She was contacted by a Bigfoot person, saying he wanted to visit. Irene agreed, but didn't know what she was agreeing to. Just as she was turning around at the sink, vegetables in one hand, granddaughter in the other, a six-and-one-half-foot-tall white Sasquatch physically appeared three feet away. It was illustrating the reality of teleportation. Whether the creature teleported from a space ship or from the forest was not clear. Although Irene was delighted by the surprise, her granddaughter began to freak out. Then, with a loving look on its face, the male Sasquatch stretched out his hand and gently placed his finger on the child's head. Instantly, the child became relaxed and started smiling and acting equally delighted by this unusual visitor. This might indicate a form of "telepathic hypnosis" that Lummi Indians and other tribes describe in their folklore. He did something psychic to the child to make her feel at ease.

The Sasquatch begin to feel more at ease while building a trust, and then exhibit more unusual psychic behavior around those they are monitoring. On several occasions, an astral Sasquatch deliberately grabbed and touched me, which was startling. Then I would hear a laugh in the room from one of them, and think: "Oh, it's you." Perhaps the creature was bored, or perhaps just mischievous. It is done in fun. This is another paradox wherein a sober-looking monster-like creature is also a fun-loving trickster at times.

One day, while I was map dowsing, I discovered a vortex at the edge of the Wilson's property. It was exciting. A vortex would answer a lot of questions concerning anomalies. This meant nothing to the Wilson family until I explained that it was a major porthole where the Sasquatch, ETs, and other entities enter and leave this dimension. It was then that Irene told me that she had shot at some black "wolves" or exceptionally large, unusual-looking "dogs" that were chasing her cattle in the pasture. She said that their look and behavior seemed somewhat abnormal as a small pack of huge black canines is not a common sight in that area. Upon interviewing the family that lived less than 100 yards from the vortex, the woman indicated that she and her family often see strange lights in the field and have heard frightening howling and growling sounds in the night. The most unusual experiences she reported were two instances wherein they had seen large colorful snakes near the vortex while they were picking blackberries. She said the snakes were six- to seven-feet long and as big around as a one-pound coffee can. The serpents were a gaudy yellowish-green and orange colored. The woman was shocked when she almost tripped over one of the snakes and could not figure out where such an oddity had come from.

After relating the vortex information from this interview to the Wilson family, Mr. Wilson said he remembered something he had discovered back in 1953. He said that he had opened up a flume to release water into one of the canals leading into the pasture when he noticed an unusual "fish" was stuck in the opening. When he retrieved it, he became frightened, as he had never before seen such a strange species of fish. Did this species of fish come through a vortex from another dimension? After looking at the sketch he made of the 15- to 18-inch primitive-looking fish, I guessed that a vortex could be an explanation.

Based on astronomical influences, the nucleus of a vortex moves along a vortex line. Whether it goes into a person's house or into water makes little difference, as it will annually move back to the original point. Wherever the nucleus is located is the gateway for anomalies to manifest, which might be an explanation as to how this bizarre-looking fish entered our world. I have seen this situation numerous times. The "water-monster" phenomenon worldwide could also be explained by aquatic vortices.

I once map dowsed three thousand miles away for a Bigfoot researcher in Georgia. Psychically, I discovered a vortex in a field not far from a dead-end road in what was the beginning of a huge forested area with several streams, lakes, and reservoirs—a very unique survival situation for a group of clandestine Sasquatch. I indicated for my associate that this was a key source for Bigfoot/UFO activity. When he interviewed the people in the last two houses on this dead-end street, they related incidents wherein they had seen space ships, Bigfoot-people, and other alien animals in the same field that I targeted as having the mysterious vortex. I have seen a repeated pattern when a vortex is involved. This is how elusive phenomena enter our world and magically leave again without being caught. So the doors to a real-life "twilight zone" do exist. Most Amerindian cultures knew about and once utilized these vortices.

Many events occurred on the ranch that were very perplexing to the Wilson family. ETs would occasionally appear suddenly on their television, whether it was turned on or off. Sometimes a message was given; sometimes not. In the spring of 1994, Irene met with a male Sasquatch in the forest. While talking, she was shocked to see a woman who appeared to be in her forties walk out of the woods and stand beside the Sasquatch. Before she could say anything, a female Sasquatch with a newborn infant joined the group. When Irene spoke to the woman, she discovered she had a difficult time making her words come from her mouth. Soon everyone was communicating telepathically.

The woman with the Bigfoot said her name was Sally and that sometime in the late fifties, when she was five or six years old, she was taken by the Bigfoot people. After living with them for a short time, they told her they would return her to human civilization, but that she had rejected this offer. As the years went on, they made several offers, but she was very content living her life with these beautiful nature people. Irene said that Sally looked very unkempt. Her hair was knotted and messy, and she wore mismatched clothing that looked like odds and ends that people had left behind at wilderness campsites. She encountered this woman twice.

I became very excited when Irene related the "wild woman incident." Previously I had heard stories of women and children who were purportedly kidnapped by Sasquatch, but I had never put any credence into these stories. Yet I know of an elderly gentleman and a manager of a store in Seattle who claim to have gone with the Sasquatch people and returned safely. The manager refuses to discuss what transpired after he was taken. Something clandestine is happening of which science is completely unaware. UFO abductions are well known, but apparently abduction by hairy giants is a new and valid area to explore.

One of the final experiences that Irene had is what every researcher desires—a reliable witness observing a Sasquatch in or beside a spaceship. The following episode has also been documented by MUFON (Mutual UFO Network) researchers and published in their newsletter.

In the spring of 1989, Irene was at home during the daytime hours with her three-and-one-half-year-old granddaughter. The child walked into the living room, took her grandmother by the hand, and said to come quickly, leading Irene to the back door. When she stepped outside, she could see a transparent outline of a spaceship slowly materializing. The ship was 75 to 100 feet in diameter and it was approximately 150 feet away from the house, she told me. Irene stood watching until it appeared to be a solid object in her field.

Initially, she saw no openings in the ship. Then, suddenly, windows and doors appeared. Through a window, she could see a Sasquatch looking out at her. In the doorway stood a very human-looking man, wearing a silver one-piece suit. Irene said he looked so human he could have easily been one of us. She observed the solid space ship for a few minutes, then it slowly faded back into another dimension. The purpose of this short visit remained unclear to Irene, but I suspect it was merely another way the Starpeople "communicate" by illustrating the reality of interdimensionalism and by revealing to her unequivocally, physically, and unquestionably the reality of a Bigfoot/ET/UFO connection. Again, the pattern is clear! Many of us would like a photograph or a "grand tour" of a spaceship ourselves, or some type of more definitive, scientific proof by a credible person. If empirical scientists work with reliable percipients like Irene they may also have an opportunity to experience a greater truth. Holistically speaking, they will then become experiential scientists in order to "graduate" by validating elusive phenomena for themselves in a *more complete* empirical way.

An extraordinary event involved the Wilsons at the end of February 1987, which led to independent scientific analysis that would lead any objective observer to conclude that the Sasquatch are not only intelligent, but they also can be literate to a degree. There was a week of mild weather on the Oregon coast. The Wilson family planned to take their adult children and grandchildren for a Sunday afternoon picnic by a small pond in the coastal mountains. After lunch, Mr. Wilson took everyone on a hike while Irene stayed and cared for the three infant grandchildren. It was quiet and peaceful as the babies napped. Suddenly, Irene was distracted by a noise and looked up to see four male Sasquatch—two adults and two juveniles—less than 100 feet away from her. As the two giant Sasquatch walked up to her, she whimsically asked, "Do you know Jack Lapseritis?"

"We know of him!" one answered. Before she could continue, one of the creatures knelt down beside the sleeping infants as if to get a better look at them. Irene thought to herself, "I hope he'll be careful with them." It was at that moment that the creature, having read her mind, turned abruptly and glared at her. The nine-foot Sasquatch, the only one with blue eyes, was standing beside Irene. He gently placed his hand on her shoulder, giving her a kind, reassuring look. "The children are very special, very beautiful," he said.

Toward the end of the visit, Irene asked the Sasquatch: "Who are you people?" To her amazement, one of the creatures knelt down, picked up a stick, and, digging the point into the soil, drew four characters from an unknown alphabet. Irene was deeply puzzled. Why didn't he merely tell her? What's the big secret? Or, was the clever being, by his actions, showing Irene that although he appeared to be a primitive-looking anthropoid, he was actually a very intelligent person?

When her husband and the rest of the family returned, Mr. Wilson covered the "hieroglyphics" (as they labeled them) by turning a basket upside down and placing it on the ground over the letters. He later returned to the site and made a plaster-of-paris cast of the characters for posterity. When I eventually had an opportunity to examine the message, I traced it onto paper and sent a copy of it to Dr. Barry Fell, a linguist who was formerly at Harvard University and is presently Director of the Epigraphic Society in San Diego, California. The only details I conveyed to him were that the characters were from northern Oregon. Here is Dr. Fell's reply in its entirety:

**The Epigraphic Society**
*an incorporated tax-exempt public foundation*
*6625 Bamburgh Drive*
*San Diego, California 92177*
*Telephone (619) 571-1344*

June 5, `87
Dear Jack Lapseritis:

The inscription is in the old Spanish (pre-Roman) Iberic alphabet and the language is Iberic (closely related to Arabic).
It reads

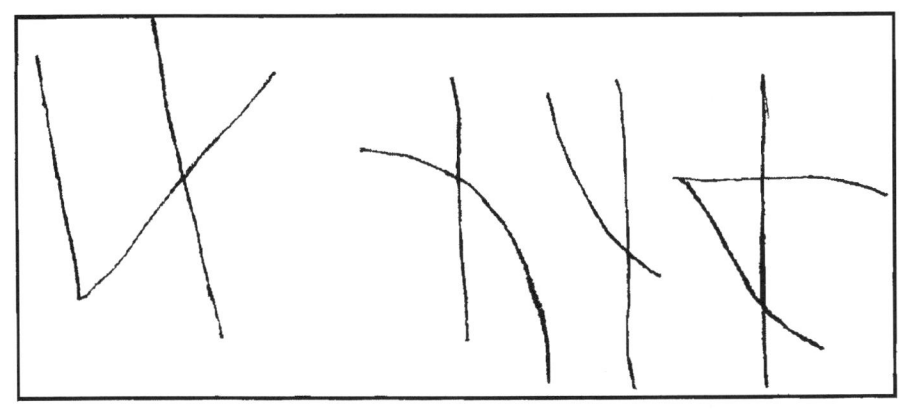

to be vocalized as *ayat waqa*. This is the same in Arabic and means "protective signs." The place is evidently a site that was to be treated as inviolate for some reason. If you can send us a photo and more details as to locality we could publish your find in ESOP. I enclose details of the current volume (15) of that journal. Many short reports, such as yours, go into the section called "Forum."

Sincerely,

Barry Fell

Dr. Fell was unaware that the Sasquatch, as a nature people, routinely tell contactees that the Bigfoot are "protectors of the Earth." The "site" of which Dr. Fell writes *is* Mother Earth, which the Sasquatch tell us should "be

**99**

treated as inviolate." This message is consistent with "folklore" from Indian tribes in North America.

I have known the Wilson family for more than ten years now, and I personally have found them to be consistent and unfailingly honest. So I rule out a hoax. Their guess that the characters might be Egyptian hieroglyphics is as reasonable as any other uninformed guess.

The bigger puzzle is: Why did the Bigfoot write in Spanish-Iberic? Was the Sasquatch merely showing off a few words he learned? If so, where did he learn a language older than the Roman empire? Did Bigfoot observe the early humans, just as they observe modern Americans today? In any case, is this behavior that of a wild animal, or is it that of an intelligent nature person, a representative of a uniquely evolved, ancient race of interdimensional psychic beings that passes cultural learnings across generations? And can a "murdered" Bigfoot corpse ever answer such anthropological questions?

# Bigfoot In New England

*OVERVIEW*

In September, 1961, in the rugged White Mountains of New Hampshire, a couple claimed they were abducted by a group of alien beings from another world. They were taken aboard a flying saucer and given a physical examination. The experience was so staggering and impressive that the couple was forever haunted by the event. Their abduction is one of the most exhaustively documented cases in the annals of ufology. Their story, as presented in the book, *The Interrupted Journey,* by John Fuller, and the movie, *The UFO Incident,* is one of the most convincing reports on record.

At the time of the abduction, Betty Hill was a social worker with a college degree, and Barney, her now-deceased husband, was a respected government postal worker. Since 1961, Betty reports observing hundreds of UFOs in her native New Hampshire. Because of the apparent reality of these experiences, she once stated: "The subject of UFOs is always the last thing I think about before falling asleep at night and the first thing I think about when I wake up in the morning."

Betty Hill and I have had many conversations about the Bigfoot/UFO connection, and she firmly believes, without a doubt, that a direct correlation exists between the two phenomena. The following is her story about Bigfoot in New England.

*EPISODE*

"My first introduction to the possibility of Bigfoot occurred back in the 1960s in my mother's backyard. Her home was located in the country, and behind her house is 33 acres that runs down and borders along the railroad tracks. The land contains brooks, swamps, cedar trees, and many other kinds of trees. A group of us were outdoors in her greenhouse one night when we heard a noise just a little beyond where we were sitting. All of a sudden, running up from the swamp area was some huge animal. We did not see it, but even the ground was shaking, and whatever this animal was, it was making verbal sounds similar to a monkey.

"Now, one of the men who was in this greenhouse with us teaches survival to Boy Scout groups, and they are frequently in areas where there are bears. He immediately ruled out the possibility of a bear and suggested that, to prevent a possible attack by the animal, we all pick up sticks and beat the ground to keep it away. So we did this. We all ran for the house, dragging my mother along with us, who wanted to stay out and see what kind of an animal it was. After we were in the house, for at least a half hour we could hear this animal circling the house and making odd sounds. While in the house, we could feel the whole ground shake from the weight of the creature. We did not see it, however. Later, after we had not heard the animal for a while, I went outside, got in my car, and drove around on some of the backwood roads behind the house. I couldn't find anything. The next day I went back to where the incident had occurred and there, on the edge of the swamp, in the mud, I found a huge print of a human-like foot. I tried to make a cast of it out of plaster of Paris, but the ground was too wet, and it would not harden.

"A few months later, in the fall, I was visiting at my sister's home, which is directly across the street from my mother's, when her next-door neighbor came running in all excited. He said that a huge animal had just run between her house and his house. The ground shook and the creature made strange sounds as it ran along the edge of the brook. He had called the police just in case someone had lost an elephant. The police came, and nothing was found. However, the next day I went back again, and we found birch trees, two or three inches in diameter, that had actually been uprooted, and others that had been broken off. Whatever this animal was, it made loud crashing sounds, although nobody saw it.

"One of the most interesting reports of Bigfoot in New Hampshire, to my knowledge, happened in Hudson. I don't remember the date of the incident. There was a large open area in the town, and on weekends different merchants would come with their trailers to sell different kinds of merchandise. People would come from miles around to get bargains. Well, one Friday night, this man and his children were in his camper-trailer. They were parked so that he could get an early start the next morning. As they were sitting there, all of a sudden the trailer started rocking back and forth. The traveling merchant assumed it was a bunch of hoodlum-kids trying to have some fun, so he threw open the back door to yell at them, stepping right into the arms of a Bigfoot! Stunned and frightened, he ran for the cab of the camper-truck, jumped inside, and watched Bigfoot stroll across an open area, climb over a fence and walk off into the woods. The man immediately drove to the police station and reported the encounter. A party was organized to look for the creature. It got a lot of publicity—newspapers and press of all kinds—and people came from all directions to look for Bigfoot.

"In the meanwhile, one of my associates who collected UFO reports and lived in that general area volunteered his services to go around and knock on doors asking people: 'Have you seen Bigfoot?' He was amazed at how many people told him 'yes,' they had. One of the most unusual sightings was from a woman who told him that on summer nights she would sit on the couch in her sunroom porch watching TV and, out of the corner of her eye, would see Bigfoot standing outside the window watching TV as well. She insisted that the man-creature did this on numerous occasions. Whenever this happened, she sat still and pretended she did not see him.

"The next report from New Hampshire that I received was from an anthropologist who was head of the anthropology department at one of our large colleges. This was in the early winter of 1975. He contacted me and wanted to know what I knew about Bigfoot. It seems that the university had been contacted by a woman who reported an incident in which she was out in the woods, walking along the shores of a lake with her dog, when the dog ran out onto the ice. The ice broke, and the dog went into the water, paddling helplessly and trying to get out. To her amazement, while she was standing there trying to figure out how to get the dog out of the water, a Bigfoot came running out of the woods and into the water. It picked up the dog, put him on the shore, and wandered off into the woods. She immediately called the anthropology department and reported this. When the head of the department went out to look the area over, he located big footprints in the sand along the shore.

"Soon after this, in the summer of 1975, I was visited by two state troopers who wanted to know what I knew about Bigfoot. They had received some reports of a UFO landing or crashing in New Hampshire's Ossipee Mountains. Planes had gone out, and search parties investigated on the ground, but nothing had been found. The Ossipee Mountains are real wilderness without even a pass through them. After these UFO reports, the state police began receiving reports of Bigfoot in the area. They were wondering if there were dangers associated with the creatures, because a group of men were thinking of camping out in the mountains and seeing if they could make contact.

"The state troopers did tell me that there had been one family who had met Bigfoot face-to-face. This was a young couple who were building a summer place in the Ossipee Mountains. The builders were there during the week, and they would go up on weekends and work around the place. They would pitch a tent, eat their food, camp out, while the work was being done. One Saturday morning when they were working around the building, they spotted Bigfoot suddenly coming out of the woods. He looked around, walked over to their car, smashed the window in the back, reached in and took out their basket of food, then wandered off into the woods. The state troopers said the couple never went back up there. They sold the partially-constructed building at a great loss. The area where this happened is also the area where the woman told the anthropologist about the dog being rescued by Bigfoot.

"I have a vacation home in the Ossipee Mountains and I'm there occasionally during the summer. If I get up there in early spring and there's snow on the ground, I always check for Bigfoot prints, and, quite often, I find them along the stone wall behind my property. Also, interestingly, October is known as UFO month in this area.

"Another report from New Hampshire happened at a home that is located on the shores of a lake in the general area where I go out to observe UFOs. Three children were lying on the living room floor watching TV when they suddenly looked up toward the window and saw Bigfoot looking in at them. The next morning, the family went out to take measurements. Because this was one of those houses that is on different layers, they figured out that for Bigfoot to be able to look in the window, he would need to be at least nine feet tall!

"There was a woman who teaches a course on psychic development and UFOs at the University of Massachusetts at Amherst. She and her husband were driving home one night when suddenly a tire on the front of the car went flat. Her husband got out to change it. While she was sitting in the car, she heard this rapping on the back window of the car. When she turned around she was startled to see a Bigfoot pressing his face up to the glass looking inside at her. She yelled to her husband. He quickly jumped in the car, and they sat there with the doors locked for a while until Bigfoot ambled off into the woods. The husband hurriedly changed the tire, and they went speeding home. She told me this experience herself.

"All of the other sightings I have from Massachusetts occurred in one place, out by Springfield in an area called The Meadows. This is a huge market garden area used by the growers there. It's fenced in and has gates which are kept locked. This woman, Kelly, whose father owned most of this land at The Meadows, had been sitting in the sunroom one summer night and had seen a UFO land in The Meadows on their property. The next day, Kelly obtained the keys to the gate from her father. She went in and found a large circular area of flattened grass. On one side of this was fine sand and, in the sand, she found one large human-like footprint! She looked all around but there was no second print, just one. She felt it was as though the UFO, or whatever the craft was that had set down there, had landed, and Bigfoot had stepped outside and put only one foot on the ground.

"Kelly called me and wanted to know what she should do. I told her to get back to The Meadows and make some plaster casts of the print. She arranged for a neighbor to go with her. The two of them went down with plaster-of-Paris and made a cast of this print. While they were doing this, something really strange happened. A small black helicopter began circling the field, coming in closer and closer to them. Then it started darting at them. They were so frightened that they picked up the cast and ran for home, with the helicopter following over them. This lady said that she had a beautiful cast of a footprint. Since it was still really clear in the sand, I suggested that she go back with paraffin wax and make another cast to see if any details would show up that were not in the first plaster cast. Later that day, Kelly made arrangements with another friend to go with her. This friend had a movie camera and planned to film the area. While they were out there, using a candle and a tin can to melt the paraffin wax and pouring it into the print, along came this mysterious black helicopter again. It began circling them, darting at them, and they got into a panic. This time they had gone out to the area in a car. They ran back to the car, jumped in, and tried to start the motor. At first it wouldn't start, but when it finally did, they drove out of there and went back to the house, with the helicopter again following them. At this point, Kelly called the police and reported that she was being harassed by someone in a mysterious helicopter. As for the cast of this foot, it is a little over 14 inches long and eight inches wide across the ball of the foot. It has *four* toes and it was apparent that there was some kind of infection or something in the foot. Kelly showed the police the cast that she had made of the footprint.

"At a later date, people who lived in a certain area on the banks of the Connecticut River next to The Meadows began to have Bigfoot encounters. In one incident, Bigfoot was looking in some people's windows. They ran to the windows and watched the creature walk over and look in the garage windows. They quickly called the police and reported it. The police came out and found footprints. At that point, they contacted Kelly because they knew of no one else who had ever had any information about Bigfoot. Kelly called me and said, 'What do I do now?' At that point, I suggested the police contact Lee Frank, a Bigfoot researcher in New York. He came out and, even though it was wintertime and there was snow on the ground, he camped out in the general area to see if he could see Bigfoot.

"There was tremendous publicity. People were coming from all directions. Hundreds came down to the area to get themselves a Bigfoot. In order to quiet things down, the police publicly stated that the whole thing was a hoax, that the mystery had been solved, and that it had been the prank of a 14-year-old boy who lived in the general area. Because of this statement the whole neighborhood was in an uproar. People who had been on TV and in the press telling of their sighting of Bigfoot, were furious that the police were now saying it was all a hoax done by a 14-year-old boy. At that point, the police demanded to see me. Most of these people are Sicilian Italians, and they were furious!

"When the weather got warmer, I went to visit. They had found big prints leading from the Connecticut River up a very steep bank, and these prints led up to windows of houses and garages, and around cars. They would circle the general area and then head down back to the Connecticut River as though the creature had returned to the water there, maybe swimming.

"One man told me that while he was sitting in his living room, he looked up and Bigfoot was looking in his window. He got a very good look at him. The only way he could describe him was huge, tall, rugged, with a hairy body and the *face of a man*, long straggly hair, and a beard. When Bigfoot saw that he was being observed by the man, he backed up, went over and looked in the garage window, and then wandered off. This man was yelling to members of his family to come and look out the window to see this creature. After I interviewed the witnesses, we all went out to an area where footprints were leading to and from the Connecticut River. They said these prints were about five feet apart. We all tried, under the best of conditions, to take steps that would be five feet apart. It was absolutely impossible for any one of us to do this, regardless of height. Also, the steep bank of this river is such that in order for a person to go up and down without slipping, one has to hang onto the trees that are growing out of the bank.

"After I had talked with all the witnesses, I dropped into the police station and talked with the chief. He admitted that all the witnesses were furious, and that it was not of their doing—the whole situation was getting way out of hand and the way things were going, somebody was going to get seriously hurt. So they thought it was time to put a stop to the whole thing.

"Over the years the police had received many reports of Bigfoot. They believed he traveled up and down the Connecticut River, and that somewhere north of this area there were some kind of man-made tunnels built under the ground that had some purpose at one time—I don't remember what it was. They believed that Bigfoot was possibly staying in these tunnels. Over the years, they had made casts of the footprints of Bigfoot on many occasions. The chief believed that there could be some serious danger associated with this creature because (he said this was not known publicly; this was given to me on a confidential basis) near these tunnels near the river where they believe that Bigfoot would stay at times, they had found animals that he said had been mutilated far beyond the point of death. The bones and the bodies of these animals had been pulverized, as though they had been crushed by a tremendous weight. They found the body of a large German Shepherd dog which had all its bones pulverized! He said it was frightening, and they didn't want to take any chances with people when it was unnecessary. So this information was not made public.

"While I was there meeting with these people, I did a lot of listening. People kept saying to me, 'Go see Joe, who owns the gas station.' Before I left, I went to see him at his station. Before Joe bought the gas station, he had owned and operated a car-crushing business. He had all his heavy equipment set up down in The Meadows and he had a trailer down there that he used as an office.

"One night he and some buddies were riding around town. He said that in those days they tended to be hell raisers and the police knew it. It seemed that no matter where they went there was a police cruiser. It was a hot night and they decided to get some beer and go down to Joe's trailer on the banks of the Connecticut River. They figured it would be cooler there. They took some chairs outdoors and were sitting outside the trailer drinking beer when suddenly they heard a great rustling of trees and branches. To their amazement, a

Bigfoot came out of the water. It walked up the bank into the clearing and stood there looking around. The huge creature saw these piled up bodies of crushed cars and stood there looking at them for a moment. Then it bent over and picked up one of the crushed car bodies and started walking off with it. Joe said that at this point, he and his buddies had gone into a state of shock. They couldn't talk; they couldn't move! They were standing there watching this Bigfoot carry a car body around as though it was a trinket, when he knew it weighted at least 1500 pounds. Bigfoot walked about 30 feet with the crushed car body in its arms. Then it stopped suddenly about 25 feet away and looked up, noticing the men sitting outside the trailer. The creature dropped the car body and stood there looking at them. Joe said Bigfoot then put up its hand and scratched the top of its head as though it was very puzzled. It stood there for a few minutes more, shrugged its shoulders, then went back to the river and swam off. Joe said they had spent all evening trying to avoid the police, but as soon as Bigfoot left, they fell all over each other trying to be the first one to reach the phone to call them.

"The police came out and made casts of the footprints, looked the area over, noting the body of the crushed car that had been moved. Joe said that the amazing thing about this creature was, first of all, that he was really tall—eight feet, or maybe a little more. He made it very clear that the creature *did not* have fur; it had HAIR! It looked like it had human hair all over its body. That was one of the things that really startled him. He expected that, as an animal, it would have fur. He further described the Bigfoot as having a *human face with long hair and a beard*. The hair covering its whole body was the same type of hair as that on its head! Joe said that within a week he had cleaned out his business, sold the car bodies, got rid of the equipment and the trailer. He then bought a gas station in the middle of town in one of the most densely settled areas he could find. He said that he had never returned to The Meadows.

"Another report comes from a woman named Lorraine who lived in a house located way back from the road and bordered on The Meadows. Lorraine had a large vegetable garden for her own home use, of which she was very proud. At one point, she was awakened in the middle of the night by horrendous snarling and growling sounds, like animals fighting. She did not turn on her light, but got out of bed and actually crawled on her hands and knees across the floor so that if anything was looking in the window it would not see her. She went into the bathroom and looked out the window where she saw two Bigfoot creatures fighting in the middle of her vegetable garden.

She became terrified! They were growling and snarling, fighting and clawing. She said that most of the time they were rolling around on the ground. When they did stand up, she could see that one was probably about two feet taller than the other. She could see that they were two very tall, massive, hairy creatures with rather long faces which were hairless, except for beards like human men, definitely not like an ape! After a while, one of them ran off, and, finally, the other one also left. The next morning she went out and found that most of her vegetable garden had been totally destroyed. Within a month, Lorraine found another rental home and moved away from that area.

"These Meadows are in the center of many UFO sightings and landings. I have gone over there myself and have stood and watched the UFOs flying around, and coming in and landing. Over the years we were actually able to pinpoint a pattern in their activity. They would come in every two weeks and would stay for three or four days. Then they would just leave. Fourteen days later, they would return.

"Another strange thing happened on the Connecticut River. I don't think there was ever any publicity about this, although people who lived in the area all knew about it. My informant said that at one spot in the middle of the Connecticut River there was a good-sized island that was uninhabited. Then suddenly one day it was inhabited by small, prehistoric-appearing people. They don't know how many of them there were, maybe 50. They lived on the island for three years. No one ever succeeded in getting near them. The police had gone out to the island on boats and had gone onto the island. These small, primitive people could outrun anyone. They would take off running and then could not be found. There were many caves on this island, and it was believed that maybe they were hiding in the caves, but the police just could not find them. Anthropologists went to the island and could observe them at a great distance but couldn't get close to them. No one ever succeeded. It is not known how they lived or what they did for food. No fires were ever seen on the island, but they lived there year-round for approximately three years. Then, just as suddenly as they appeared, they disappeared.

"It was as though somebody had picked up a group of early cavemen and had set them down on the island in a New England countryside. Planes and helicopters had flown over the area, hoping to get pictures, but these little people—they're not really tiny people, but maybe four feet tall or so—would just take off running at such speeds that no one could even get pictures of them. These prehistoric-looking people would be there one instant, then would start running and in the next instant they would just disappear!

This went on for three years. The main hobby of the people who lived in the area was to go out and park along the banks of the Connecticut River, hoping to get a glimpse of these unusual people. Some people waved to them and tried to show friendliness, but just could not approach them.

"After the little people left, teams went out and searched the island, thinking that maybe some great catastrophe had killed all of them. But there were no signs of them, not a trace. The main mystery is how they survived the winter in a harsh New England climate without fire and without clothes —just sparse hair covering on their bodies. Their food supply was also a complete mystery. The chief of police said that he himself had seen them, not close, but through binoculars. I wish I had known about this while it was going on. I would have loved to have gone out and attempted to see these little people. The information about these little people was given to me by the same police chief who gave me the information about Bigfoot.

"It is important to note that I promised the people I interviewed that I would protect their confidentiality in order to get them to talk with me. They told me that I could use the information they offered if I promised not to use their names. Incidentally, all of these Bigfoot experiences happened within a three-year time period, between 1975 and 1978. I am not aware of any reports before that and I've had no further reports since that time."

# Spiritual Keepers

*OVERVIEW*

In early 1987, I received an exceptional letter from a man in Texas who had a Bigfoot encounter and swore he would never tell anyone about it. After a lengthy correspondence and a few telephone conversations, Ed eventually came to Oregon to be interviewed so I could document his unique telepathic conversation. He had struggled with the encounter for years. We finally developed enough trust so that he could share his personal story.

*EPISODE*

"I've been an interstate trucker for a number of years, hauling out of the Eugene-Albany (Oregon) area to the east coast, southeast and into Texas. The company had opened up a terminal in the Eugene area. There were times I got tired of driving a truck—occasionally getting into what we call a burnout situation. In the early summer or late spring of 1964, I decided to take some time off to go up into the mountains. I'm a rock hound. I like working the rivers and streams looking for gemstones and items like that. I was exploring the area called the North Fork of the Willamette River, approximately 60-65 miles east and north of Eugene. Everything in the area was in bloom. After being out on the river for quite some time—I guess four or five days—I set up camp. Soon after, I began feeling a little uneasy. As I cooked my evening meal, I started to smell something strange. It wasn't really a sickening smell, but more of a musty, damp odor—like a dog that had been out in the rain, but not quite as pungent. It was just around sunset—about 6:30 or 7:30. I could still see the sun just over the edge of the mountains to the west. I knew there was about another one-half to three-quarters of an hour of sunlight left. As I ate, I kept smelling the strange odor. Looking around, I noticed some kind of being out in the trees about 25-30

111

feet away and thought to myself, 'Gee, what is that thing?' It didn't appear to be an animal. It looked more like some kind of humanoid, about seven to seven and one-half feet tall and about six or seven hundred pounds. It appeared to be very stout and strong looking, with long hair the color of ebony, I guess. It wasn't really red and not brown either. The hair color reminded me of the people down in the valley, or people in the South Pacific Islands—more of a copper-tone brown. The face had some hair on it, mainly on the cheeks, like sideburns, and on upper lip, like a moustache. It also had fairly long hair growing from the chin, looking like it had never been clipped or trimmed. At that time I hadn't heard anything about Bigfoot, Sasquatch, Yetis, or whatever.

"I suddenly felt something in my head, psychically, like this being was talking to me, yet it wasn't speaking any words with its mouth. It just seemed as if the words were coming to me, but no sound was coming from the being. It seemed to be reading my thoughts and I was reading its thoughts. I offered it something to eat and then sat down.

"The creature first said: 'Don't be afraid; I'm not going to harm you. I just want to rest and sit for a while. I just want to be with you for a while.' I was thinking to myself, "Gee, I'm hearing this thing talk to me and it's not moving its lips or anything." I was sort of apprehensive, but I wasn't scared. The creature sat down on a log about 15-20 feet from me. I again offered it something to eat, which it declined with a wave of its hand. The hand had five digits, like a human hand—not like a bear or some other type of animal. I've heard it said that the Sasquatch are just animals, but I don't agree. This was some type of humanoid person I met. Maybe 'person' isn't the right word, but it was definitely humanoid. It was tall and bulky—not fat, but muscular and huge! When it moved over out of the direction from which the wind was coming, the smell seemed to disappear. It didn't really make me sick, but it was quite noticeable. Because of the hair on its face, I couldn't really see the color of its eyes, but they looked like humanoid eyes. They were large cavities, like the eyes of a human, but larger. And they were oval, not slanted like the eyes of Japanese people. It had a medium- to small-size nose, which slanted down like a human's nose. It was not like the pug nose of a gorilla or monkey, it was more like my nose. The face was not at all like a gorilla. It didn't really look apelike, but the arms were gangly and quite long. A human's arms usually come just past the hips, but the creature's arms were longer, about eight or nine inches above the knee when it was standing. When it walked, it had a sort of stooped posture and a lumbering gait. It didn't walk very fast when it approached me, probably because I was apprehensive, but I got the feeling that it didn't mean to harm me; it just wanted to 'talk.'

"As it began to get dark, we just sat, talking about things in general. The being was sitting on the log near to me, sort of in a slouched position, with its arms on its legs. It was asking me what I was doing there in the wilderness.

"Earlier in the day, I had run across a deer that had been shot with an arrow. The arrow was still in it and I could see that it was in pain and that it had been there for quite some time. I caught the animal and tied it to a tree. I cut the arrow out and treated the deer, then gave it some of my oatmeal, mixed with water. It ate the oatmeal, but I could tell that it was sick. I then set up my camp near to where I had found the deer.

"I had caught a couple of fish and was cooking them as I sat communicating with this unusual being. At one point, the being asked: 'Why did you help the deer?' Seeing this injured animal, I had wanted to heal it. I used to hunt quite a bit, but I had quit because I hadn't been able to kill anything for quite some time. When I saw the injured deer, I felt sorry for it. Using what I'd learned from my medical training, I doctored up the deer as best I could. Apparently, the creature had observed me caring for the deer, and that was why it felt it needed to approach me. It had never seen this done before—a human caring for a wild animal. He told me he had seen deer with half the carcass wasted, left to rot. I told him: 'You may think I'm corny, but this is my philosophy in life: If I see an injured person or an injured animal, I will try to help it.'

"The creature replied, saying: "Well, I've seen what you have done," referring to the injured deer. I got the impression that the creature felt my love for this deer. I told the Bigfoot creature, 'Well, you know, I help anything that is injured.' The creature asked me where I was going. I told him what I was doing and where I was headed. He seemed to understand. Evidently, he had run into prospectors before. Then he said, 'You have no gun.' I said to him: 'I'm not out here to kill anything. I've brought my food with me instead.' I had enough supplies to stay out for two or three weeks.

"I was not afraid as I sat there communicating with this being; however I was somewhat in a state of shock or apprehension. When a guy is coming at you with a knife—now that's fear! But it wasn't this type of fear, like when a wild animal is coming at you. It was more of a feeling of apprehension, like 'Hey, what's going on here?' We conversed back and forth, and when he asked me where I was going, I took a stick and drew a river in the dirt and pointed at it. I don't know if he understood me or not. This type of communication takes time, and, before I knew it, two hours had passed. I don't remember much of what we talked about because it was 20 years ago, but I do remember the amount of time that we spent communicating. I told him my name, not knowing if names meant anything to him or not. He got up and walked around, kind of looking around the camp. Then he walked over and looked at the deer and sort of patted it. The deer appeared to be shaking. It was probably the first time the deer had seen a creature of this kind. Suddenly, the Bigfoot creature turned around, sort of waved, then dropped its arm down, and walked off into the woods. I heard noises right away and had a feeling that perhaps there were more of these creatures nearby, maybe a family of them.

"The being seemed to be most interested in why I had helped the injured deer, as it seemed to know that people hunt and kill deer, sometimes for the meat, but sometimes just to take a little of the meat and leave the rest. When the being communicated to me, it wasn't like a regular conversation; it was more disjointed, with the questions kind of jumping around. With a little difficulty, I was able to make myself understood to this creature. When I said, "No gun. I don't need a gun. I'm not out to kill; I'm out just for enjoyment," I don't think he understood the meaning of the word enjoyment. I told him that I go looking for gemstones. I reached into my pocket and pulled out a couple of stones I had picked up. It seemed as though he couldn't understand what I wanted with these stones. He was standing about two or three feet away from me, and a little behind, when I showed him the gemstones. I turned and sort of touched him, noticing that his hair was very coarse. It wasn't really like fur, though—more like hair. I guess the creature got scared when I touched it, as it stepped aside very quickly. It started to leave then, and I said, "Bye." But he just turned around and waved his hand up, then put it back down. Apparently he had seen people wave good-bye and knew what it meant. Then I heard some noises, like grunting and branches breaking, in the woods about 500 feet away. That's when I realized there must have been more than one Bigfoot creature out there. I wondered if perhaps the others thought I had tried to hurt this one and they wanted to let me know they were there and that they would protect him.

"When the Bigfoot creature left, I was tired and went into my little pup tent and went to sleep. When I woke up in the morning, I could see by the numerous footprints all around that the creatures had been all through my camp. The footprints of the creature I had communicated with the night before seemed to be the largest. I don't know if it was a family of these creatures or just a bunch of males, but there were different size footprints. I know one of them had to be pretty small, because its footprint was about the size of a size-eight shoe, just a little smaller than mine. Maybe it was a child or a young Bigfoot creature. The footprints had five digits, like toes: a big one and then some smaller ones. I could tell by the footprint that, instead of being arched, like a human foot, the feet were totally flat. Apparently, they walked like humans, going up on the toes, not a shuffling-type walk. I could also tell by the depth of the imprints in the ground that the creatures were quite heavy, even the youngest one. I compared the depth to the depth of the footprints I made with a 30- to 40-pound pack on my back. My body weight is about 185 pounds, and even with this 30- to 40-pound pack, my feet barely dented the ground when I walked. I figured that the being that made the smaller footprints, the ones that were about the size of a size-eight or size-nine shoe, must have weighed 250-300 pounds. The larger footprints were about 1-1/2" deep. They were not like bear or ape prints; they were definitely made by a humanoid-type foot. There were at least three sets of tracks, maybe more. Besides the smaller ones, there were some that were about the size of a size-twelve or size-thirteen shoe, and then another set that were humongous. I'm not sure, but I think those largest ones were made by the creature that visited me. I didn't have a tape measure, but I would say that those largest footprints were about 18 inches long. I could tell that the being that made them was very heavy, as it had really sunk into the soft ground. As I walked up along the river, I spotted more Sasquatch tracks there; some were old and some were very fresh. I don't want to give out the exact location where they were, though.

"I realize that I've had a very unique experience, something very rare. This humanoid-type being had been observing me for a while before it approached. One of the reasons I know this is because whenever I set up camp, I always dig what is known as a 'cat-hole.' All my trash and garbage are buried there. When I have empty cans to discard, I always open up both ends and flatten them out, turning the lids in, so that no animals will be injured by them. When the Bigfoot creature was communicating with me, it asked: 'What is this you do? Why did you do that?' I didn't understand what he was asking, so he went over and dug up some stuff I had buried. When I realized what he was asking, I explained to him that by taking out a can and opening it up, I could get the sharp edges out. Then I took a piece of a tree limb and cut the bark off of it, showing him how it could hurt. He shook his head as if to say, 'I know, but then why do you do this?' I then said, 'So the animals and other beings in the forest cannot get injured by what I leave behind. That's why I buried the garbage. When I put my fire out, I bury it also. See? And you can barely tell that anyone spent the night here.' He seemed to understand what I said, but yet, in a dumbfounded way, also seemed to be telling me, 'I know what the man is trying to say, but I can't figure it out.' He seemed to get the gist of it, though.

"These beings actually seem very intelligent, as far as I'm concerned. They are very much like me, but they are unable to speak. The being I encountered seemed to communicate in a way that was strange to me, by speaking *into my head*. And I would communicate back by speaking into his head. Before I could say anything out loud, he seemed to know exactly what I was going to say. This was an entirely new experience for me. Like I said before, I wasn't scared, just apprehensive.

"The being kept repeating something about the trees, about cutting the trees down. I took my hatchet and pretended like I was going to cut down a tree. Then I pointed at myself and said, 'I don't do this.' He then wanted to know who did and why. I drew a house in the dirt and he seemed to understand what it was. I tried to show him that the trees are used to build houses and I think he understood. He seemed to have some fear about the cutting down of the trees. I won't really say that their existence was being threatened, but their territory and the environment in which they lived was becoming out of balance, and they can somehow feel it. Because they live so close to nature, they seem to have a psychic knowingness about this. They are a type of nature-people.

"All throughout Oregon, this 'raping' of the land is going on. When the logging companies move out, there is nothing left but the bare Earth. I think the Bigfoot creature was trying to understand why modern man takes and takes all this timber and all these beautiful trees off the land just to build a house. When I communicated with him, I deliberately acted like a simpleton so I could better understand his way of thinking and his values. The Sasquatch people seem to have picked up language by hearing human beings talk and gesture. In this way, we were able to communicate with each other by projecting words into each others' minds and by gesturing, and by my drawing pictures in the dirt. I picked up through our communication that the Sasquatch people are very concerned about the environment. It seemed that the area that I was in was one of their main areas of travel. When I was up in that region, I saw plenty of signs that they were there. Besides the footprints, some old and some very fresh, I also ran across carcasses of animals that had been killed. Some were three or four days old. I'm convinced that they were killed by the Sasquatch for food because blueberries and other edible berries weren't out yet. I saw the tops of other spring plants and flowers that appeared to have been pulled out of the ground and discarded after the roots were eaten. There is a lot of what is called Jerusalem artichoke growing in that area. It is a tuber that is palatable to most types of primates. I think they're delicious. I could tell that the foliage on the top of these plants was from the previous year. Some were starting to grow, but the Sasquatch had apparently pulled them out to eat the artichokes, because I'd find pieces of bad ones on the ground, yet the rest of the plant was missing. In several areas, it appeared that they had pulled up large amounts of these plants to keep for sustenance. Another edible herb that grows in this area is Indian cabbage, also known as skunk cabbage, because it smells like a skunk. The roots of this plant are very edible. I've eaten them myself in a soup called 'swamp cabbage soup.'

"As I said, the being seemed to be very concerned about the rate our environment is being unnecessarily destroyed. I couldn't really grasp exactly what it meant. I understood about the environment to some degree, the trees and so forth, and realized that a tremendous number of species of animals in the world have disappeared because their environment was destroyed, leaving them with nothing to eat and no place to go. We nearly lost the American bison as a species. Because of our somewhat demented social values, we have directly caused the extinction of several of our native animals. Knowing that they will never return, we must bear the shame caused by our actions. This I understand.

"I understand the timber industry's right to harvest timber, but to rape a piece of property by leaving it completely barren is clearly wrong. Selective harvesting is the answer. I'm not a timber engineer, but anyone with common sense can see this.

"I find it somewhat humorous that the creature was unimpressed with my rock collection. He couldn't understand why I was collecting these rocks. When I wet the rock and showed him how pretty it looked, he seemed to comprehend that. He telepathically communicated: 'Oh, now I understand what you're doing!' Then I showed him how I take some of the rocks, the ones we call thunder eggs, and break them open to see what they look like inside. The Bigfoot creature didn't seem to have a particular interest in this stuff, gemstones or any kind of metal, like gold.

"The day after my encounter with the creature, as I headed up the trail, I had the feeling that I was being watched. I also felt something else, and I'm not sure if it was a concern on their part for me, or an apprehension of me. It seemed as though they were thinking, 'Well, is this guy really doing what he says?' I picked up some gemstones and different things along my way. I came out of the area a different way.

"I didn't say anything to anyone for many years about this incident with the Bigfoot creature. A few years ago, however, I read something about some person who wanted to go out and shoot a Bigfoot. I guess he thought the only way to prove that they exist is to shoot one, cut it up, and bring it out of the forest. I don't agree with this at all. I feel it's downright murder! These beings are definitely humanoid. Even their teeth are like ours, no fangs or anything wild looking. Also, when I communicated with the being, he would sometimes grin when he answered some of my questions. That's how I was able to see his teeth; some were yellowish and worn down.

"Although I knew the being was male, I didn't really notice any genitalia. I didn't look at that area for that particular reason. I didn't want to be impolite or offend him in any way. That part of his body was the furthest thing from my mind. There was hair over its entire body, some of it four to five inches long, maybe even longer. It was matted with pieces of branches and leaves in it. It wasn't really dirty, it was just hanging sort of loose. I was looking at its feet most of the time. I could see that down around the ankles there was hair and just a little bit on the tops of the feet, but none on the sides. The front of the legs had less hair than the backs. As I said, its feet were basically the same as mine, the same shape, with a big toe and everything. Its hands were more or less like a human's. Its thumb was similar to my thumb, but longer and closer to the first finger. When he closed his hand, the thumb automatically grasped to the inside, like a person's. I could never guess what the age of the being was; I wouldn't even try.

"Its appearance wasn't really scary, and somehow its demeanor conveyed to me that there was nothing to be afraid of, although I'd never encountered anything like it before. All I can say is, I saw what I saw! If people want to believe me, then fine, and if they don't, then that's fine too. Since that time, I have done some reading about the Bigfoot creatures. Based on what I've read, I've decided I don't want my name used in connection with this story, because I don't want people to come up to me and tell me I'm crazy. Of course, I understand that anyone who would do this would be someone who is narrow minded and who has had limited experiences in life.

"I think that science can prove the existence of Bigfoot if the scientists are honorable by trying to communicate with them, and then they would come forward. But if they are going to start sticking needles in them or putting lights in their eyes, or dissecting them in some impersonal way, that's wrong. I could see cutting a little hair off here or there if one were to speak with them and make an exchange. This is enough proof to me. Why commit murder for the sake of science when the being is a humanoid? A nonviolent approach is what is necessary.

"I think the Bigfoot's purpose in life is to live, just like we do. I don't think they're destructive. I have not seen where it has taken down acres of trees or plowed blacktop down through the middle of the forest. It seems to coexist peacefully with its surroundings. If anyone were to shoot one of these beings, I believe they should be charged with murder. I don't think it would be fair to them or to us as human beings to do this when I'm certain there are better, nonviolent, ways to prove their existence. We've put a man on the moon, we've got spaceships that go up there; surely if we can do this, we can approach the Sasquatch phenomenon in a peaceful, humanistic way by communicating with them first. They are not animals; this I will say! It's just not human to kill something else human just to prove that it exists.

"Over the years, I moved to Texas and continued my adventures as a rockhound. Then, in 1987, a good friend of mine—a captain of a commercial fishing boat in Miami—invited me to vacation in Florida and to go out on his boat to watch the operation. It sounded like a nice change, so I went. The incident I describe below took place near Bimini, at the edge of the Bermuda Triangle. I agreed to never reveal the captain's name or the name of the vessel. He does not want publicity, nor do I, because the following event really happened.

"It was early November. The captain of the fishing boat would drag for bottom fish—different kinds of fish—and also for shrimp. The boat went a little to the north, by northeast, of Miami, approximately 60 to 80 miles. We spent the night around the island of Bimini, which is in the Bahama chain, and he was fishing in approximately 40 to 60 fathoms of water with a dragnet. After several good pulls of fish, the fishermen noticed that the pull on the net on a particular pull was different. They pulled the net up on the deck and emptied its contents. Then they do what is called "culling of catch"— getting rid of unwanted things. It was during the culling that everyone present was shocked to see a funny-looking 'sea-being' in the net. It was somewhat of a humanoid-type being in that it was an upright creature. It had a round head, with an area like a ridge down the center. The ridge

**119**

seemed to be more pronounced toward the front, then slowly disappeared toward the back of the head. The skin was a greenish-brown, with a little of a blue tint. As the creature came up on the boat, still tangled in the net, the captain let the net down on the deck to try to free the creature. We could tell that the thing, being out of water, was affected by the hot sun. It made sounds like some kind of language we could not understand. The amphibious creature began reaching out, trying to catch water which was washing across the deck from the deck holes. It tried splashing water on itself, but to no avail. I took the deck bucket, filled it with water, and slowly poured it on the creature. After that, it seemed less frightened—not really at ease, however. Nobody seemed very scared—only a little apprehensive. The part we were cautious about were the arms, although they weren't really arms as we know them. They were just appendages coming out, with no elbow, just a sort of hand, similar to a lobster's claw but with odd-looking fingers, on each arm. The digit finger was approximately one-half to one-quarter of the way to the hand. Four were webbed. The feet had four digits, which were webbed also. Overall, the creature was approximately four and one-half- to five-feet tall and weighed about 150-200 pounds.

"Six people witnessed this creature: the skipper, me, and four others. Two of the others were from one of the islands—the Bahamas, I guess. The captain and the two other witnesses were American citizens. While the captain and crew were trying to untangle the creature from the net, I took some pictures of the creature with a Polaroid camera and some with a 35-mm camera. It literally tore the net to pieces with its claw-like appendages. The crew was trying to untangle it so it could be thrown back overboard, but then the captain told them to try to save it. He wanted to bring it back to shore. When this half-fish, half-humanoid creature was finally untangled, it was in a very weakened state—not really unconscious, but barely able to move. The crew was able to get it into the empty bait tank and the tank was filled with water to keep the creature wet. The being struggled to get out of the tank, and we all watched as the captain placed the vented tops onto the tank and securely fastened them down. He then summoned the U.S. Coast Guard from Miami. A Coast Guard helicopter arrived, and one of its officers was lowered down onto the boat. He took a look at the creature, then, using a portable radio, he reported his findings back to his superior officer. We were met by a Coast Guard vehicle approximately eight to ten miles from shore in an area known as the Sea Channel Buoy, or the approach buoy to Miami Harbor. Some Coast Guard personnel came aboard the boat. Using a net, they moved the being to the holding tank of the Coast Guard vessel. The officer who seemed to be in charge asked if anyone had taken any pictures of the creature. I told him I had taken some pictures and had also recorded some of the sounds made by the creature. All my equipment was then confiscated—the Polaroid photos, the 35-mm camera, the Polaroid camera, and my tape recorder. Although I didn't understand this procedure at the time, I later came to understand, after talking with various individuals, that the government was taking the creature somewhere to perform experiments on it in order to determine what it was. All of us who had been on the boat that day were told not to say anything to anyone about what we had seen. I thought this was kind of ridiculous, because I think that if we have information about anything that comes from the sea, or from space, or even from inside the Bermuda Triangle, the public should know about it.

"When I returned to Texas, I discovered that I had another tape recorder with me—a micro-mini tape recorder, which I had in my pocket and had forgotten to mention to the Coast Guard officials. I found that it had picked up the sounds made by the creature as well as the conversations with the Coast Guard personnel. The recording included all the people's names and what they were saying. I had a recording of the Coast Guard personnel telling us what they were looking for, asking for all the photographs, cameras, etc., and telling us not to say anything about the incident. Shortly after my return to Texas, I called a friend on the telephone to let him listen to the tape. A couple of days later, I had to leave town for a few days. When I returned from this trip, I realized right away that someone had been in my apartment and that the cassette tapes documenting the evidence of this sea creature were missing. All of the notes, drawings, and tape recordings that I had made regarding this shocking encounter were also missing. Because my apartment was located on the 11th floor of a 15-story building, it would have been impossible for anyone to have entered from the outside. They would have had to enter from inside the building, using a special key.

"I checked with the personnel in the office of the apartment complex to find out if they had given my apartment key to anyone and was told that they had not and that, as far as they knew, no one had been in my apartment during my absence. My next-door neighbor, an 86-year old woman, told me that she had heard some men in my apartment while I was gone. She had heard some noises and, when she came out to see what was going on, a man in the hallway told her not to worry about it and to go back into her apartment. I have no idea who it was or why they wanted these other tapes.

"Before I'd left to go out of town, I had sent a letter, along with some copies of drawings I had made of the sea creature, and some tapes, to my friend Jack Lapseritis, who is a scientist. I had sent him one of the tapes at his request, and a letter asking him if he could identify any of the words, or sounds, being made by the creature. Some of Jack's associates were involved in analyzing and interpreting languages. But he never received the tape or the letter. He also had not received several other letters I had sent to him. During that time period, Jack had also sent me some material that I never received. It was obvious that our communications were being monitored by some agency.

"I still had one tape in my possession, which I had taken with me when I'd left town after returning from the boating adventure; however, I later noticed that this tape had been tampered with. It was as if someone had erased the sounds made by the creature from the tape. I don't know if this was done by a computer or what, but I now can't make heads nor tails of this tape that had previously contained the sounds made by the sea creature. All of the written information I had concerning the incident has disappeared.

"I have never before in my life seen anything like this creature—nor had the captain or any of his crew members. It seems fascinating to me that such a being could be living 300 feet below the surface of the ocean. It didn't look like an air-breathing creature, yet it didn't have the typical type of gills found on most sea animals, however. Its ears were shaped somewhat like gills. It seemed to be more frightened of us than we were of it.

"A week or so after my return from Miami, a grocery store tabloid called *The Sun* displayed on its cover a sketch of a creature that very much resembled the creature we had seen. I was shocked when I saw it. Except for the fact that the creature shown on the tabloid cover was wearing a shirt or some kind of clothing, it had the same shape as the creature we had seen. The structure of its head and neck were the same. I have no clue as to where this newspaper had acquired this information or the sketch.

"Mysterious happenings then began to occur in my life. In 1987, just before Christmas, I was awakened from a sleeping state by an unusual feeling. It was as if I had telepathically received a message to call a phone number with a Florida area code. I called the number and the voice that answered said, 'Hello.' I said: 'This is going to sound strange, but something happened to me just a little while ago. I was sleeping, when all of a sudden I awoke and was told to call this number. Who are you? What is going on, and why have I been instructed to call you?' The voice on the other end of the line replied, 'Well, don't worry about it. Everything is going to be all right. You don't have anything to worry about. But when you go to the northwest to see Jack, explain this to him.'

"Several hours later—around 5:00 in the morning—the phone rang. A person, whose name I still do not know, said, 'Ed, don't worry about anything. But I want you to listen to something.' He played a recording of my voice making a phone call to him. The person on the other end of the line then said, 'Do you recognize this voice?' I was aghast. It was my own voice! I said, 'What's going on here?'

"Then the voice of the caller said to me, 'Well, don't worry about it. Jack Lapseritis will explain all of this when you get to Oregon.' I'm convinced these people in Florida were the 'good ETs.' Jack said he doesn't know of anyone in Florida and has not mentioned my name to anyone in any state! It's a mystery to me how this person got my name. How did he get me to communicate—telepathically? The voice on the phone was a man's voice— not a stern type voice—just kind of mellow sounding.

"I cannot disprove, nor can I verify the existence of flying saucers, UFOs, space people, or Starpeople. I cannot say 'yes;' I cannot say 'no.' I am an educated person and have read several pieces concerning UFOs that made sense. I do know that everything and anything is possible. I do not believe that we should harm any of these beings, or people—or whatever they are. When we first encountered the sea creature, we, of course, were somewhat afraid because of its unusual shape and menacing-looking claws. Whether it was of this Earth, another dimension, or outer space, I cannot say. In our world today, anything is possible!

"I believe that with love anything is possible. Love is God; God is love. As an amateur writer, I have written about love. I do not write about spacecraft or strange beings. I write about love—love for my fellow man and love for all living things— the trees, the flowers, the grass, the animals and birds. I feel that because of my affinity for nature, my respect for other living things, and because I practice unconditional love—always giving to others and sending out loving vibrations within a very negative society—the space people have been drawn to me. One of the cosmic laws is 'Like attracts like.' Love is a very high vibration and because the space beings exist in a very high vibration, they have been attracted to me. It seems to be some kind of dynamic like that!

"This way of thinking—this way of living one's life—began in my life when I was quite young. As a boy, I knew Dr. Leo Buscaglia and his family. Dr. Buscaglia is now a professor at the University of Southern California and has written a number of books about love. He is a very dear, loving person and teacher. I have incorporated much of the teachings of Dr. Buscaglia into my everyday life.

"For example, have you ever actually hugged a tree? I have! Have you ever said to a flower, 'You're beautiful—I love you!'? It sounds kind of silly at first, but trees and flowers are living things. To me, living things mean love. I am talking about love as caring, as concern for others, as the joy of life! Love is a feeling of oneness with all living things. Everything on this Earth is related to everything else. The tree is related to the ground. The ground is related to the grass. Some animals need grass to live. Birds need trees and seeds to live. And now, with the subject of ecology, if given a fair approach, this 'theory' of interconnectedness can be proven scientifically.

"Einstein said, 'Everything is relative.' I believe this. I hate no one. I am a Christian. I accept people on an equal plane with myself— including other humanoid types! I feel that the only one above me is the Lord, God. So, if I do not like a person, or I get a negative vibration from them that may be harmful to me or my way of thinking, I still remain polite in my interactions with them, whether they are male, female, child, or adult. I still treat them with respect, even if they have hurt me. I still love them on a spiritual level. I do not judge them. I judge only myself. This is all I can do."

In addition to Ed's testimonial, the following information also illustrates why the Bigfoot people are spiritual keepers of Mother Earth.

The Great Lakes Woodland Indians wrote a book for Indian students for the purpose of learning and understanding their own culture. The information itself was gathered from Native American elders on reservations in northern Wisconsin and Minnesota and published as *The Mishomis Book* by Edward Benton-Banai. Though the material is in story form, it was given as *fact*, not as folklore, as many anthropologists would prefer to view it. The value of the story is that it gives the reader an Indian perspective, keeping in mind that some tribes have a different view of Bigfoot and what it culturally means to them. Note how some of the statements in the story parallel many of the experiences witnessed by contactees in this book. In the story, a classic scene is depicted involving a young brave named Waynaboozhoo going out into the wilderness on a spiritual quest in search of himself:

"Waynaboozhoo dozed off but soon awoke with a start as if someone or something had prodded him. He looked around slowly. Even though he did not see anything, he knew he was not alone. Suddenly he noticed that just out of his direct eyesight was a being—

a huge, dark figure with red eyes that peered out of a shadowy face. Again he felt his fear rising to an uncontrollable level. He wanted to run. He thought fleetingly of defending himself—of fighting—but violence was unknown to the world at that time. He was able to control both his fear and terror but still he felt a new, strange sensation. What was this strange feeling that possessed him? For the first time in many years, violence was evident on the Earth. But with Waynaboozhoo it was only a thought. He was able to put it aside. Violence, which is the twin of peace, must always be secondary and subservient to peace just as it was with Waynaboozhoo.

"The shadowy being spoke:

"'I am Bug-way'-jinini [wildman]. Some of the people who follow you will know me as Sasquatch or Yeti, but they will seldom see me. It will be forbidden for them to look into my eyes. Some will not ever know of me. Many will not believe that I exist. I am your oldest brother!

"'I have been with you on your journey. I have been ahead of you at times and behind you at times. Sometimes I have watched you walk by. The Creator sent me here to guide and care for those who become lost. I am to watch over those who go into the forests, swamps, hills and mountains to gather medicines and other things. If those who seek the medicine roots, bark, and berries will ask me in a good way, if their thoughts are good, and their concern is for others, I will help them to find the medicines they seek. I shall know their thoughts. Also I am to help those who choose to meditate, pray, and fast in the *bug-way-ji'* [wild and natural places]. I am the caretaker of all these places—the deep forests, swamps, mountains, and deep valleys. I am natural man. I am to be the different one, different in all ways, I shall not build a home or gather in *o-day-nah-wing'* [towns]. Nor will I assemble with my own kind in tribes or nations. I will make no trails. Nor will I build *ji-mon'-nug* [canoes.] I am to be alone in the quiet solitude and majesty of the natural world of the Creator. I shall know of man's presence, and I will know his thoughts. But only the Anishinabe will know me. I am not to desire the companionship of Anishinabe or others...but only the Anishinabe shall know or honor me.

"'Little brother, I have watched your journey and have known your thoughts. I will tell you of some but not all of the things you have wondered about. First, you must always treat the natural Creation with respect. When you must come through my territory, honor those places with Tobacco and good thoughts. Be not in fear. In that way you shall not become lost or confused and no harm will befall you. Be always in wonder and awe of all these natural works that you see; they are the hand and thought of the Creator, Gitchi Manito. These works, whether they be mountains, glaciers, waterfall, the deepest swamps, or the wildest places, should never be changed, diverted, or disturbed. They are to remain as they are now just as I am to remain in my natural way.'

"Waynaboozhoo did not need to voice his thoughts as he visited with Bug-way'-jinini and they conversed through the night. Bug-way'-jinini continued to tell him many things that he had previously wondered about.

"'Here upon the Earth is a plane—a place marked by time. Nowhere else in the Universe is time necessary. Remember that time belongs to the Creator and to none other. It is the one thing that is beyond the reach of man. None shall ever see it. Very few shall ever get to know it. Do not concern yourself with it. If you do, it will become an obsession, and in the end you will be slave to it.

"'I know of many things that have puzzled you: the time you looked into the sky and wondered about the clouds; the time you felt rain drops on your face and looked into the distance to see rain falling in torrent; the time you felt warm and cold drafts of air sweep across your face; the time when you saw the heat dancing in waves over the plains.

"'Here upon the lap of our Mother the Earth is a place and time that hangs between eight levels of elements. These elements are unseen but are as real and necessary for life as the water you drink. Of these eight elements, four are above the Earth and four are below the Earth. These elements are the things that must work together if life itself is to be. All these things working together lift the water into the clouds. Your oldest uncle Noo'-din [the wind] then blows this water to where it is needed. There it falls to the ground to nourish the grasses, flowers, and other beings who are dependent on it for life. Beyond this, there are elements that work together to change the seasons. The seasons are the evidence of time.

"'Someday, when the time comes according to the Creator's plan, the cup of life will be measured by time. But even though time will be a part of life, life cannot exist without the other things we have spoken of. Remember, the cup of life is water and the cup is measured by time.

"'If you should climb to the highest place, you will feel the absence of the air which is necessary to draw into your body in order to live. Likewise, if you would go into the Earth, soon it would get pitch black and there would be only poisons to breathe and draw into your body.

"'As you walk on your journey, remember that there is a purpose to all things. There is a reason for the gentle rains and gentle winds as well as their opposites.

"'Accept these things I give you. The evidence is all around you. See it, know it, accept it! Accept this knowledge as a 'Way of Knowing.' Accept it as you accept the knowledge of your own shadow. When your shadow is cast on the ground you are able to see it. But even though you do not see it at times, you know that your shadow is still there. Your shadow represents your relationship to Grandfather Sun and the Four Directions and thus to the Universe.

"'It is time for you to continue on your journey. I will be with you, little brother, wherever your steps may take you. There is one last thing I wish to leave you and then we shall never talk again.

"'You have a twin brother whom you have wondered about and whom you would seek. This I tell you: He is your other side in all things and in all ways. He is with you...do not seek him. Do not wish to know him, but understand him.

"'You will walk the path of peace...he would not.
"'You are kind...he is not.
"'You are humble...he is not.
"'Your are generous...he is not.
"'You seek the good in things...he does not.
"'You shall respect others...he will not.
"'You will seek the goodness in others...he will not.
"'You are the light...he is the darkness.
"'Know that he is with you, understand him,
"'But do not seek him!'

"With that, Bug-way'-jinini left Waynaboozhoo and vanished like a shadow into the woods."[1]

---

1. Benton-Banai, 1979, pp. 44-47.

Every time the beings told me something about nature and how disgusted they are with "people in the outer world," I could not help thinking of how surprisingly similar Amerindian religio-philosophy is to what the Bigfoot believe and frequently talk about. One Indian's words especially remind me of what the Sasquatch frequently talk about. In a sense, the following quote is their urgent message to humanity. It is an excerpt from a presentation by the great orator Chief Seattle in 1854 to a group of white men who kept insisting he sell them Indian land. The wise chief knew that Europeans view land and resources in an irreverent and detached manner. The Bigfoot say this is their planet. It was given to them to populate by the friendly ETs who brought them. The Bigfoot say they are the Keepers of Mother Earth. The Starpeople and Bigfoot people have both expressed that they understand and accept that all of us are an integral part of the Great Oneness, and like the traditional Amerindian tribes, wish for all world nations to understand and practice basic respect for every living thing in God's Universe. Chief Seattle could easily have been speaking for the Sasquatch and ETs when he spoke on how he felt about the destructive white intruders:

"We know that the white man does not understand our ways. One portion of land is the same to him as the next, for he is a stranger who comes in the night and takes from the land whatever he needs. The Earth is not his brother, but his enemy, and when he has conquered it, he moves on. He leaves his fathers' graves behind, and he does not care. He kidnaps the Earth from his children; he does not care. His fathers' graves and his children's birthright are forgotten. He treats his mother, the Earth, and his brother, the sky, as things to be bought, plundered, sold like sheep or bright beads. His appetite will devour the Earth and leave behind only a desert.

"I do not know. Our ways are different from your ways. The sight of your cities pains the eyes of the red man. But perhaps it is because the red man is a savage and does not understand.

"The air is precious to the red man for all things share the same breath—the beast, the tree, the man, they all share the same breath. The white man does not seem to notice the air he breathes. Like a man dying for many days, he is numb to the stench. But if we sell you our land, you must remember that the air is precious to us, that the air shares its spirit with all the life it supports. The wind that gave our grandfather his first breath also receives his last sigh. And the wind must also give our children the spirit of life.

"You must teach your children that the ground beneath their feet is the ashes of our grandfathers. So that they will respect the land, tell your children that the Earth is rich with the lives of our kin. Teach your children what we have taught our children, that the Earth is our mother. Whatever befalls the Earth befalls the sons of the Earth. If men spit upon the ground, they spit upon themselves.

"This we know. The Earth does not belong to man; man belongs to the Earth. This we know. All things are connected like the blood which unites one family. All things are connected....

"Man did not weave the web of life, he is merely a strand in it. Whatever he does to the web, he does to himself.

"Even the white man, whose God walks and talks with him as friend to friend, cannot be exempt from the common destiny. We may be brothers after all; we shall see. One thing we know, which the white man may one day discover—our God is the same God. You may think that you own Him as you wish to own our land, but you cannot. He is the God of man, and His compassion is equal for the red man and the white. The Earth is precious to Him and to harm the Earth is to heap contempt on its Creator. The whites too shall pass; perhaps sooner than all other tribes. Continue to contaminate your bed, and you will one night suffocate in your own waste."[2]

---

2. Watt, 1934

# PART TWO

©1998 by Corey Wolfe

# ANALYSIS & IMPLICATIONS

# The Bigfoot/UFO Connection

"Wake up, wake up, my friend; we are here," a gentle, eerie voice commanded. Lying in bed facing the wall, I instantly opened my eyes and felt an *overwhelming* "presence" in the bedroom. Turning around, I was fascinated beyond delight as my eyes beheld two living apparitions, very much "alive," of apelike men, which I immediately could see were the Sasquatch people. Without fear, I lay there and looked with great wonder, knowing I was privileged that these interdimensional nature-beings were sharing who they were by revealing their presence while in the astral state. Since September, 1979, this non-hallucinatory experience has occurred to me a few hundred times. Sometimes it occurred in the company of multiple witnesses who experienced the same phenomenon, which, at times, included telepathic communication with these apparitions.

After years of diligent searching for what I believed to be a giant prehistoric primate with limited intelligence, I was faced with a situation for which my academic background had not prepared me. This chapter explains my own personal struggles and deep concern for the direction these discoveries were leading me, in a world where an association with psychic phenomena could easily bring public and scientific condemnation. During these years of data collecting, I was haunted by the dilemma of how to present the facts to a world so skeptical and insensitive to the possibilities of metaphysical revelations.

I was astounded the first night I encountered the astral visitors. It was a magnificent revelation. It was an unmistakable reality that I experienced with three of my physical senses: *hearing* a Sasquatch communicate with me, *feeling* a vibrational energy of living presence from them, and *seeing* two ghostly figures whose features moved in a physical manner. Because I experienced this astral phenomenon with three of my senses, I know it was not a hallucination. In several other encounters, I, and others, were actually "touched" by the astral body of a Sasquatch—that is, the hand of the being was felt physically. This has happened to me so frequently that I now know that their astral energy is indeed powerful enough to affect physical matter.

Rolling over in bed, I moved closer to these living spirit-like forms that I easily recognized as astral bodies. Parapsychology researcher Dr. Charles T. Tart, University of California at Davis, defines "astral travel" or "out-of-body experiences" (OOBE) as:

...a universal human phenomenon in the sense of having been experienced in every time and culture, although only a very small fraction of people ever experience it.

In an OOBE, a person experiences his consciousness existing outside his physical body. The effect of an OOBE on a person is almost always a conviction of survival after death, and this is probably the origin of the concept of a soul, a central doctrine in most religions.

Current physical science defines such experiences as meaningless, but solid evidence now exists that challenges that part of the belief system of modern science which denies the reality of OOBE's.[1]

Since I had previously read about the phenomenon, I was familiar with what was occurring in my bedroom that night. The apparitions projected a deep sense of love, peace, and curiosity to me, and I gratefully accepted it, void of all fear. I was fascinated! What was there to fear when interdimensional beings were placidly visiting me? The two Sasquatch were both males, one about seven to eight feet tall and the other approximately four feet in height. The smaller one appeared extremely shy, seemingly uncomfortable about being so close to me. He gave me the impression that astral travel was new to him and that standing at the foot of my bed was the closest he dared be to an Earth human.

The larger creature had a remarkably interesting face, which looked half-ape, half-man! That face had an air of control and intelligence, and the eyes studied me in an inquisitive manner. In its effort to scrutinize me, I was surprised to observe the bottom half of the translucent body float through and below the bedroom floor until the being's face was only three feet from mine. This gave me a perfect view of the head. The aliveness and movement

---

1. Tart, 1977, p. 87.

*My sketch of the apelike Bigfoot whose astral aspect often appeared to me in my bedroom in Wisconsin.*

of the pupils in the eyes thoroughly intrigued me, indicating that I was indeed viewing something very extraordinary.

The cranium of the larger Sasquatch was shaped more like that of a gorilla than of a man; it displayed a sagittal crest over the top of its head. The younger Sasquatch lacked this feature. Also, a slight protuberance above the eyebrows indicated a distinct supra-orbital ridge—an outstanding feature exaggerated in most prototypical reproductions of Neanderthal man. The mandibles were large and thick, forming a wide, prominent mouth with thin lips. The nose was short and the nostrils wide, semi-Negroid in shape, yet proportional to its face. Cheek bones were high and noticeable. For some reason, I paid little attention to the ears but vaguely remembered they were anthropoid. Also, I cannot remember the precise shape of the chin itself. What impressed me the most, and was distracting in a positive way, was the intensity of the psychic vibrations that transmitted its mood, feelings, and presence into my consciousness. It was a most vivid and revealing experience.

When I shifted my body to get a closer look, I received a curt response. The adult Sasquatch abruptly turned its body with the right shoulder toward me, in a protective stance. This response surprised me. With its head partially turned, it looked at me through the corners of cautious eyes, clearly expressing its timidity. The pupils rotated away from me, then back, as if wondering what I would do. The skin on its forehead wrinkled in a frown as if it was uncomfortable with my overture to get closer. Still, it telepathically projected kindness.

When I sat up to get a better look at the juvenile, he instantly put his entire back to me and then peeked over his shoulder with a wary glance, a signal I interpreted to mean, "We are close enough." It is baffling that beings possessing such extraordinary powers of survival and elusiveness should be so vigilant when in a non-physical dimension where apparently they could not be harmed by me.

After about two minutes, during which we closely observed each other, the Sasquatch apparitions slowly faded, disappearing before my eyes. The vibration of their presence also subsided. But what made them come to me at that time?

The previous day, a friend had taken me to visit an Indian family who had recently acquired farm land. I had never met this family before, and they had invited a bona-fide medicine man to discuss the blessing of the land. It sounded like a pleasant meeting. I accepted.

My friend Carl accompanied me into the Wisconsin countryside where we were to meet the Indian family. Upon arrival, Carl and I were escorted to the back side of the field where brush and small islands of trees intermingled with about five acres of swamp on one side, and woodland on the other. After social introductions and a pleasant chat with my new Indian friends, I began wandering about the property. My thoughts were tranquil, while enjoying the peacefulness of the country. Then I received the shock of my life!

"Greetings, I am of the Sasquatch people, and I am here watching you, and I have been watching you for many years now," a kindly voice said with a coarse and slight accent.

I quickly looked around in disbelief. There was no one in sight. Again, an *inner voice* spoke to me, saying: "As I said, I am of the Sasquatch people and have been watching you for many years, longer than you know."

I saw nothing and began thinking that it must be my imagination.

"No, you don't understand. As I said, I am Sasquatch here watching you and have been doing so for many years now," the voice repeated.

Again I looked around and saw nothing. My head became light, and I was soon in a daze, as if physically sedated. I was deeply puzzled. Before I could compose myself or grasp that I was experiencing genuine telepathy, a second, more sophisticated voice spoke to me: "Hear me. I am a person from the stars, and I too have been watching you for a long time now."

"But where are you? I can't see you!" I asked in my mind, totally incredulous with what I was experiencing.

A controlled and tempered voice replied: "At the moment I am in a UFO, as you people call it."

Placing a hand above my eyebrows to block the autumn sun, I scanned the sky to the end of the horizon but saw nothing. Thinking to myself, "But I don't understand where the UFO is," instantly produced the same reply from the being, verifying that he was clearly reading my mind.

Shocked and in disbelief, I no longer wanted to be involved in confusing mind games, so I quickly returned to the group of Indian friends who were sitting casually in a circle. It was my intent to escape this clutter in my mind. Once again, I was shocked. The telepathy continued even when I stood by the group of Indians. It was apparent that no one else responded to the voice of Sasquatch in my head telling me he is my guide and has been monitoring me for years. And I clearly remember my thoughts as I struggled: "This is crazy! Is this for real? No one will ever believe me. Can this really be happening to me?"

"Over there would be a good place for a sweat lodge," an Indian elder remarked.

"No, not there," the head-of-house answered in a disapproving tone.

"I think that's an excellent place; I agree with Wallace," another Native American commented in support of his friend.

"Nothing will be built there; that piece will be left alone. Our friends, the Starpeople, have been landing their ships there, and I don't want to disturb their activity," the head-of-house sternly spoke in a decisive manner.

Those words really jolted me, so I turned and bolted for the house!

Later, on my return trip to Milwaukee, Carl warmly related his visit. Feeling withdrawn, I unintentionally ignored him. I was still in a state of confusion. As he spoke, I smiled politely, nodded occasionally in agreement, but said nothing. Half-way home Carl realized I was paying little attention to what he was saying. Suddenly his jocular tone of voice changed and he became serious.

"Jack, I have something important to tell you and you may not believe me—but there are Bigfoot creatures out on that property, and UFOs are dropping them off!"

"Stop it, Carl, you're freaking me out!" I loudly retorted. At the time I did not want to hear the truth. None of this was a part of my then-limited view of reality concerning this phenomenon. A belief in a relationship between Bigfoot, telepathy, and UFOs was incompatible with my sense of order, logic, and science.

Nevertheless, Carl went on to say that he visually saw an astral apparition of Sasquatch following me everywhere I walked on the property. He insisted it was ten to twelve feet tall and showed considerable interest in me. He also claimed he was overwhelmed by the sensation that a UFO was indeed present. His entire story instantly startled me into facing the reality of the encounter. *Independently*, Carl experienced something similar. I thought: "Could two people independently have the same experience and still be sane?"

It was the following night that I began having astral visits from the psychic Sasquatch. One Sasquatch apparition was a female that was the mate of the large male and mother of the juvenile. For a time, the large male did not return to visit. When he returned one evening, I immediately recognized him. It was like recognizing a new human friend after meeting him only once before—his features and telepathic vibration were that distinct.

The weekend after the telepathy occurred on the farm, I began camping there every weekend. Ellen, my new girlfriend, was dumbfounded by my fantastic story. She commented that it sounded like science fiction. My insistence that it was true was met with frequent teasing and a rational explanation which she conjured up that made it more believable for her. I challenged her, and one weekend she agreed to camp with me. She accompanied me to the property, and, after setting up the tent, we huddled around a large fire made by the Indian family to warm us on a cold autumn night. We chatted, and the head-of-house spoke of God, Mother Earth, the destruction of our environment, and discussed his philosophy of life and the Indian way.

Soon a giant silhouette was sighted about 65 feet away, peeking from behind a cluster of trees and brush. It was Sasquatch—my first physical sighting! After it ducked behind the trees, I telepathed and asked it questions, but it would not answer. For a while I thought I might not be "thinking at it" properly, that it was not receiving my words. Then I asked Ellen to assist me. I explained how to telepath by visualizing him as she spoke in her mind. Suspiciously, she agreed. We both requested that the Bigfoot man visit us during the night to assure us it was indeed our friend.

Shortly before retiring, six of us observed a UFO flying over the house. Within 20 minutes, one of the Indians became startled and yelled out. About 50 feet from the group, just over a knoll, he'd seen a 12-foot Sasquatch run from the open field into the cluster of trees where I had first seen the giant before telepathing. Soon after the sighting, the Indians walked back to the house for the night. Ellen and I crawled into the tent and fell asleep.

At exactly 2:45, a voice abruptly woke me saying: "Wake up, my friend, I am here as you asked." The telepathic words were so powerfully abrupt that I instantly sat up in my sleeping bag and heard the thumping of heavy footsteps, like that of a giant man walking up to the tent. The creature stood there for about one minute, then nonchalantly walked away. I scrambled for my shoes and climbed outside to get a look. The creature was gone. In the dead, dry grass were footprints leading to the tent.

"Wow, what an experience!" Ellen shouted. She had not moved all the while, so I had assumed she was still sleeping. She was exuberant and claimed he had telepathically awakened her, saying: "Wake up, my friend, I am here, as you asked." Splendid! As a social scientist, I considered this information to be vital. The mental telepathy independently perceived by another person verified my experience. Yes, it *was* "genuine." I remember a feeling of relief and thinking: "I guess I'm not crazy after all."

Ellen said she could smell a faint musky odor when the Bigfoot creature approached the tent. Many people think Sasquatch stinks because it never washes its body, but I discovered that to be untrue. The pungent odor is similar to that of the musk glands of a skunk. When a Sasquatch is threatened in any way, or senses fear, or is startled, or perceives a violent intention in the mind of an oncoming person, it secretes a powerful odor that deliberately stuns the olfactory nerves in the nose. It is the creature's benign way of communicating to others, saying: "Stay away; don't come near!" And it works. This is what I have discovered, both through personal experience and from what the creatures have told other informants who were privileged enough to talk with them. In all the years I have encountered them, *not one time* have I ever smelled this stench that others describe. Some people have told me it was so strong it made their eyes water. My deep love of nature and lack of fear around animals have proven to be major factors in attracting the psychic Sasquatch without triggering its release of scent.

That same morning, the head-of-house and I talked and it was then that he told me his personal story. Since the five-member family moved to the farm that summer, they had observed round, glowing objects in the sky, occasionally hovering directly above the high-tension lines on the adjoining property. On a few occasions, they claimed the saucer-shaped craft landed on their property. But no one ever investigated to see what they were doing. At times, other Indian visitors would stand out in the yard at night, observing the same phenomenon.

The times the UFOs landed were most significant. Usually the family was in the house watching television. Then the dog would go berserk, barking, whining, and cowering as if trying to escape some terrible foe. Sometimes, an ominous-looking figure of a giant man would peep in the windows. On the first few encounters, the teenage boys grabbed a .22-caliber rifle and ran outside to face the intruder. Each time they were mystified as to where the stranger had fled. Once the two boys saw a seven-to eight-foot "man" run into the barn and heard him climb the steps to the second floor. The youths cautiously tiptoed up the stairs. They heard a thud from someone jumping to the ground from the second level. One of the boys ran to the side of the barn just in time to see a Sasquatch duck around the other side.

When they reported the incident to their father, he immediately banned all guns and counseled them as to the nature of the being. He told his three sons to accept the Sasquatch as a spiritual friend, that the creatures meant no harm, and that they were conducting some task for the benevolent Starpeople who were on the flying saucers. The sons accepted this, as the entire family of five saw the spaceships land and, within an hour of the landing, a Sasquatch would boldly stand at their window. Sometimes one or two other Indians would be there to witness the Bigfoot/UFO connection. Since both phenomena were experienced simultaneously, the Bigfoot's presence and UFO landings were viewed by the family as a single phenomenon. Traditional medicine people had told the head-of-house of this association many years before. The Indians came to accept that reality as a part of universal nature. I was told both phenomena existed previous to the coming of the white man and were here before the Indians occupied the North American continent.

The head-of-house later shared with me his first encounter with the Bigfoot on the Oregon-California border, just south of Klamath Falls. In 1959, while working in northern California, he went on a camping trip one three-day weekend. He was hiking on a forest trail when he met a Klamath Indian who was on his way to a sacred medicine bowl located on a cliff above a tiny wilderness lake. He was invited by this fellow Indian to join him in traditional prayer. Soon they arrived at an obscure lake and began the sacred pipe ceremony on a secure rock shelf at the edge of a precipice. Just after sundown, to his amazement, three Sasquatch appeared at the lake and commenced to swim about, undaunted by the sight of two human beings. There were two adults and a juvenile. He said he was flabbergasted at the gracefulness and speed of the creatures' swimming ability, especially that of the youngster. The Klamath Indian told him that he saw them there often and considered himself to be their friend. He added that the creatures knew it was a sacred place where they could bathe openly, unmolested.

One night the head-of-house and I were standing on a hillside behind the farm discussing native Amerindian philosophy. Soon, we observed a round, low-flying object with pulsating red and green lights silently gliding across the sky.

"My God! That's a UFO!" I stammered in disbelief.

My Indian friend continued to speak as if it were not there.

"Do you think they know we're here?" I continued, babbling in amazement.

He turned and, looking up, confirmed that this was the type of starship he had often witnessed landing on his property and transporting the Sasquatch.

I asked the Indian: "If they can read our minds as you say, the Starpeople must know we mean no harm and won't tell the authorities. Then why don't they land so we can speak with them?"

Solemnly and with a firm glance, as if I had asked the most asinine question, he curtly replied, "Why would they want to talk to an ant?"

That was not the expected response, yet I imagine Einstein would have been bored beyond his limits if he attempted to discuss the theory of relativity with a primitive Dani tribesman of New Guinea.

There are many reasons to believe in a Bigfoot/ET/UFO connection. Seven percipients were directly told by a Sasquatch that they were friends of Starpeople or were involved with them. Mrs. Jones's new friend would not discuss the matter with her even after observing a ship hovering above the trees at a time when the creature was coming nearly every day.

In Wisconsin in 1979, five members of a family would stand in their farmyard at night, often with two or three friends, and observe spaceships hovering a few feet from high tension lines. After the craft would land out of sight and everyone would go back to the house, within 30 minutes one or two Sasquatch would be standing outside the house, looking in the windows, observing them. The head-of-house said it happened three times, possibly four. I corroborated his story when I received permission to camp in their back lot on weekends. I also observed a spaceship twice (but not on the high tension lines) and later a Bigfoot would approach my tent. I had a girlfriend at the time who witnessed this and even experienced telepathy on one occasion. She had a difficult time believing in my experience with telepathy until one of the creatures spoke to her.

In 1989, White Song Eagle also corroborated an incident when I was living in Oregon and she was living in Indiana. At the time, I was having frequent psychic contact from both the Bigfoot people and ETs. One day, when an ET spoke to me, I asked him to please contact White Song. Two days later, White Song called and said: "You'll never guess what happened!" I replied, "The Starpeople came to see you!" She was shocked and asked how I knew, and I explained that I requested it. White Song told me she was awakened by an ET and observed a ship in the field between her house and a neighbor's. The next day her neighbor told her that he saw the UFO out there around 3:00 A.M. White Song contacted a reputable UFO investigator the next day who came over to assess the area and get statements from the two witnesses so it could be officially documented. I always seek to verify by cross-referencing or receiving supporting data from independent sources. This helps to rule out chance or subjective coincidence. There are clear patterns for all the anomalous attributes that form a solid case for a psychic Sasquatch.

Interestingly, three days before White Song came out to Oregon to check on some Bigfoot areas, a Sasquatch walked up behind my car at the gate to the estate, but remained invisible. I asked him to connect with White Song when she came. He hesitated, then said, "We'll see. I'll think about it." Then, with heavy thumps, he walked off into the forest. I did not expect such an ambiguous answer. I was chagrined. Yet, when she arrived, he came to her the following day while she was out hiking by herself. There is a kind of wonderful craziness about the phenomenon whereby a person never views this world the same way again. So often people expect the Sasquatch to either act like a grizzly bear or to respond as we might. They are definitely humanoid and, like any other being, have their own personalities, cultural values, and emotional hang-ups. Keep in mind, most of them still do not want to bother with the kindest of us. Like most indigenous peoples of the world who experienced colonialism/westernism, they find us difficult to trust.

In June 1983, near Shawano, Wisconsin, eleven witnesses in two cars clearly saw a spaceship in a field and when it shot into the air, a giant ape-like figure was seen by all walking into the woods. It is important to note that a week before when I was there, a Sasquatch told me that a ship would be dropping off some of his people in the area near midnight, two days in a row. That is why the two vehicles were driving around so late. I spent three days interviewing each person and every one told precisely the same story. Eleven people have no reason to fabricate. And four or five years earlier, a part of that family observed Sasquatch in their pickle patch and later two spaceships landing beside the farmhouse. The Bigfoot/UFO connections became more and more obvious over the years.

In March 1987, in Oregon, I telepathed to a ship from the deck of my house and, within 30 minutes, a Sasquatch medicine woman astrally appeared, gave me a healing with a powerful "electrical" energy and left.

In May 1993, near Tucson, Arizona, a spaceship landed outside my house in the desert one night while I was away and my wife was asleep. Moments later, a Sasquatch literally walked through the solid doors of the house and into our bedroom, looked at my wife, then left.

In September 1981, in Michigan, a spaceship was seen landing in a field in the exact area where the inhabitants of several farms were having numerous encounters with a Sasquatch. In the Medicine Mountain episode in Oregon, for an entire week a tiny spaceship would land beside my tent while the sun was setting on the horizon. Immediately after it left, Sasquatch would walk up to my tent. Each time, through my yellow-tan tent, it was very easy to view the ship as well as the Sasquatch as it squatted to look at my water jugs and as it gently stepped over my tent strings. Also, those involved in the Ohio incident, as well as others in Massachusetts, all reported many times the correlation between spaceships appearing on one day and then Bigfoot creatures thereafter. The consistent redundancy of reports becomes overwhelming.

The Jeffery family and friends saw Bigfoot, ETs, and UFOs, all in separate encounters but always in the same area, near a primitive campground. Irene Wilson is the only person on file who claims to have seen an ET (that looked human) with a Sasquatch inside the materialized spaceship in her field. I personally have seen ships at her ranch and was contacted at least a dozen times by Bigfoot over a five-year period, so I have no doubt about her veracity.

One Indian woman whom I interviewed, told me of an incident that happened on a reservation in the Dakotas. She said there was an area where the Bigfoot and UFOs were frequently seen and where strange happenings occurred. Her people were afraid to enter this zone. Every time she left Minneapolis to drive home to visit her family, she had to drive through this part of the reservation. She said she experiences an eerie feeling each time she drives through the area.

Once, after visiting her parents, she was returning to Minneapolis driving through "the zone." She reports that she could see what appeared to be a UFO landing in a flat area off the road about a half mile ahead of her. She became terrified! It was late at night and, as she drove down the lonely stretch of highway, a huge apelike creature stepped to the edge of the road and telepathically told her to pull over and stop the car. By now the woman was panic stricken! This sent such a chill of fear through her that she stepped on the accelerator and sped away. While this was occurring, she quickly looked off the road and noticed a glowing saucer-shaped object sitting on the ground.

I interviewed her for a period of four-and-a-half hours and it took me some time to convince her that I would not publicly reveal her name. She had been struggling with this experience for some time and was unable to discuss it with anyone. Her live-in boyfriend became irate whenever she attempted to share it with him. The Indian woman was grateful for my patience and understanding, and it became apparent that she experienced a catharsis during our conversation. By the time we said good-bye, she acted very relieved—as if a great burden had been lifted from her.

I must note that I never share my own encounters with the percipient until after the interview is complete. That way, the information remains empirically objective and thus untainted. As William James said: "It takes only one white crow to prove that not all crows are black." At present, I have 76 white crows—76 percipients who claim to have had the same type of anomalous experience, and who repeatedly conclude that Sasquatch: 1) is humanoid, not an animal; 2) is benign, not a crazed monster; 3) has profound psychic abilities; 4) did not evolve on planet Earth; and 5) is directly associated with UFOs and their occupants.

All of these documented cases are major reports and many of the minor ones sound very similar. By now the reader must be wondering, with such an enormous amount of data collected over the years, what were all the other researchers doing that the truth did not come out sooner? In many ways, each Bigfoot researcher was doing his/her part of the puzzle. All the physical/material data is equally needed, because Bigfoot is both a physical and a non-physical nature being.

# ETs, Sasquatch and Psychic Healing

During my years analyzing UFO reports, I became aware of how ET experiences have fundamentally changed the lives of those they have contacted. The psychic healings that contactees sometimes receive illustrate some of the "normal" abilities of the psychic Sasquatch and of the ETs themselves. Physical, mental and spiritual healing effects can come from either the ETs or the Sasquatch that work with them. Their methods may be practiced in different psychic forms and the results are dramatic as you will see in the following examples.

In February 1987, I had a herniated disc. It was the most excruciating physical pain I have ever endured. The orthopedic surgeon said it was the worst case of an injured disc he had seen in 30 years of practice and that surgery was the only method of treatment. I, however, refused to undergo surgery. Realizing I had no alternative, I became filled with anxiety. Unable to walk, I was confined to a wheelchair when not in bed and spent most of the hours of each day lying flat on my back. Friends and neighbors came by with food and helped out with the laundry.

The cottage where I lived, along the North Umpqua River, was situated in an area known to be a flight line for UFOs. Occupants of every house for a half-mile span along this river had reported seeing spaceships on numerous occasions. This was validated by associates who visited me, even though they doubted what I initially told them. When I returned home from the visit to the orthopedic surgeon, I began telepathing to the Starpeople. Out of desperation, I repeatedly cried out for help for the next three or four days, but received no answer. Distraught from the intense pain, I became extremely frustrated. On the evening of the fourth day, as I reached up from my bed to turn off the light, I sensed a presence in the room and then heard what sounded like the shuffling of tiny feet. Although I was lying in a rather precarious position, I was able to turn my head in the direction of the footsteps. To my amazement, I saw three space beings, each measuring about three and one-half feet in height. They had chalky-looking skin, large dark eyes, and they were wearing one-piece space suits with a belt at the waist. They spoke to me, saying: "We are here to heal you." I anxiously replied: "Please, come ahead. Thank you and God bless you!" They then rendered me unconscious.

I am unsure how much time elapsed, but I do remember hearing some of the telepathic conversations that transpired between these space beings as they performed the healing. At one point, I was awakened by their conversation that seemed to "leak" into my mind. Looking up, I saw one of the ETs behind me, holding a cylinder-shaped object in its right hand. All I could say was, "I love you," then I became unconscious again. What does one say when humanoids come to heal you? They didn't ask me if I had health insurance, or tell me they were going to carve into my spine. I honored them by exhibiting the two highest forms of respect I knew: by telling them "I love you" and by saying "God bless you." That was how I demonstrated the deep gratitude I felt towards them.

The method of healing that the Starpeople used that night was not explained to me. However, they did say it had something to do with electromagnetism, that it charges the system like a battery until the body is efficaciously healed. Apparently, the intensity of the electromagnetic charge is in direct relationship to the amount of healing.

Ten and one-half hours later, I awoke from a very restful sleep. In the previous weeks, I had been able to sleep only about an average of four hours per night. I felt incredibly rested, in fact, ecstatic. The pain in my lower back and legs was gone! The proof of the experience came when I stood up and walked toward the bathroom with only a slight limp.

The next evening at bedtime, as I turned off the light, the three tiny space beings again appeared. I was delighted. They told me that they needed to work on me again to complete the healing. I thanked them and, stretching out on my bed, fell into a state of relaxation. The following morning, I awoke to find that my limp had completely disappeared. In a matter of 48 hours, I was able to again walk normally. I was scheduled to see the doctor that day. The look on my physician's face as I walked through the door was a sight to behold! He stood before me, patting his bald head and moving his mouth, but no words were coming forth. He was speechless! He then began to utter, "I don't understand. But…but…what happened? I don't understand!" I evasively responded, "All I've been doing is taking my vitamins!"

Two and a half weeks later I had to drive to San Francisco on business. After driving eleven hours each way, I began to again experience some pain

*My sketch of one of three 3-1/2-foot-tall ETs that came into my bedroom to heal me two nights in a row, at a time when I was unable to walk due to a ruptured disc. I surprised my doctor by walking into his office the next morning.*

in my lower back. Upon my return, I found that I was beginning to limp again. I thought that perhaps by walking I could work out some of the stiffness and kinks in my back. I was wrong; it only got worse!

That evening, I stepped out onto the deck in my bathrobe. Looking out at the stars I was delighted to see a spaceship about a half-mile away, conspicuously hovering over the mountain closest to my house. I began telepathing, asking the occupants of this spaceship to send someone down to heal me, as my back was again beginning to cripple me. I repeated this request about four times with no response. I then demanded that they give me some kind of answer or acknowledge that they were receiving my plea by flashing their lights or moving their ship. Then both the blinking lights on the spaceship began to flash and the ship moved to three different positions in a triangular pattern. I understood this to mean: "Yes, yes, we hear you!"

I went back inside the cottage and went to bed. I turned off the light, expecting that the space beings would appear, as before. Nothing materialized. About 35 minutes later, I felt a powerful vibratory energy just behind me in the room. As I turned my head to see who was there, I felt an intense tingling sensation, like an electrical energy, move up and down my spinal column. It seemed to hover momentarily at the base of my brain, then finally moved all the way down to my coccyx. Looking up, I was surprised to see a half-materialized female Sasquatch shaman facing the bed. I thanked her and said, "God bless you." She replied, "Be well." The last thing I remembered was a flood of love energy inundating my entire being. When I awoke the following morning, the limp *and* the pain were gone!

In May of 1988, I had another unique healing experience. I had been suffering from recurring migraine headaches. My head felt as if it were in a vice grip. The headaches continued regardless of what medication I tried. After a while I began to wonder if I had some serious complication such as a brain tumor. I ruminated over this possibility for several days and came very close to making an appointment to see a doctor. Then, one night as I was traveling home through the foothills of the Cascades, I spotted a spaceship along the occasionally busy flight line near my cottage. I stopped my car, turned off the lights, and stepped out of the vehicle. I stood outside the car, and for at least one full minute I telepathically asked the occupants of the spaceship if they would send a doctor to give me a checkup. I received the reply: "We hear you. We will ask."

I continued on home, crawled into bed, and approximately 45 minutes later an ET doctor made a house call. Just as I was drifting off into sleep, a brilliant white light flashed beside my bed. I then observed a humanoid figure, approximately five feet tall, manifest out of the flash of light. It was a magnificent visual experience! The physical figure appeared to be a male, and his face appeared to be almost human-like. He was bald-headed, with an exceptionally large, square-shaped forehead, high cheek bones, a somewhat pointed nose, and he was wearing a layered white frock. The kindly being stretched both arms out to me, while looking at me with very piercing eyes. The last thing I remember before slipping into a state of unconsciousness was the Starperson smiling as he leaned toward me. His face seemed to be filled with wisdom or some kind of omniscience.

The next thing I remember was waking up the next morning with one foot on the floor and my body lying in an angular position in the bed. Although I was perplexed at my strange position, I quickly began organizing my day and soon became very busy. Not knowing why at the time, I somehow felt compelled to call a muffler shop to make an appointment to have my car checked. After doing so, I could not remember why I had called, as my muffler was not making any noise or malfunctioning in any way that I was aware of. I kept wondering what had prompted me to make the appointment. I got ready to leave, then, as I sat in my car with the motor running, going over my list of errands to do in town, I suddenly became aware of fumes from carbon monoxide. As I smelled this, my annoying headache returned. Aha—what a revelation! The ET doctor who had visited me the night before had obviously diagnosed evidence of carbon monoxide in my bloodstream, a poisonous gas that was leaking from the exhaust system. He had treated the source of the medical problem and not the symptom, as would have been the case with an allopathic physician. In a post-hypnotic-type suggestion, he programmed me to call a muffler shop the following morning. That's why I didn't know why I had called. Once fixed, there were no more headaches.

Another healing incident that struck me humorously was with a woman named Trisha, in Nashville, Tennessee. I sent my portfolio to her because she was a promotional agent. One morning, about two weeks later, wondering if she would accept me as a client, I called her to discuss the matter. Although she maintained a professional manner, she sounded somewhat sarcastic, as though she did not take me seriously. She seemed to be politely poking fun at me as she said, "Your portfolio reads like a fairy story in an enchanted forest." Assuring her that my work was authentic did not seem to impress her. I soon realized that our conversation was being psychically monitored by the

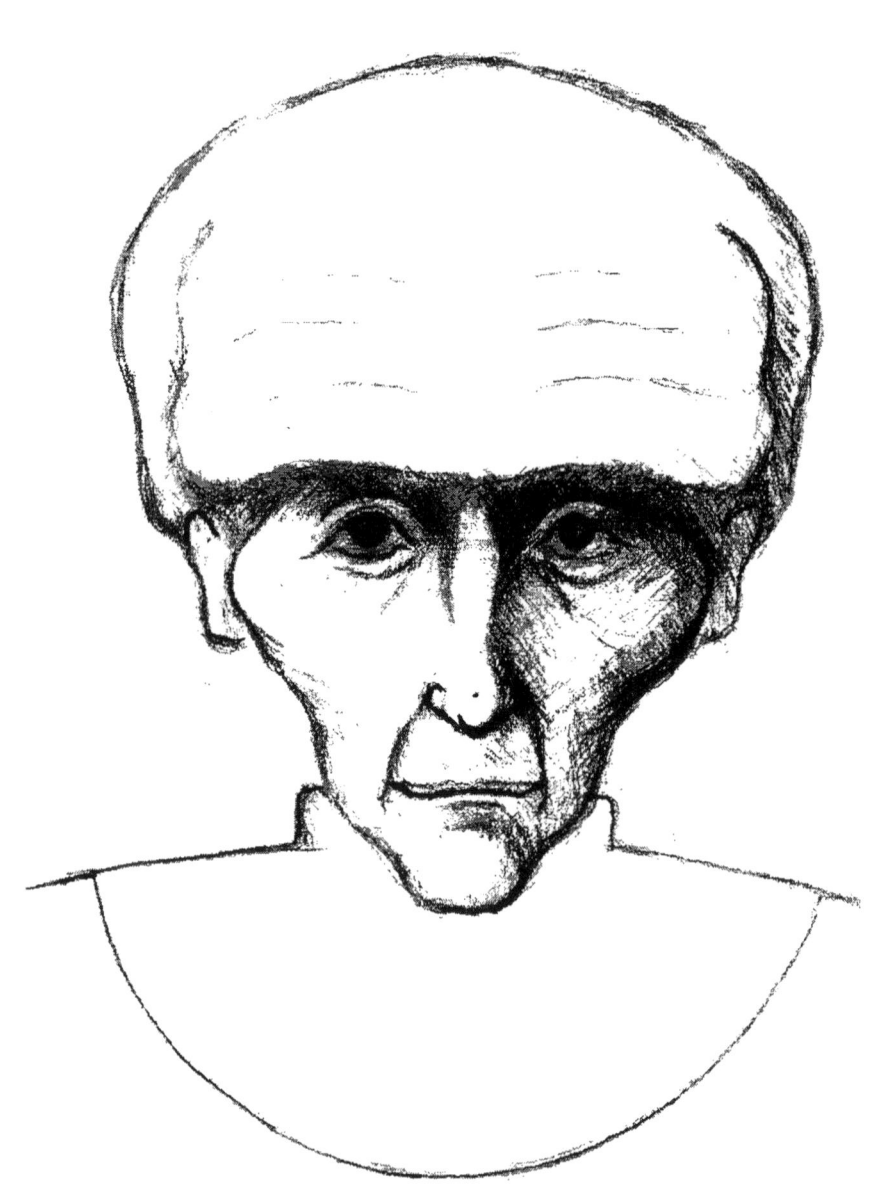

*My sketch of an ET doctor who physically appeared in my bedroom when my headaches were terrible.*

Starpeople, but I said nothing about it. As Trisha proceeded to tell me that she didn't believe in ETs or Bigfoot, her voice was suddenly blocked out by some strange electronic sounds, and the phone went dead. She called back within a minute and stated that she didn't know why the phone went dead and that the sound was very strange. Being honest, I told her it was the ETs. She snickered, then got back to business, saying she would call me in a few weeks. Trisha said it would take that long to decide if she wanted to take me as a client. This conversation occurred about 10:00 A.M.

At 8:00 that evening, I received a phone call from a woman whose voice was unrecognizable to me. Her voice was soft and humble as she asked if she could speak with me. It was Trisha. She related to me the following incident. She claims that after completing our telephone conversation that morning, she had two more business calls. Each time, the same electronic noise was heard, then the phone went dead. During this time, she felt as if someone was watching and following her around the home office. But nothing was visible. Then she began to feel weak and dizzy, and, because she could no longer concentrate on her work, she decided to lie down for a short nap. She became unnerved when she entered her bedroom and found that several of the large crystals she kept in a bowl on her nightstand were neatly scattered around the room. This was perplexing to her, as she lives alone. As she lay on her side in bed, a deep fear ignited in her, when she felt an overwhelming presence in the room. She felt "someone" crawl onto the bed behind her and cuddle up to her, conforming its body to hers in a "spooning" position. She finally got up enough nerve to look behind her, but could see no one there. She was so upset by this incident that she could not do any more work for the rest of the day.

That evening, she had a dinner date with a man she was just getting to know. Just as she was about to leave the house, her adult daughter arrived for a visit. When she saw that her mother was leaving, she said she would just stay there and watch television until Trisha returned from dinner.

While at the restaurant, Trisha said she still could not resolve in her mind the bizarre incidents that had occurred to her that day. Her mind was not on making conversation with her new beau. On several occasions, as they sat chatting, she clearly felt someone tap her on the shoulder. Each time she turned around, no one was there. Her back was, in fact, facing a corner of the room. Her gentleman friend asked several times what was wrong, but she declined to share the experience with him. As the annoying tap on the shoulder persisted and her friend persisted in asking what was wrong, she finally gave in and told him the entire story, starting with our phone conversation. By the end of dinner, her companion was completely "turned off" by her honest sharing of these unusual events and announced that he did not want to see her again.

When Trisha arrived home, she found her daughter extremely distraught. She explained that, while watching television, she had heard voices and laughter in her mother's office. Knowing that she was alone in the house, she became alarmed and slowly approached the closed office door. When she opened the door to the dark room, she was instantly entranced at the sight of three balls of intelligently controlled light floating around the room. The lights then stopped and each one floated down, landing on a large manila envelope on the desk. It was later discovered that this manila envelope contained my portfolio. Trisha sat down with her daughter and explained to her the strange occurrences of the day. After her daughter left and Trisha went into her bedroom, she again found crystals strategically placed around the room. It was then that she decided to call me to relate these confusing events and to state that she now believed in ETs and would take me as a client.

This was a unique healing experience for this woman. She had finally let go of her fears and accepted the benevolent, invisible Starpeople. This report illustrates how the Starpeople function by communicating indirectly with certain fearful participants in order to personally give that witness "experiential proof" to heal their fears.

I recall a trip I made from Oregon to California. I drove south along the coastal route and intended to take the interstate back up to the center of the state. The Sasquatch interjected, saying, "No, take the coast. You will meet two women, and your meeting will be helpful to all." I had learned not to intellectualize such messages or to seek a rational explanation.

Against my initial decision to go inland, the following morning I drove the coast. While I waited to be served breakfast at a roadside restaurant, two women entered and sat across from me, paying no attention to my presence. After receiving my meal and saying my usual grace before eating, I noticed the two women giving me a warm smile of approval for praying in public. Within minutes, the three of us were enjoying breakfast together.

After sharing with them that I had been conducting Bigfoot research, one of the women quipped, "Tell me, are they from outer space?"

I gave a brief explanation and decided to mention the creatures' ability to project themselves astrally and how they have often guided me.

"Can you ask them to heal me?" the other woman inquired. "I have a medical problem and need some help."

No sooner had I explained that it was not that easy for me to do, when my whole body began to vibrate, indicating to me that the Bigfoot people were indeed there listening. I was again surrounded by an energy of great love.

Her eyes wide with disbelief, the second woman exclaimed with a look of shock on her face, "Oh my God, something is happening to me—they're here; I can feel them. Bigfoot is giving me a healing." She was overjoyed. Although we had talked for less than five minutes, my caring, invisible friend somehow knew this woman could handle the experience. She was very happy and grateful, and the attitude of both women was immediately changed.

Situations such as this have happened to me dozens of times. Just when I think I will be scoffed at by someone, the Sasquatch intervene and *prove* their interdimensional existence to the person. The price I pay for sharing my honesty with others has often been rewarded with direct support from the psychic Sasquatch. It is their way of saying, "Of course we are here; can't you feel us?" Not only would their physical appearance frighten most people, but perhaps these beings only spend a limited portion of their lives in the material Earth dimension! Perhaps they are here only 50% of the time—or possibly only 10%. Maybe it is easier for them to relate to us from another plane of existence. We are wise not to impose our ethnocentric values and limited thinking on them, as their reasoning is vastly different from ours.

The two women and I later discovered we had mutual business interests and we helped each other in our endeavors in a most fruitful way. Taking the coastal route proved the Sasquatch's advice to be correct.

Another incident occurred in Tucson, Arizona, in November 1991, while I was receiving acupuncture. During the healing session, the practitioner stopped three times, gazing around the room with a puzzled look on her face. Finally, she related to me that there were Sasquatch people in the room with us, observing from the astral dimension. She said there was one large one, well over ten feet tall, who was the leader, and two other shorter ones, seven and eight feet tall. The woman asked them what they wanted and why they were there.

The leader replied, "We are here to protect Kewaunee. Why are you hurting him with those needles?"

"I am not hurting him; I am healing him," emphasized the acupuncturist.

"It doesn't look that way to me," the Sasquatch retorted.

The woman asked, "What do you care what I'm doing to this person? Who is he that you should be so concerned?"

"We are his guides and protectors and we monitor Kewaunee all the time to help whenever we can. He has helped us in the past in another life, and now we are working together on a spiritual mission," the Sasquatch related.

Once the Starpeople saved my life while I was on a short trip into the Oregon wilderness. Just before the trip, the ETs had made contact, and I could feel them monitoring me as I drove along a narrow, dangerous road beside a 60 foot drop-off. Suddenly, I lost control of the car. As I approached a hairpin curve, I frantically pumped the brakes without effect, and my vehicle went over the side. My first thoughts were: "This is it; I'm dead!" Fear turned to shock when I found my car hovering in mid-air. It then swiveled and landed back on the road, pointed in the direction I had been traveling, but on the other side of the hairpin curve! Although I did not have any telepathic communication from a spaceship, I could *feel* the presence of the Starpeople monitoring me. I remember reading an article in a UFO magazine back in the early seventies that described a contactee's car being lifted off the road to avoid an accident with a tractor-trailer. At the time I read this, I remember wondering why the UFO contactee had fabricated the story about levitation. My thinking had not yet evolved enough to realize that the levitation was a part of the UFO phenomenon.

Another incident in Tucson involved my landlady and her daughter. I had just moved into the house. On the evening of my first day, I was introduced to Dawn, the landlady's 19-year-old daughter, who was nine months pregnant. The next morning, I called my landlady at her place of business to ask a question. She was crying when I called, and she related to me that she had just spoken with Dawn on the telephone. Dawn had developed eclampsia, a toxic blood condition that kills one in every two hundred pregnant women who are diagnosed with it. In the phone conversation, Dawn had reported to her mother that her face was red from an increase in blood pressure, that she had edema and was weak and dizzy. Dawn had called the hospital for an ambulance, but she had been told not to worry, because her blood test had not been completed yet, and that would determine if she needed an ambulance. She was told that most likely she did not have the dreaded eclampsia when, in fact, she did. She then called her mother, fearing that she was going to pass out or die.

As I hung up the phone, I felt terrible and helpless. The hospital didn't want to send an ambulance until the tests were completed, but Dawn might have been dead by then. I sat down and, in less than a minute, I left my physical body and located Dawn. I was immediately aware that her life was in danger. Upon "popping" back into my body, I instantly burst into tears, as I knew she was in serious trouble and could easily die. I just didn't know how I could help her, and this bothered me deeply. I then attempted to psychically call my friends, the Starpeople, to see if they would intervene and heal Dawn. Within one minute, an ET voice said, "We hear you; we will go."

I jumped up and ran to the phone to call my landlady. Once again, in an apologetic tone, I said, "Do you remember last night when I told you I was writing a book on Bigfoot and ETs? Well, in desperation to help Dawn, I just contacted them and they're going to her house to heal her. I know this must sound crazy, but what I'm saying to you is true. I'm just trying to help."

My landlady repeatedly thanked me without questioning. I suggested to her that she close her business and go to assist her daughter. When I chatted with her later, she seemed pleased about what had transpired at my instigation. She related that when she arrived at Dawn's house, she expected the worst. To her surprise, her daughter was perfectly fine, with no symptoms of eclampsia whatsoever. How could that be? The mother told Dawn that their new tenant was in touch with space people and was going to send them to help her. The daughter remarked that she knew all about it because the ETs had just left. They had given her a healing, and she was fine. She said that three beings appeared to her like living shadows walking around the room. When I asked, "You mean they were in another dimension?" Dawn excitedly replied, "That's it, that's it!"

Two more witnesses will objectify the reality of what is being documented in this chapter. One healing episode I will never forget took place at the home of a Hopi Indian elder in Sedona, Arizona, in January 1991. I had serious liver cancer, and, although I was in pain, I had no interest in being treated by allopathic medicine. I had not yet decided what holistic health approach I would use. Retiring to the guest room for the night, I climbed into bed and shut off the light. Within minutes, I felt a powerful presence. At the foot of the bed stood four 6-1/2-foot-tall Kachinas. In the Hopi Indian tradition, Kachina spirits are actually a race of Starpeople who guided them to the sacred land where they now live. Two beings stood in front of the bed and two in back, and they began telepathically communicating to me with great wisdom and compassion, saying, "You have cancer and will die if you do not treat yourself soon. But that is your choice. You can choose to live or die; you have the power. Yet, you are needed during this time of the Great Purification when turmoil and destruction will reign. You are an herbalist and understand natural healing. Use the herb chaparral and you will recover quickly so you can continue to do the work of the Creator. All of this is your choice; we make no judgment or demands. It is your life. We are here to be supportive and offer guidance and knowledge. It is your will to accept it or not."

The Kachinas spoke with me for nearly an hour. I was impressed by their kindness and compassion. Two days later, I collapsed and was bedridden for five weeks. During this time, I blended other potent herbs with chaparral and took them four times daily. Five-and-one-half weeks later I was mountain trekking! A check-up three months later proved negative for cancer.

Native Americans have also spoken of memory stones from the Sasquatch people. These stones are powerful and healing and I was fortunate to receive these gifts directly from Sasquatch.

In December of 1995, while living in Tucson, Arizona, I went outside in the early morning hours (1:15 A.M.) because I could not sleep. There, in the clear night sky, was a large, glowing object close to the horizon. The light did not in any way look like the planes that frequently fly over. Whenever I see a craft, I always start by saying, "Hello ETs and Bigfoot people," and then tell them what I want. In my mind, I initiated the communication, asking them if they have any means of helping me financially for my projects. Such a request was more an experiment to see how they would react, as I thought it would be fun to ask. I repeated my odd request three times, then became bored after ten minutes when no one replied. I went back to bed.

The next morning I had already pushed the seemingly insignificant incident from the night before to the back of my mind. After all, I have seen well over one hundred of such ships over the years while looking for Bigfoot in the wilderness. When I walked into the kitchen, I noticed a red smooth kind of "gemstone" sitting on the counter. Since I live alone, I wondered how something so bright and obvious had arrived on my counter. I had a busy day planned, so I laid it back on the counter and forgot about it. Two days later, when I awoke in the morning, I became somewhat unnerved when I saw two red gem-like stones side by side. I was perplexed! How did they get there and where did they come from? How could anyone get into my place at night when I have a 90-pound dog in the house? Again, my busy schedule consumed me and soon I left the house to start my day.

Two more days lapsed and there were three stones sitting on the counter. Then I began piecing two and two together, starting with the spaceship I had observed earlier in the week. If the stones were from the Starpeople, were they worth anything? I took them to the International Gem Show to find out, but was disappointed when I was told they were unusual, yet they were just glass, probably with some gold in the center, the gemologist related. By the week's end, another had materialized and I had in my possession four red gemstones. My interest was in finding out what their significance was, as I had learned they had no monetary value.

Julie, a new friend of mine at the time, stopped over to look at the stones. She has a strong interest in both Bigfoot and UFOs, but is not a researcher and had never encountered anything unusual over the years. She became excited while examining the "gifts" that had materialized in my place. Just before leaving, I gave Julie a small medicine bag with a delicate cord to put around her neck. She felt the bag to see if there was anything in it, but it was empty. Julie gratefully placed the bag around her neck as I escorted her to the car. She held a button in her hand to later sew on a shirt for me, and decided to drop it in the bag so as not to lose it. I stood a mere two feet from Julie, watching her fingers disappear in the bag. In a second, she let out a startled cry as she lifted a red gemstone out of the bag. It literally "aported" or materialized from another dimension in front of our eyes, with Julie as my witness! That made five stones. Within the next two weeks, another red one, plus a large clear white stone also manifested.

During this time we took the stones to a respected psychic to get her opinion on the anomalous stones. She was helpful, but unable to reveal anything specific. But, within two weeks, the psychic told me about a Native American medicine man from Idaho who told her about the red "gems." She never mentioned my name to the shaman. She said she knew a man who was having red gemstones materializing in his house, and she asked him if he had ever heard anything about such a phenomenon. His answer was immediate: "Anyone who receives such a gift is to consider themselves very special. The person should treasure the stones because they are rare to receive. They are called "memory stones" because each stone is individually programmed like a miniature computer with a message to the receiver to guide them with certain spiritual information. The information will not help anyone else except that person and each stone will reveal its spiritual value and power over a period of time."

When the psychic asked the Indian elder where the stones are from, he quipped: "They were given by the Sasquatch people!" When she asked how he knew the red stones were from Bigfoot, he replied: "Because I have a whole drawer full of them!"

Then, a week later, a friend called to tell me that an associate of his who was skilled in Amazonian herbology was visiting from Florida. My friend thought we should meet to discuss his research since I am a master herbalist. I agreed, and we met at a local restaurant. During the course of our conversation, the red memory stones were mentioned. Everyone then wanted to see them. I laid one of the seven stones in the hand of the herbalist. Fascinated, he held the stone between his finger and thumb up to the light. The stone remained in his hand a full fifteen minutes, possibly more, as he continued to study it at different angles to the light while we casually socialized.

Before he returned the stone, the man reported to me that he had sustained a serious injury to his left shoulder four months earlier and was in pain 24 hours a day. But, while holding the memory stone in his left hand, he felt an odd electrical sensation go up his left arm, then was startled when he realized that all pain had instantly ceased from his injured shoulder! When we departed an hour later, the pain was still completely gone, he reported.

Presently, I meditate with the memory stones daily to see what new avenues of cosmic information might transpire. Who knows what might be gleaned?

# The Interdimensional Bigfoot

The Sasquatch can traverse other dimensions by materializing and dematerializing at will. At times, it will be only halfway into another dimension so if you were to shoot at it, you would shoot into space and trees, as its physical body would have made the "transfer" into a less dense etheric dimension. What often remains is the "red eyes" literally peeping through an electromagnetic field, whose frequency displays the color red when seen from this three-dimensional side of reality. When a Sasquatch "blips" into another dimension while walking on snow or in mud, the *proof* is that the physical tracks abruptly end as if the creature vanished into thin air—and, in reality, it truly did, by entering another, "lighter," less dense dimension. This phenomenon has been reported frequently by researchers and percipients. The sentient creatures use other dimensions both to hide from danger and to spy on humans while reading their minds.

Still, the present scientific paradigm requires repeatability, reliability, statistics, and physical proof. But the paradigm is incomplete, non-holistic, and thus distorted, lending to misinformation and unacceptability when a researcher attempts to apply it to "elusive" phenomena. With these inadequate standards, it becomes frustrating. I experienced mental telepathy with: ETs, the Bigfoot people, a bear, a snake, twice with a hawk, three times with a raven, once with a 130-pound domesticated wolf, and often with Comanche, my Black Labrador. Sound absurd? You bet! Telepathy isn't something I was looking for, since I didn't believe it was a real phenomenon. I remained in denial for two years while operating on a strange new "frequency" called PSI. As a social scientist and trained hypnotherapist, I know enough about the mind to know that none of what I described above was hallucinatory! It is merely a wonderful new reality that I am enjoying and learning from and want to continue to share with others who are also open-minded and willing to learn.

It all started the very day in September 1979 when both a Sasquatch and a Starperson telepathically spoke with me. My life has never been the same since. Apparently, I had an additional sense awakened within me, and I am convinced that I went through a "spiritual-psychic transformation." A part of my mind was stimulated and opened by these beings. The people I documented objectified my reality; at times two or three of us experienced the phenomenon together.

I no longer fear sharing these anomalous happenings publicly, because I sincerely feel I am fulfilling an academic *and* spiritual responsibility as a social scientist to report the truth as I experienced and perceived it. Education is the key. Avoidance breeds ignorance. We are involved with highly intelligent human-type beings that we know little about, and it is important to respect them unconditionally for who they are, without fantasizing the monster hypothesis.

Once, two friends visited me in my Milwaukee apartment. While I was kneeling down arranging some photographs on the coffee table, Ralph said: "My God, there's a monkey looking over your shoulder!" I looked around and wondered what he was talking about. I waited for the punch line, but it never came. Ralph squinted his eyes in an effort to see better. His companion said she observed a ghostly outline but could not make out the features. Then I knew what they were talking about—it was probably the young Sasquatch that projects to me on occasion. But why could I not see him this time? It did not make sense. Nevertheless, it did further objectify the psychic reality I was previously experiencing alone, and that was important. Here it was confirmed again by two more people who did not know I had encountered an astral Sasquatch.

Over the next three years, Ralph reported to me that he had five more astral encounters with the psychic Sasquatch. He told me that sometimes a ten-foot-tall creature would appear in his living room with its head lowered to avoid going through the ceiling into the upper floor. It would look around the room, intermittently glancing back at Ralph, who would be spooked by the huge size of the large male. He said he would wave his arms at the apparition and say: "Go away, go away! Jack is not here right now; don't come around me. I like you—but Jack's not here!" Ralph is a warm, good-natured man, and I am sure the Sasquatch was amused at his innocuous gestures. After all,

Ralph was not searching for them nor did he desire to interact with them in any way. The apparitions were as much a shock to him as they were to me.

Numerous times, as I was having a telephone conversation with someone not involved in Bigfoot research, the other person would report that an astral Sasquatch manifested before him. I now believe the creatures appeared to others in order to objectify their interdimensional astral reality to me.

Not all astral encounters were mundane. Once I was talking with a psychologist friend when an astral Sasquatch appeared, touching me on the shoulder. Its psychic vibrations were so intense that it temporarily paralyzed my vocal cords. My friend thought I was having a stroke. The experience was rather embarrassing. When the paralysis subsided, he told me he *felt* a third person in the room during the strange episode. To avoid further embarrassment, I told him that the loss of my voice was caused by an Indian spirit guide that follows me, thinking it may not damage my credibility as much as mentioning a Sasquatch! Because he insisted he had felt *something*, the man accepted my explanation, marveling at how the phenomenon had physically affected me.

When I arrived home that evening, before going to bed, I took off my wristwatch and then attempted to remove my ring. When I had purchased the ring six years earlier, it was a bit large for my fingers and always loosely flopped around, the gemstone inevitably ending up on the underside of my hand. I bought it because I liked the style, but now I could not remove it! It was firmly stuck, and there was no logical explanation for it. After using soap and water, I finally removed the ring and then examined the thick silver shank. The once-round shank was now bent into a crookedly shaped oval. Just the day before, I had cleaned off some grime that had adhered to the base of the gemstone. At that time, the sturdy shank was perfectly round. Only a good whack with a hefty hammer could have bent it like that. The whole matter was very disturbing. I began to review what had happened earlier that evening. The Sasquatch had touched me on the shoulder on the same side of my body as my ring hand. It seemed that the electrical impulses that vibrated through my body were powerful enough to paralyze my throat in the middle of a conversation, but also, in a Uri Geller fashion, my ring had become bent in the process. It is unclear what the creature meant to accomplish by charging my body with that much psychic force. I cannot help but think that the creature did not realize that the input of energy would have such a profound effect on me or the ring. This was the third time my voice had become paralyzed when I was touched by a Sasquatch; however, I had not been wearing a ring during those previous times.

As the years progressed, the astral Sasquatch phenomenon did not go away—in fact, their visits increased. People were stunned when they would be standing talking with me and then see a giant apparition appear behind me. Crazy? You bet! For a long while it was embarrassing for me to try to explain that what the person was witnessing was in no way imaginary. The interdimensional beings seemed to watch over me, observe me, and at times communicate with me via feeling and verbal telepathy. Much of the time when I travel in a car, visit a friend, talk on the telephone, or go shopping, they are there. I *vividly* feel them and, occasionally, other people do as well. In the presence of psychics, without relating to them my research, several have said: "Are you aware that one of your guides is a Sasquatch?" or "Did you know you are being monitored by Bigfoot?" Mostly, they seem to guide me in decision-making when it directly relates to linking up with someone I have not yet met pertaining to my research. When these happenings occur, I put my scientific knowledge on the shelf and patiently watch where these mind-boggling events take me. Because they do not go away, I have no choice but to embrace it and fearlessly "go with the flow."

It's interesting and ironic that the Bigfoot people consider *us* primitive! They wear hair instead of clothes, plus they have a strikingly different anthropoid structure compared to the modern human or the non-bipedal gorilla. The Bigfoot can pass on cultural information to subsequent generations just as we can, only it is through mental telepathy. These beings are more polite and respectful than we are to our own people. On rare occasions, they have mentioned prayer and God, which is a characteristic that anthropologists use to separate *humans from non-humans*. The use of tools is still another such characteristic. There is no evidence showing that the Sasquatch are tool makers, but they are tool "users" judging from objects they have been carrying (a kettle, a flashlight-type device, a rolled-up blanket-like object, and so on). Based on my research, the Sasquatch are *clearly* a people with culture as defined in anthropology.

Mental telepathy is the primary tool that these beings are using to make us aware of other realms so we will change our consciousness. One woman whose telepathic skills enable her to communicate with Sasquatch is a Cherokee medicine woman Dhyani Ywahoo who helps others to be more spiritually aware of a living planet and more attuned to the Universal Flow. Her words seem to touch at the very *essence* of our existence as to why we are here, the temporariness of our physicalness, and the awareness that our soul-selves are the real substance that directs us to our purpose in life. Here she shares her understanding of the Sasquatch:

I think the people who have really touched me very deeply, and in fact have stayed and protected me are the Bigfoot people, the Sasquatch. Even when I'm on another continent, if I'm in a jungle or something, they're there. They're an extremely loving people with a real sense of honor, respect, loyalty and caring. They're like dolphins in that their consciousness is unified so they can feel what's happening with their whole race and the people they care for. Human beings have made things so distorted that Sasquatch children are dying and the forests, the places where they live, are dying from the acidic rain. The hearts of the Sasquatch are really open. When you meet one of those people, it's a complete meeting, a full contact with the whole essence, the whole nature of the being.

I've always known they were there and at first they would leave little things for me or let me see them in the Carolinas. When I was in the Himalayas, the Nepalese people would say, "She brought those American Yetis with her." But the first really powerful meeting where we could just acknowledge our purpose and our time as one was three years ago in the Rockies where I went and spent seven days with them. It was very wonderful.

Well, there were two other people with me. The man had a nervous breakdown, and the woman, who is very strong, was okay, but her husband never recovered. At first the Bigfoot people would come to the tepee, but after the third night it was too hard for them. Paul would lose consciousness and Mona would come in her subtle body, and one particular scene of going off in a spaceship just did it for the man. His consciousness has been so expanded that everyday reality is difficult for him and there was a great lesson in that. He was a businessman, and now he just prefers to meditate. His nervous breakdown was a build up—it was a renewal for him.

Now, I try to visit the Sasquatch every year, and some of them have moved near to Vermont.[1]

Like myself, this spiritual woman is having similar experiences, but on a more in-depth level. Nonetheless, the Sasquatch interdimensionally demonstrated that they can astrally project anywhere, even to the Himalayas, where other spiritually evolved people could see them in an apparitional form.

---

1. Burlington, Vt: "The Movement".

These reports clearly illustrate the psychic abilities of the Sasquatch and how they apparently attach themselves to certain people who are trying to make a spiritual contribution to humanity. Once a Sasquatch telepathed to me in my home in Melrose, Oregon, saying only: "I am here." I had not had any direct contact with them for seven months, and this introduction pleasantly surprised me. My home was located at the foot of the towering Callahan Mountains which formed a dog-leg of the Coastal Siskiyou range. Three nights earlier I had spotted a glowing UFO following me at a distance. It then navigated to the summit of the Callahans. Arriving home, I telescoped with my zoom-lens binoculars and excitedly watched the craft slowly descend behind the mountain. Most likely, the Sasquatch had exited from this same ship.

Twice I went outside and stood in the bitter cold, beckoning the creature to step out and talk. Nothing. No response. Each time when I returned to my desk to proceed with my paper work, it psychically interrupted me again. Then it pounded on the side of the trailer, producing a loud and powerful "thud" to assure me it was indeed outside. The second time it "vibed" me with love energy but refused to converse.

This situation happened often, and it still frustrates me at times. They let me know they are there, then ignore me. The way they seem to "play games" on occasion mystifies me. I am a serious-minded individual and like tending to business. Maybe that is it—maybe I am not light-hearted enough for their taste. Several reservation Indians have used the word "trickster" to describe the sometimes prankish Sasquatch. So there is a light side to them, even if they do look frightening.

A short time later I went to bed. After snapping off the lights, I immediately heard the familiar heavy footfalls of a giant biped walking past my window along the length of the building. Suddenly, they stopped. Five seconds passed, then my spine started to quiver. The heavy stomping continued, but this time it was *in my living room* and was coming down the hall toward my bedroom! I was baffled at how the creature entered through a locked door. I had not heard the bulky glass door slide open.

I lay there in awe, wondering what to expect. In a few seconds I saw him. The Bigfoot creature was on the astral plane, yet affecting the physical surroundings. His physical body was outside, but his consciousness projected this living apparition or soul-self. This nonphysical state is as real as the material body, only it is freer and capable of passing through walls and doors. He stood over me, looking down, and I began telepathing by asking his name. No answer. I turned my head momentarily to pull the blanket around my shoulder, and when I looked back the eight- to nine-foot creature was gone.

"Ka-boom!" The foot of my bed bounced hard as the Sasquatch deliberately sat on it. I have to admit that it temporarily startled me. Perhaps I bored him, as no exchanges of words ensued. I sensed a playfulness. My telepathing proved fruitless. Within minutes, the Sasquatch apparition disappeared. Almost simultaneously, the sound of heavy footsteps resumed outside, gradually fading into the forest.

In the summer of 1985, I visited a certain mountain within a 20-mile radius of Roseburg, Oregon. I encountered a male and female Sasquatch and used dowsing rods to track them. Within minutes, I located 17-1/2-inch-long, fresh tracks in the big timber where I heard the creatures moving ahead of me. That was the verification I needed. Stalking them was out of the question, because I consider it an act of aggression. Besides, it forces them to flee. My methodology has always been: 1) map dowse to target an area, 2) field dowse to verify and explore, and 3) set up camp to allow the Sasquatch to come to me. Most Sasquatch families do not want any contact with the outside world, but some are genuinely curious and like to observe people. A rare few actually make telepathic contact with a person.

On the mountain where I located the Sasquatch family, I learned that there was a total of three creatures. Sometimes members of other families would visit, but generally three creatures stayed within the vicinity of the mountain, migrating on occasion. The Sasquatch told two different percipients there are seven races or species of their people worldwide, some less evolved, and mentioned the Yeti as having more animal qualities. The Himalayan Yeti is more primitive, yet like all other hominoid types, they too have psychic ability as a survival mechanism, one percipient was told.

Twice on my visits to the mountain area, I brought a block of salt from the farmers' co-op. I began frequently camping out on the mountain. During the day I could hear the Sasquatch sneaking around. The sound was distinctly that of a biped walking about. One evening I drove my car up the old wood road to where the creatures congregated and could "feel" them picking up my vibrations from about two miles away. My body began vibrating, and soon I felt an intelligent presence accompanying me in the vehicle. (Since then, both the Bigfoot people and ETs have telepathically spoken to me dozens of times while I was in a car. Once I had a passenger with me and, after the being ended our telepathic conversation, my companion turned to me and said: "That's strange. I feel there's someone else in the car with us. It's not one of your weird friends following you, is it?")

My automobile was parked at the edge of an isolated trail for the night. With my knapsack on my back, I hiked up into the giant stand of timber of western cedar and Douglas fir. The atmosphere was friendly. Telepathically, I was told there were a male and two female Sasquatch present, and that I was welcome. The communication was very clear. They requested that I not camp in the timber but out in the open instead. I agreed to do so. Two of the beings repeatedly struck a hollow log with sticks, to a very eerie beat. The sound came from a level area in the forest, approximately two acres in size. The rest of the terrain was rugged and very steep. The Sasquatch told me they were conducting a ritual next to a vortex on this "shelf." I did not fully understand, but I knew this area was sacred territory to them, and so I respected their request. Clairsentiently, I could feel love and peace flowing from them. Though they were less than 50 feet from me, the Sasquatch remained invisible.

While telepathing to them, I laid a block of salt on the butt of the log. I honored them. This was their home and I was their guest. Then I heard what sounded like someone tip-toeing behind me. I did not look. The other two Sasquatch could easily be heard slowly moving about in the forest in front of me. Again, I felt very welcomed. When I turned to walk the 35 feet or so, back-tracking my steps to the main trail, there on the path was a bouquet of flowers that was not there just ten minutes before! I felt female energy. It was indeed a kind gesture of thanks for my bringing the salt.

After pitching my tent, I paced the trail in the dark, playing a harmonica and wondering if there would be a specific reaction to my music. The dirge-like drumming continued without my interrupting a beat of it. The Sasquatch did not come out to talk face-to-face. After an hour, I crawled into my tent for the night.

Less than ten minutes passed before I heard footsteps coming from the forest into the clearing and up to my tent. I looked through the customized peep-holes on each side of the canvas, but there was no one in sight! My interdimensional friend chose to remain incognito. I climbed out of the tent and briefly surveyed the area, verifying my initial findings—there was nothing in sight. The slow banging of hollow logs in an odd rhythmic fashion continued. I heard twigs snap and bushes rustle a few feet behind the tall brush at the perimeter of the forest. Then, about six feet behind the tent, I heard what sounded like someone loudly clearing their throat in a distinct, almost guttural growl.

I investigated by taking a step closer to the sound, while telling the being that I desired it to appear. My request was ignored. After turning around, I heard a shuffling of feet a short distance behind me and once again a sound like clearing a throat. My body vibrated with their presence as I looked out into the star-filled night.

In his book, *The Path of Power*, Sun Bear, a Chippewa Indian medicine man, says:

> In the Feather River country of California, I met a medicine man named Calvin Rube, who was a servant of Sasquatch, the ones we call the "Bigfoot" people. He was a chief of the Wichipek tribe, and when we were learning about Sasquatch he'd go up into the mountains, make his prayers, and Bigfoot would come to him, either in person or in spirit. The Bigfoot would speak to him; he would teach him. You see, we Native Americans believe that the Sasquatch is a superhuman being, a spirit keeper who can change form or disappear. The Bigfoot has knowledge far beyond ours, and he is protector of the forest.[2]

When Sun Bear says the Sasquatch came to Calvin Rube "either in person or in spirit," he means physically, in person, or in out-of-body travel, in which it appears as an apparition. Because that form or dimension is the real consciousness of the physical self, it *is* the "real" Sasquatch in its freest expression and form.

Scientist Dan A. Davidson of Arizona has a similar theory pertaining to interdimensionality. He offers three *possible* explanations about the creatures' adeptness with invisibility:

> 1. The Bigfoot are able to project a mental suggestion into the mind of the observer which clouds the observer's perception using telepathic hypnosis. This effect can be demonstrated with hypnosis and mental suggestion. This is also prevalent in the Indian rope trick where a chela (student) of the guru (teacher) supposedly climbs a rope which the guru has thrown into the air and seemingly hangs there suspended while the chela climbs the rope and disappears. Movies taken of this scene, which everybody swears they witnessed, shows the guru toss the rope into the air and it immediately falls to earth; whereupon, the chela walks up and pretends to start climbing the rope. The chela then

---

2. Sun Bear, 1983, p. 58.

walks off the staging area. Everyone 'sees' the chela climb the rope but the camera doesn't. The explanation is mass hypnosis or mental suggestion, which is the first stage taught by a master to his chelas to learn mastery of the mental forces.

2. This explanation is a little more involved from a physics point of view. We have all seen a simple electric fan where the motor is off and the blades are at rest. If the fan is energized, then the blade spins at such a high rate that it becomes invisible. The real Yogi Adepts and the Ascended Masters (e.g., Beloved Jesus or Saint Germain) are able to control the vibration rate of their bodies by causing the cells of the body to vibrate at a rate which is either visible or invisible to the observer(s). Thus, the Masters can appear and disappear at will. People who are clairvoyant can adjust the vibratory rate of their nervous system so that they can see light vibrations which are above the visible spectrum, which means they can see in 'higher dimensions.' Thus, a true clairvoyant can see and communicate easily with beings that are vibrating at a rate which is invisible to the so-called normal person. For those who have some degree of clairvoyant capability, this is an obvious possibility.

3. This third explanation is even more involved technically than #2. This explanation is vastly simplified for the non-technical reader. It is an established fact that the earth has a natural 'resonant' frequency which varies around 7 to 8 cycles per second or hertz (Hz) as frequency rate is termed in physics. In addition, our time/space continuum is continually being created by the conditions that we are immersed in. Another way of saying this is our universe as we observe it is being created before our eyes, but because of our mental conditioning, we do not observe the process. Because we are all immersed in this natural frequency of the earth and our time/space condition, all our perceptions of sight, sound, hearing, etc. are all in synchronism with the earth resonant frequencies and the biased conditioned mental view that we have. From a physics point of view, if a being (human, Bigfoot, or ETs) was able to change the natural synchronistic frequency of their body so it was no longer in resonance with our world as we experience it, then it is theoretically possible that we wouldn't see them, and in fact they may not even "register" in this world. Examples are (1) when the Bigfoot would leave no footprints in our 3 dimensional world, (2) when a Bigfoot leaves prints in the snow and then suddenly the footprints end, or (3) when a Bigfoot peaks out from the safety of another dimension and all a

witness sees is glowing red eyes. They would, in effect, be operating in a different time/space dimension.

Since I have not had the experience, like Kewaunee, of seeing or experiencing a Bigfoot, I don't have a feeling from such an experience as to whether any of the above explanations are valid. Since many of the reports that I have read suggested that the Bigfoot are somewhat odorous (i.e., they smell badly by our standards), I would pick explanation number one. The Bigfoot live close to nature and very likely have a strongly developed emotional body. The emotional body is the same as the subconscious mind and the Bigfoot could have a strong ability to project mental suggestion. So called 'normal' humans also have very powerful emotional bodies but because of mental and emotional conditioning most people have suppressed and/or never learned to be in control of their emotions. Primitives that live close to nature tend to be more in tune with using their emotional body as a sensory and creative function because many times their survival depends on a higher sense perception[3].

Mr. Davidson's explanation in #1 was told to me by two separate Native American medicine people, and can be found in accounts of telepathic hypnosis in the literature. Sasquatch are very adept at mind control but rarely use it. More often, they dematerialize using methods #2 and #3. Some dematerialization and materialization happen as fast as the click of a light switch while at other times the living image "fades" so one can see right through the creature. And, at times, the percipient sees only glowing red eyes. So, I concur with Mr. Davidson and feel strongly that all three areas of projected hypnosis and quantum physics are being utilized as an innate psychic survival mechanism by these clever nature-beings.

Professor Fred Reines, a prominent physicist who worked directly with Dr. Robert Oppenheimer on the first atomic bomb, stated in 1982, that: "Our universe is only one-tenth of the whole, nine-tenths are made up of invisible mass." If our physical universe that is composed of ten billion or more galaxies is only one-tenth of reality, then what of the missing nine-tenths? Contemporary physicists now believe that subatomic neutrinos and neutrino-like particles constitute the other nine-tenths. These elusive particles, though smaller than those of an atom, have mass yet can easily pass through any physical matter. Researcher George C. Andrews, in his book, *Extra-Terrestrials Among Us* (1986), perceives the situation thus:

---

3. Davidson, personal communication.

The atoms our physical bodies are composed of contain protons, neutrons, and electrons, as do all other atoms in the physical universe perceptible to our senses. The atoms of our physical bodies also contain much finer and faster-vibrating neutrinos and neutrino-like particles.[4]

These finer and faster-vibrating particles compose the substance of the bioplasmic 'spirit' body that is joined to our physical body by an invisible magnetic cord which breaks at the moment of death. The bioplasmic body is the butterfly that breaks loose from the chrysalis of the old worn-out physical body when we die. We are in this world, but we are not of it. We come from, and return to the dimension of neutrinos and neutrino-like particles that the nuclear physicists have recently discovered, the same dimension that Sir William Crookes and Sir Oliver Lodge postulated the existence of a century ago. The so-called supernatural and paranormal turn out to be natural and normal after all.[5]

Norman Friedman, in his 1990 book *Bridging Science and Spirit*, also says:
One of the most significant contributions to contemporary physics was Einstein's discovery of the equivalence of mass and energy. A fundamental equivalence we have seen in this examination is that of matter/energy and consciousness. This means that all existence is a form of consciousness and is alive in some sense; inert or dead matter is an illusion. As Seth points out 'Scientists say now that energy and matter are one. They must take the next full step to realize that *consciousness* and energy and matter are one.'[6]

The paraphysical Sasquatch and Starpeople learned to psychically control the trigger mechanism that allows them, literally, to traverse other dimensions. Over the millennia, psychics have assured us that we, too, have the same capacity if we only knew how to use it. Andrews continues his discussion by sagaciously saying:

There may be a correlation between this invisible nine-tenths of the universe and the puzzling fact that approximately 90% of the human cerebral cortex is unassigned. We use only about one-tenth of our potential intelligence. If we were able to use our full brain capacity, would the invisible nine-tenths of the universe become visible to us? Is the dormant 90% of the cerebral cortex comparable to equipment that is ready for use, but is not yet connected to its power source?

---

4. Andrews, 1986, pp. 240-241.
5. Andrews, 1986, p. 241.
6. Friedman, Norman, 1990, p. 286.

What is the mental connection that needs to be made in order to complete the circuit and activate our dormant potential?[7]

Transcending to higher spiritual standards will allow history not to repeat itself, and thus move planet Earth out of the immature stage of political and environmental chaos in which we are so dangerously floundering.

There are abundant indications that this invisible nine-tenths of the universe is swarming with life, and is just as real to its inhabitants as this world is to us. If they wish to interact with our physical dimension, they have to slow down their rates of vibration. In this context, consider the following statement made by a UFO contactee after he had been abducted and returned.

The Sun is a transmitter and the Earth is a receiver on a specific range of frequencies. UFOs can share the same space with us, as they operate outside our normal range of frequencies, interacting only when they wish to. A nuclear bomb is a miniature Sun, which emits energy on all spectrums, not just the Earth range of frequencies that humans are sensitive to. Therefore nuclear war would annihilate not only terrestrial humanity, but also many forms of intelligent life inhabiting dimensions we normally have no awareness of or contact with. So no wonder we are being visited by aliens.[8]

Michael Talbot, author of *Mysticism and the New Physics*, comments about UFOs and these can easily be applied to the Bigfoot phenomenon since they both are "ultradimensional."

It demonstrates that we're foolish to believe that what we perceive of as reality is all there is to reality...I think we exist on one channel, and it's quite possible that if we went to an alien planet we might not see any civilization there, but if we could move up a channel, it might be filled with civilization...But they could just as easily exist on channels here on our own planet, or they could exist on levels of reality that may not even be organized. Their universe might not even be composed of planets and suns—they may exist in some region that has a structure so foreign and alien to ours that we couldn't conceive of it at this point because we've never encountered reality organized in that particular fashion.[9]

---

7. Friedman, Norman, 1990, p. 286.
8. Friedman, Norman, 1990, p. 286.
9. Talbot, 1987, p. 19.

Everything is interconnected. Push the first in a lineup of dominoes, and you set off a series of reactions that affect all the other dominoes—in this case, our entire planet, solar system, and the invisible time-space beyond.

Even though I and other contactees continue to experience the reality of interdimensionalism, it must be understood that, for percipients, it is *not* a theory; for us—*it is fact*! It has been revealed to contactees "experientially," through all our senses. If we cannot live in peace with ourselves, other races, as well as our animal neighbors, how can we ever expect to get along with unusual-looking alien beings?

# A Genetic Experiment?

As a largely Christian nation, most of us were raised "creationists," that is, believing that God created the Universe and planet Earth was first populated by Adam and Eve, who started the human race. Theologians use the Bible as the word of God to substantiate faith in their beliefs. Scientists, however, claim the "evolution theory" that humankind's predecessors were a series of apelike hominoids that eventually, through Darwinian natural selection process and genetic mutation, branched off and developed into full-fledged *Homo sapiens sapiens*—modern man! Establishment science uses skeletons and artifacts to substantiate that our highly developed brain and nervous system evolved over three million years and only reached cosmic maturity 35,000 to 100,000 years ago.

Could it be that God (whoever She/He/It/They may be) created the Universe and put evolution in motion? Then all living things would be *co-creators* with God, and each of us would be a universal expression of God, acting out some grand plan within a physical body with God's "image and likeness." Certainly there is logic to that. But were Adam and Eve real people as told in the holy scriptures? How could two people populate an entire planet and physiognomically create all the diverse races we have today? Who would Adam and Eve's children marry? Each other? Their parents? How did they migrate to the different continents to genetically differentiate and evolve into other unique nations, languages, and cultures? The fact is, neither science nor religion can adequately and pragmatically answer these questions! There are just too many "missing links" to properly form a sequence of coherent logic, unless one entertains another possibility— the "extraterrestrial intervention theory."

In 1985, I was told by a Sasquatch that they consider themselves the *first* "people" to populate this planet and that they were brought here millions of years ago by their friends, the Starpeople! He said there were "no humans" on Earth except themselves. There were bipedal human-types that the Bigfoot considered "animals" because the creatures were so unevolved that they had not yet discovered fire. The Sasquatch said that they eventually taught these primitive Earth hominoids how to use fire. Could they be speaking of *Homo erectus*? There is no evidence that *Australopethicus* had that ability; *Homo erectus* was the first. Interestingly, *Gigantopithecus* and *Homo erectus* lived in an overlapping time frame of existence as well as in the same geographic region—China.

When I asked a Bigfoot, "What about Adam and Eve?", he replied, "I don't know anything about Adam and Eve. If you want to know about them, you'll have to wait and ask our friends the Starpeople, because they are they ones who brought them." This was shocking to me indeed. He went on to say that we hairless humans were *seeded* later, each race being released on a continent best suited for its survival. This includes *Homo neanderthalis* and *Cro-Magnon*.

"Does that mean you are the missing link?" I asked.

"No, you people are the missing link. You don't know where you've come from or where you're going!" he retorted with a chuckle.

Interestingly, there are numerous "missing link" stories from oral traditions of many cultures around the world. The Dogon tribe of Mali, West Africa, say that they initially came from a planet in the constellation Sirius. Long before modern humans had the technology to build a powerful telescope to study the heavens, the Dogon people knew the precise position of all the celestial bodies within the Sirius system. How is that possible *unless* direct knowledge was genuinely given them by interstellar visitors from Sirius hundreds, if not thousands of years ago?

In Robert Temple's book *The Sirius Mystery*, he relates the Dogon's detailed knowledge about a star that is invisible to the naked eye and so difficult for astronomers to observe that it was not "discovered" until 1970. The elders told anthropologists that this knowledge was imparted to them by Starpeople who visited their region of our world. The Dogon, prior to 1970, told scientists that Sirius B (1) is small, (2) is a heavy star, (3) is white, (4) has an elliptical orbit and (5) has an orbital period of 50 years. All five of the above statements were later *proven to be 100% correct!* How is that possible?

## A Genetic Experiment?

Maybe we should start giving "primitive" people more credibility when they tell us their "folklore."

Australian aboriginal medicine woman Lorraine Maffi Williams speaks of extraterrestrials as a distinct part of her tribal history. It is not a fireside story for skeptics, but is presented here as an integrally factual segment of her culture. She says:

> According to our people, we came from another planet which suffered galactic disintegration. When we came to Earth, we were given the responsibility to look after the Earth so that would not happen as it did on the other planet.[1]

This is similar to the oral tradition of Amerindian tribes in both North and South America, and from tribes geographically isolated from one another. Williams continues by explaining how our world was and is being environmentally abused by insensitive technocratic cultures.

> The Planet Earth was in very big danger. I say "was." You see, we also have planetary helpers—I call them brothers and sisters from other planets. They just threw their arms up in disgust with us human beings here on Earth about how we destroyed our Earth, our home. Somewhere along the line, they got together and said, "We're not helping them no more. We're finished with them." But God, the being of love and light, said, "I will not let you destroy my Earth." So the planetary helpers came down to Earth to help us restore the Earth and put the energy line grids back.[2]

Their culture is based on this information that they believe to be factual. Likewise, the Cherokee Indians claim ancestrally that they are from the Pleiadian system. Other Indian tribes, like the Great Lake Woodland Indians, speak of originating from outside the Earth. These are not metaphors or something mythical. The Torojas tribe of Indonesia also claim to be from a planet somewhere in the Pleiades constellation and their day-to-day lives revolve around rituals that purportedly have an extraterrestrial origin. All these years, anthropocentric science has been relegating this information to "legend" and "folklore" instead of investigating and correlating this global phenomenon. Science needs to pay closer attention to ethnohistory if it wishes to discover the real truth.

Though this particular subject may open Pandora's box, I feel it only fair to relate what the Bigfoot creatures told me and others about humanity's

---

1. Macer-Story, 1989, p. 48.
2. Macer-Story, 1989, p. 48.

genesis. The Sasquatch people told four separate witnesses that their ancestors were brought here by more advanced beings millions of years ago on spaceships during the age of the dinosaurs. They also claimed that their people lived through the Ice Age and a gigantic world flood. No specific details were given in order for one to match up geological time sequences and make better sense of the percipient's data. I admit such statements lack (1) proof from the Sasquatch and ETs, and (2) a complete background check and testing of each witness's veracity, yet these shortcomings do not invalidate the data.

Geological Engineer John Morris, in his book *Tracking Those Incredible Dinosaurs And The People Who Know Them*[3], discusses at length the Paluxy River enigma in Texas, where human-like tracks are commonly found in limestone deposits *beside* footprints of dinosaurs! Nearly 20 photographs presented in the book aid the reader in examining this unbelievable correlation. Anthropologists have long stated that human ancestors evolved over three and a half million years ago. Paleontologists tell us the dinosaurs became extinct about 65 million years ago, and that humans never saw a living dinosaur, because the time period was millions of years apart!

The most remarkable feature in several of the photographs in the book are the numerous "giant" human-like footprints—many actually resembling those of a Sasquatch! The length of most of the footprints range from a normal human size to some measuring 15" long, with several intermittent sizes in between. One reaches 30" in length. However, many of the tracks are not clear enough to make a positive identification, and most are considered by conservative scientists to be made from a hitherto "unknown" *bipedal* dinosaur. Sounds like an interesting rationalization. For example, the 30" track is thought to be either a foot slip or a track from an elongated foot. Yet, I have personally found Bigfoot prints that look like those tracks. How does one explain that? Clearly, these tracks could belong to the ancestor of one of the several races or species of Bigfoot creatures that exist.

Footprint shapes and anatomical features vary. From all over America, Sasquatch reports have included finding footprints with anywhere from two to six toes on a foot with every variation of length in between.

The Paluxy River giant "man" tracks were reported to have a stride as much as 55" between footprints, with a foot length between 17" and 20" long and 6" to 8" wide. One is reported to be 23-1/2" long by 11" wide. The

---

3. Morris, 1980, pp. 1-3.

most impressive I have noted in the series has five clearly indented toes that look identical to those of a Sasquatch. In fact, the anthropological evidence is normal for a Sasquatch stride. Sasquatch footprints have been reported up to 24" long, although the average print seems to be approximately 16" long and 5-1/2" to 6" wide. The reported stride is between 55" and 72" long, depending on the height of the Bigfoot. None of this is presented here as a proof, but it is circumstantial evidence that may explain one possibility for some of the tracks if we are to believe that the Sasquatch words are true—that they really did live during the age of the dinosaur!

It is vital to note that fossilized big-footed prints from a giant humanoid have long been found throughout Australia. In the book *Mysterious Australia* (1993), author/scientist Rex Gilroy shows a photograph comparing two plaster of Paris casts—one of a fossilized footprint he found in 1977 in the Carrai Range of New South Wales, the other one from a Yeti taken in Nepal. The comparison is remarkable for, at first glance, the two seem like they are from a right and left foot of the same creature. The only real difference is that the fossilized track is from Australia's Ice Age, whereas the Yeti track was cast a few years ago by a still-living bipedal hominoid. At present, Gilroy has at least 5,000 Bigfoot-type reports on record, with numerous "fresh" manlike footprints up to 20" in length and there are more still being reported in present-day Australia.

There are many pro-Creationist books written that state that the fossil records are not adequate enough to support evidence for a Darwinian evolution of *Homo sapiens* on this planet. *Ape-Men: Fact or Fallacy?* by M. Bowden points out the numerous contradictions and suppressed materials that are not congruent with some of the paleoanthropological evidence. The implication of his argument is that we were simply created by God.

If *Homo sapiens sapiens* did not evolve here on Earth, then perhaps only the animals and plants did. If this radical notion is true, then Darwinism may still prevail with natural selection but with the introduction of an exotic species—*Man!* This concept is further complicated by the statement made by a Bigfoot that *all* modern hominoids were transported here for experimental purposes, including *Homo neanderthalis*, and *Cro-Magnon* man, whereas *Australopithecines* and *Homo erectus* evolved here but were more animal than human. Experimentally, these hominoids were distributed around a primitive Earth and later different races of *Homo sapiens* were placed or "seeded" climatically, the Bigfoot telepathically related.

The Sasquatch people insisted there are *no* missing links among hominoids since we are all genetic by-products of an extraterrestrial "creation!" The fossil hominoids are not our progenitors. They said, if a "missing link" exists at all, it is *us*! We are the genetic link between Earth and the Starpeople. Apparently, Adam and Eve is symbolic wording, meaning that the races were actually hybrid strains of ETs placed in tiny communities to colonize the world, according to the Sasquatch people. If the ETs manipulated their own genetic creations, then our creation story could involve the "Sons of God," *precisely as described in the Bible*. Is such an event so difficult to comprehend or imagine for such a tiny planet that sits at the very edge of the Milky Way Galaxy? Are we *that* anthropocentric, xenophobic, and nonperceptive that we cannot entertain such a possibility in the light of all the reported alien abductions, direct ET contact, and UFO sightings worldwide?

An incredibly startling find in Delta, Utah, by William Meistor in 1968 unmistakably shows the fossil remains of two human footprints from a prehistoric man *wearing shoes!* The left heel of the shoe had a fossilized trilobite embedded in it. The last living trilobite, scientists claim, became extinct about 400 million years ago. Where did this man come from to have been alive at a time when dinosaurs had not yet emerged on planet Earth? The imprinted trilobite *proves* the shoe prints are not a hoax. Do we ignore it, or do we attempt to place it in a scenario that better fits Earth's true genesis? ETs led author and experiencer Ida Kannenberg to another ancient footprint, (seen below, in the upper center) in ancient Hawaiian rocks.[4]

To aid in developing my "ET theory," I want to add that Sasquatch told six percipients that they periodically enter a portal, a vortex leading to another dimension, where there are plants, animals and people living out

---

4. Kannenberg, 1995, p. 206.

their lives. There are vortices in outer space as well as on Earth, they said. Millions of years ago it took the Starpeople approximately ten years Earth time to traverse time and space by entering a series of vortices that allowed them to "dimension-hop" and reach other planets in the vastness of space in a relatively short period of time. Today, since more vortices have been discovered and the synchronicity of their opening is better known, spaceships (UFOs) are able to travel between Earth and their home planet, in some cases, within an hour's time! This is what the Sasquatch shared. Since some race of Starpeople had to discover this first, it is remotely possible that Earth was being visited as far back as one billion years ago and thus it would explain the trilobite in the anomalous shoe print. Over time, Sasquatch and different races of "homo" were being experimentally *seeded* here. As one group began to die out, like *Homo erectus*, the Starpeople transported other more evolved races to take its place until the planet was safe and habitable for the modern human to emerge.

Hypothetically then, we may all be ETs of sorts! If so, then in what time period did the human race arrive? Zecharia Sitchin, in his well documented book titled *The 12th Planet* (1976), took on the laborious task of examining and re-interpreting Sumerian archeological finds from the oldest known civilization on the planet. He compared these ancient inscriptions from Babylon with the Torah and the Bible, and noted numerous astounding similarities. Ancient Sumerian astronomical tablets of our solar system aided dramatically in translating the full and true scientific meaning of what Sitchin discovered. The book is slow reading because of the exactness of the rich anthropological data Sitchin presents as evidence. It is an impressive volume, and will easily fuel the intellect of any open-minded anthropologist and historian because of its articulate presentation and fascinating theme.

Sitchin carefully reconstructs the pieces to the puzzle which suggest that the Sumerian culture began when the Starpeople, which he terms Nefilim and Elohim (words taken from the Bible), colonized the Earth around 450,000 years ago. Sitchin concludes that humans were genetically engineered by the "gods" around 300,000 years ago, just as the Bigfoot people indicated. Eventually, a full-blown Earth civilization emerged some 6,000 years ago. Sitchin alludes to only one race of Starpeople, whereas contactee and abductee reports suggest that many races of ETs visited throughout Earth's geological history and into modern time.

T.C. Lethbridge, a distinguished British naturalist and archeologist, who for 30 years was Director of Excavations for the Cambridge Antissarian Society and for the University Museum of Archeology and Ethnology, wrote a most compelling book called *The Legend of the Sons of God*, a title he partly extracted from the Book of Genesis. In his search for a genealogical succession in man, Lethbridge, as did many other independent researchers, discovered vital gaps in the scientific chronology as well as profoundly meaningful historic anomalies and anachronisms that were conveniently overlooked by mainstream academicians. He philosophized:

> Perhaps the most remarkable bearing on the conflicting stories in Genesis is the truly amazing series of traditions extracted by a Polynesian from the Polynesian inhabitants of Easter Island, almost as remote a spot as you could find on the face of the globe. Here is a story of Adam and Eve almost identical with Genesis, coupled with a great deal of supposed information about the planets which could hardly have been derived from any modern source and does not look like spontaneous invention. A variant of the creation story of man being made of clay and also several other figures being involved in this work is found also in ancient American Indian writings. It almost seems as if these creation stories were once spread all over the world, together with a great deal of information of an astronomical and geological nature. This is very odd indeed, *for where could it possibly have spread from?* (Emphasis is mine.) [5]

There are many sections in the Bible that could easily be interpreted as an ET landing. I perfectly understand the difficulty accepting that modern man may be observing UFOs and encountering their occupants, but it could be a very frightful notion to suggest that the superior space beings were here all along and possibly transplanted us. Still, in 1972, Lethbridge speculated about the Sons of God:

> I feel it is all most improbable. But, I do see that it could be a possible explanation of many things in ancient records and modern research which are at present completely disconnected. Such things as lost Atlantis and Mu would have their place in it, together with the mythical gods of Greece and those of many races. The mystery of why men built the megaliths would be explained and our strange questions from the Bible at least partly answered.
>
> But should this explanation be even partly correct, it could alter much that many people take for granted. Five thousand years ago at any rate there would have to have been people living somewhere

---

5. Lethbridge, 1972, p. 109.

else who were so like human beings on Earth that they could intermarry with them and produce fertile offspring. They must have been of the same species as ourselves. Apparently the Russians already think along these lines and many Americans do....[6]

Anthropologist Dr. Jeffery Goodman in his intriguing book *The Genesis Mystery* discusses three possibilities: (1) evolution, (2) creationism, and (3) intervention. He focuses mostly on flaws in Darwinism as it is applied to human origin, yet accepts organic evolution in the lower animals to explain their development. A most convincing argument is presented against evolution for humankind. Random gene mutation does not adequately explain the sudden emergence of a hominoid predecessor as it supposedly transcended into modern man. Dr. Goodman relates:

> It is indeed hard to comprehend *Homo erectus* means of transport to the Americas; we do not even know how a creature of his limited intelligence could have crossed the waters separating Java, Australia, and Africa. But *Homo erectus* was quite a widespread species, and where he appears, modern man eventually appears as well. There is no particular correlation between the areas of earliest appearance of *Homo sapiens sapiens*; there does, on the one hand, seem to be some geographic correlation between late-surviving *Homo erectus* and early *Homo sapiens sapiens*. In Eurasia, where *Homo erectus* did not survive very late, *Homo sapiens sapiens* appear last, but in the Americas, Africa, and Australia the two species overlap in time. This fact leaves us with the possibility that mankind may have made the highly improbable transition from *erectus* to *sapiens* not once, but four separate times. Perish the thought. How could four regional populations of *Homo erectus* randomly evolve to the *sapiens* level while at the same time maintaining the high genetic homogeneity shown by the major living geographically based races of the world?[7]

Goodman opts for the "outside intervention theory," stating that either God, spacemen, or a hitchhiking spirit created *Homo sapiens sapiens*—someone with superior intelligence who possessed enough power to intervene in order to "create" the present-day human. He suggests we remain open to possible multiple working hypotheses as well, as we don't know all the answers as yet.

Archeologist John Philip Cohane, who wrote *Paradox: The Case for the Extraterrestrial Origin of Man* in 1977, is another example of an academician

---

6. Lethbridge, 1972, p. 115.
7. Goodman, 1983, p. 272.

following where the evidence seems to take him whether anyone wants to hear it or not. It was scholarly and conservatively written, yet he came to conclusions similar to Dr. Goodman's.

Maurice Chatelain came to the same conclusion in 1979 in his mathematically and physically based book *Our Ancestors Came From Outer Space*, as did Yale educated anthropologist, Dr. Arthur Horn, in his bio-culturally based book *Humanity's Extraterrestrial Origins* (1994).

Dr. James W. Deardorff, a national award-winning atmospheric scientist and professor emeritus at Oregon State University-Corvallis, with over 100 scientific papers published to his credit, wrote an exquisite analysis of an ancient Aramaic document that was discovered in 1963. His book, *Celestial Teachings* (1991), is based on the content of the scrolls known as the *Talmud of Jmmanuel* (meaning the true Testament of Jesus). When the ancient script was interpreted, it revealed that *the true genealogy of Jesus was extraterrestrial!*[8]

Author and amateur historian William Bramley was a non-proponent of ufology and had no interest in the subject before his startling research revealed the profound sociological influence ETs have had on humankind's entire history. In his book, *Gods of Eden*, Bramley states:

> The UFO phenomenon has been a part of history for thousands of years. That's nothing new. What is new, and very surprising, is just how deeply the UFO has affected human society. I was startled to see the UFO emerge as a missing link for understanding some of the bigger problems of the human race.[9]

He researched to the very beginning of what historians understand to be Earth's first civilization, and he saw a pattern emerge over and over again. It began in Sumeria six to seven thousand years ago. Bramley points out the archeological finds and says:

> Like other ancient societies which arose in the Mesopotamian region, Sumeria left records stating that human-like creatures of extraterrestrial origin had ruled early human society as Earth's first monarchs. Those alien people were often thought of as 'gods.' Some Sumerian 'gods' were said to travel into the skies and through the heavens in flying 'globes' and rocket-like vehicles. Ancient carvings depict several 'gods' wearing goggle-like apparel over their eyes. Human priests acted as mere intermediaries between the alien 'gods' and the human population.[10]

---

8. Deardorff, 1991
9. Bramley, 1989, dust cover.

## A Genetic Experiment?

Ancient stories and legends from other parts of the world indirectly support the Tower of Babel story. The Japanese people, Alaskan Eskimos, South Americans, and Egyptians all have traditions stating that their earliest forefathers had either been transported by human-like 'gods' to where the modern descendants live today, or that those 'gods' had been the source of the local language or writing.[11]

What I am presenting is nothing new, as more researchers are independently coming to similar conclusions, that directly support what the Sasquatch told me. Recent books such as *The God Hypothesis: Extraterrestrial Life and its Implications for Science and Religion* by Dr. Joe Lewels, and *Gods of the New Millenium: Scientific Proof of Flesh and Blood Gods*, by Alan F. Alford, and *Everything You Know is Wrong—Book I: Human Evolution*, by Howard Pye offer much challenging information that reinforces the ET/God concept in the literature with the theme that Earth-man was indeed brought here from somewhere else.

The Bigfoot people said many times that even today they are transported to new regions of wilderness whenever hostile humans or developers enter the creatures' immediate domain. The Sasquatch insist that ET intervention occurred with all races of humans and higher hominoid types. The Sasquatch also said that seven *races* of Bigfoot have been seeded on Earth, with one race less than five feet tall and another up to fifteen feet tall. Interestingly, cryptozoologist Ivan T. Sanderson listed eight separate species of Bigfoot types world-wide, based on research data he had collected, which almost matches up to what I was told by the Bigfoot people. Sanderson categorizes the types as follows:

I. Sub-Humans
    1. Indo-Chinese-Malay, and South Chinese
    2. East Eurasian (Ksy-guk-Almas)
II. Proto-Pygmies
    1. Oriental (Sedapa-Teh-lmas)
    2. African (Selite-Agogives)
    3. American (Divendi-Sirius)
III. Neo-Giants
    1. Oriental (Dzu-Teh-Tok-Gin-Sung)
    2. American (Sasquatch-Clh-Mah-Didi, Mapinguarys)
IV. Sub-Hominids
    1. Tibet and Himalayas (Meh-Teh-Golub-yavans)[12]

---

10. Bramley, 1989, p. 39.
11. Bramley, 1989, p. 54.

Richard Thompson and Michael Cremo's eye-popping book about the hidden history of the human race, *Forbidden Archaeology*, reveals overwhelming proof that people were here walking upon this Earth as far back as 2.8 billion years ago—long before the Mesozoic period, also known as the "age of the dinosaur." Thompson and Cremo refer to the rejection of real scientific discoveries (because they don't fit into mainstream thinking) by the establishment as a form of "knowledge filtering." This means—that whatever new information or research mainstream science does not agree with (whether it's valid or not) will be *subjectively* rejected, and eliminated from text books so that its educational content will be omitted from universal reality. Thompson and Cremo document 159 instances of physical evidence (many taken directly from scientific journals), that dispute the accepted theories of the history of our planet. The objects were independently discovered in Africa, Europe, India, South America, Asia, and the Near East. Some of the findings were a coin, figurines, strange metal spheres, a cup, a metal tube, a gold chain, a metal vase, a nail, and so on, with geological dates ranging from the late Pleistocene to the 2.8-billion- year-old Precambrian Era. Amazingly, there is another fossilized human shoe print found in Nevada in Triassic rock, which is at least 200 million years old. The print was validated by a microphotographer who examined the uniform stitches on the sole, which attested to the authenticity of the sandal.[13]

In *Genesis Revisited* (1990), Zecharia Sitchin accurately compares the information received at NASA by Voyager 2 with the ancient Sumerian cuneiforms concerning our most distant planets—Uranus, Neptune, and Pluto. How could information from NASA in 1989 *perfectly match* information by Earth's "supposed" first civilization 6,000 years ago unless someone from somewhere else came to teach them? Archeologists unearthed many astronomy texts and illustrations listing stars and constellations in their correct positions in the heavens. Sitchin remarks:

> Indeed, as we continue to expound the Sumerian cosmogony, it will become evident that not only is much of modern discovery merely a rediscovery of ancient knowledge, but that ancient knowledge offered explanations for many phenomena that modern science has yet to figure out.[14]

---

12. Sanderson, 1961, p. 360.
13. Cremo, 1993.
14. Sitchin, 1990, p.18.

## A Genetic Experiment?

According to Sitchin, the initial reason the ETs created humans on Earth was to use them to mine for gold. The Sumerians indicated that one of the major places where they mined for gold was South Africa. Sitchin adds:

> In September 1988, a team of international physicists came to South Africa to verify the age of human habitats in Swaziland and Zululand. The most modern techniques indicated an age of 80,000 to 115,0000 years. Regarding the most ancient gold mines of Monotapa in Southern Zimbabwe, Zulu legends hold that they were worked by 'artificially produced flesh and blood slaves created by the First People.' These slaves, the Zulu legends recount, 'went into battle with the Ape-Man' when 'the great war star appeared in the sky.'[15]

Is Ape-Man the *Australopithecine*? *Homo erectus*? Or a Bigfoot type still in existence there today? The Sumerian records tell of a great rebellion by the mine workers—specifically in South Africa!

There is one very interesting cosmic tidbit that Sitchin reveals when referring to the "Anunnaki" (the Sumerian name for their "gods"—the Starpeople), pertaining to their influence on this planet. The Anunnaki, or Nefilim, came from the planet Nibiru, which the archeological records suggest orbits into our inner solar system every 3600 years. Sitchin says there are many words and linguistic remnants of these space people who left a powerful influence on us after they departed. For example, he states, in *Genesis Revisited*:

> Why do we call our planet "Earth"? In German, it is Erde, from Erda in Old High German; Jordh in Icelandic, Jord in Danish, Erthe in Middle English, Airtho in Gothic, and, going eastward geographically backward in time, Ereds or Aratha in Aramaic, Erd or Erty in Kurdish, and Eretz in Hebrew. The sea we nowadays call the Arabian Sea, the body of water that leads to the Persian Gulf, was called in antiquity, the Sea of Erythrea, and, to this day, ordu means an encampment or settlement in Persian. Why?

> The answer lies in the Sumerian texts that relate the arrival of the first group of Anunnaki/Nefilim on Earth. There were fifty of them, under the leadership of EA ("whose home is water"), a great scientist and first-born son of the ruler of Nibiru, ANU. They splashed down in the Arabian Sea and waded ashore to the edge of the marshlands that, after the climate warmed up, became the Persian Gulf. And, at the head of the marshlands, they established their first settlement on

---
15. Sitchin, 1990, p. 22.

a new planet. It was called by them E.RI.DU —"Home in the Faraway"—a most appropriate name.

And so it was that in time the whole settled planet came to be called after the first settlement—Erde, Erthe, Earth. To this day, whenever we call our planet by its name, we evoke the memory of that first settlement on Earth, unknowingly, we remember Eridu and honor the first group of Anunnaki who established it.[16]

Both the Bigfoot people and the ETs told three separate contactees that the Earth is a *living organism* that is being "attacked" by its own insensitive inhabitants to a point of imminent destruction. Interestingly, Zecharia Sitchin says that Earth is indeed a living entity:

But the exploration of the planetary system in recent decades has, in fact, revealed worlds for which the word 'alive' has been repeatedly used. That Earth itself is a living planet was forcefully put forth as the Gaia Hypothesis by James E. Lovelock in the 1970's (*Gaia - A New Look at Life on Earth*) and most recently reinforced by him in *The Ages of Gaia: A Biography of our Living Earth*. It is a hypothesis that views the Earth and the life that has evolved upon it as a single organism; Earth is not just an inanimate globe upon which there is life; it is a coherent if complex body that is itself alive through its mass and land surface; its oceans and atmosphere, and through the flora and fauna which it sustains and which in turn sustain Earth. 'The largest living creature on Earth,' Lovelock wrote, 'is the Earth itself.' And in that, he admitted, he was revisiting the ancient 'concept of Mother Earth, or as the Greeks called her long ago, Gaia.'[17]

The Starpeople and Sasquatch related this to me and others as *fact* and in no way was it meant as a cute metaphor. Our primitive concept of ourselves and this planet is distorted and incomplete. Keep in mind that the Sasquatch can reason and synthesize environmental data just as we can—only they do it better, because they operate on other levels that aid them in monitoring their surroundings to elude unwanted visitors. The Sasquatch can psychically "communicate" with the living flora and fauna within their environment. I refer the interested reader to Eliot Cowan's seminal work *Plant Spirit Medicine*[18] wherein he demonstrates proven methods by which humans can communicate with plants in their environment so as to invoke their healing assistance via telepathy rather than by destructive ingestion of plant material.

---

16. Sitchin, 1990, p. 88.
17. Sitchin, 1990, p. 106.
18. Cowan, 1995.

## A Genetic Experiment?

A Sasquatch told me and one other person in 1985 that by 1990 the Earth, environmentally, would be at a point of no return if we did not drastically change how we treat each other and the environment. We could avert this disaster by drastically reducing the global population and dramatically slowing down our exploitation of natural resources. Then the present resources would better sustain a smaller world population without depleting it to a life-threatening level. We are at the very brink of some stupendous calamity—something that will strongly landmark all of human history. Both the Starpeople and the Bigfoot creatures have talked about such catastrophic events occurring over the next few years. Christians might label it Armageddon. The Amerindian tribes call it The Great Purification. Because everyone and everything is cosmically connected, all living organisms will be profoundly affected.

When I lecture and write articles relating these concepts, it often angers the Bigfoot hunters because I have spoiled their violent game of shooting a monster. They can't stand the thought that Sasquatch has human traits and more natural abilities than we do. *Homo sapiens sapiens* is really very helpless in nature with no shelter, weapons, or elaborate equipment, whereas the Bigfoot people are not! What is so difficult about the conceptualizing a humanoid Sasquatch with unique psychic survival abilities? We don't have a problem with whales and dolphins using sonar to monitor their environment, or bats using biological radar. I think Henry Beston expressed himself beautifully and succinctly in his powerful book *The Outermost House*, when he stated:

> We need another and a wiser and perhaps a more mystical concept of animals. Remote from universal nature, and living by complicated artifice, man in civilization surveys the creatures through the glass of his knowledge and sees thereby a feather magnified and the whole image in distortion. We patronize them for their incompleteness, for their tragic fate of having taken form so far below ourselves. And therein we err, and greatly err. For the animal shall not be measured by man. In a world older and more complete than ours, they are more finished and complete, gifted with extensions of the senses we have lost or never attained, living by voices we shall never hear. They are not brethren; they are not underlings; they are other nations, caught with ourselves in the net of life and time, fellow prisoners of the splendor and travail of the earth.[19]

---

19. Beston, 1928, p. 25.

Today, as our environment gets gobbled up by corporate greed, the animals and oxygen-giving plants are also diminishing and disappearing along with it. These are ecological facts that should not be underestimated. Technology has truly superseded our spiritual growth to a point where our children see adults acting disrespectfully toward not only animal and plant life, but also toward one another, and therefore "imitate" this negative social behavior. This attitude is a major concern of the Sasquatch people and ETs, because now *we* are the monsters, threatening them and our environment, as well as our very own existence. They see us as immature, violent, spiritually deficient, and irresponsible.

What the Bigfoot said to me was confusing until now, because Darwinism in the scheme of evolution was a vital part of my anthropology background, which I used as a reference point. Yet it didn't match up. Sitchin says:

> The biblical tale of man's creation is, of course, the crux of the debate —at times bitter—between Creationists and Evolutionists and of the ongoing confrontation between them—at times in courts, always on school boards. As previously stated, both sides had better read the Bible again (and in its Hebrew original); the conflict would evaporate once Evolutionists recognize the scientific basis of Genesis and Creationists realized what its text really says.[20]

Much of what Sitchin has translated and what the Sasquatch said makes more sense than science monkeying around looking for a purported "missing link" in the lineage of man. Science then, in some ways, is more submerged in *myth* here than in fact. Sitchin continues by emphasizing:

> ...that Genesis represents not just religion but also science....One must recognize the role of the Anunnaki and accept that the Sumerian texts are not "myth" but factual reports. Scholars have made much progress in this respect, but they have not yet arrived at a total recognition of the factual nature of the texts. Although both scientists and theologians are by now well aware of the Mesopotamian origin of Genesis, they remain stubborn in brushing off the scientific value of these ancient texts.[21]

Michael Grumley, in his book *There are Giants in the Earth*, talks about a race of giants or possibly hairy giants found in ancient Hebrew tradition.

> ...in the Genesis story, there is an incident absent in the King James version but present in various scattered references in the Hebrew

---

20. Sitchin, 1990, p. 158.
21. Sitchin, 1990, p. 46.

Midrash which concerns a giant named 'Og' who is said to have ridden on the ark during the forty days and forty nights of the downpour that caused Noah's flood. In order to be included in the ship's company, so the story goes, it was agreed that he would, once the ark reached dry land and the waters receded, become a servant of Noah and *all* of his descendants. He (and presumably a female of his kind) were the only ones of what was a widespread race of giants who perished, along with all men except Noah and his three sons Shem, Ham, and Japeth (this also, Hebrew tradition holds, included the four women who were the wives of Noah and his three sons, making eight in all.) Or, if the 'Og' account is accurate, was it ten 'people'— eight humans and two half-humans? [22]

If this account is true, Noah and his family did not encounter any monsters, only humanoid-type beings in need of safe refuge like everyone else. There are many ancient texts and "lost" books of the Bible that are collecting dust at the Vatican or in the basement of an abbey that could fill the gaps and pull more pieces of the evolutionary puzzle more neatly in place. Sadly, many religious zealots are taught not to question the Bible, Torah, etc., but merely to accept it on faith. I believe there is room for both science and spiritual data without one offending the other. A very open mind is needed at both ends of the continuum.

We must now ask, if ETs were our genetic creator, then who created them? Do the ET "gods" believe in one God as Creator? The Starpeople, I am sure, have examined who they are and where they originally came from to form their own concept of God and religion. These emissaries are merely several steps higher on the evolutionary scale than we.

---

22. Grumley, 1974, p. 112.

# Universal Reality

Over the years, certain curious Sasquatch have been reaching out to Earth people, particularly those with a spiritual attitude, and they still do. They selectively choose people whom they meet in their wanderings and with whom they begin to feel secure enough to telepathically contact them. This is what happened to me; this is why I have found so many others who are being contacted as well. I have discovered the identical phenomenon is occurring in numerous places around the United States, no doubt around the world! But nobody wanted to talk about it out of fear, when the exact opposite is needed.

For me, the anomalies I experienced are fact, not what I believe is real. Why? Because I have been experiencing the psychic Sasquatch, ETs, and their ships for 19 years now and the anomalous behavior patterns continue to repeat themselves over and over again. So, if I thought I was hallucinating, was in denial, or somehow rationalized these anomalies away, I had nearly two decades of psychic encounters to figure it out. Plus, I have documented 76 percipients who also had the same unique experiences—and I continue to interview more witnesses every year. Anomalies are out there to be gathered as authentic research data, and they are an integral part of the phenomenon. The percipients that I documented make the Bigfoot/UFO "consensus reality."

Dr. J. Allen Hynek expressed this point to me at our first lengthy meeting in 1980 pertaining to his own research in Ufology. Before meeting him, I wondered if my making the same statement about Sasquatch studies would turn him off as to what I discovered. But it was that exact theme that made our conversation cohesive, stimulating, and meaningful. Dr. Hynek saw legitimate patterns in his area of research, just as I saw and experienced the same patterns in mine. We had a common ground because he also applied a holistic approach, letting the patterns of the phenomenon lead him to the real answers.

As in any other approach to science, analysis of anomalous data is translated into statistics. Statistics are based on mathematics, the purest of measurable science. Sixty-six percent (49 percipients) claim mental telepathy, or thought transference, with a Sasquatch and 8% (6 people) stated Starpeople were also involved with this kind of communication during contact. Three people admitted to telepathic conversations simultaneously with both a Sasquatch and a Starperson. White Song Eagle's and Irene Wilson's cases are still ongoing, though most of the ET contact has ceased, or is rare. Periodically, the Bigfoot people visit them, sharing advice and occasional guidance.

While collecting field data, often months at a time in an active Bigfoot area, I have discovered other unorthodox characteristics about them. For example, some researchers speculate that the powerful, unpleasant odor is from rotting pieces of meat stuck to the creatures' hair. From what little I was told from three percipients, and later a Bigfoot, there appears to be a gland similar to a skunk's that secretes a foul, stunning odor, warning a trespasser to "stay away." When a creature is close by, I have often smelled a faint, moldy aroma in the air. Even if they are in another dimension, it somehow leaks through into our world. However, when startled or threatened by a hiker or hunter, especially a person with a hostile attitude, the Sasquatch feels that negativity, and triggers its glands to secrete a skunklike odor which overwhelms and stops the intruder. In this way, they do not need to physically defend themselves. This is a passive way of avoiding someone.

Whenever glowing red eyes are reported from a Sasquatch sighting, it means the man-creature feels threatened and is preparing to dematerialize if it becomes necessary. At times only two red eyes are seen by a witness, with no visible body. Here they are literally between dimensions, protecting their physical bodies while still playing peek-a-boo from the safety of that paraphysical zone.

Levitation is another anomaly that has been reported. Two Oregon loggers in a truck going 35 miles per hour chased a ten-foot Sasquatch, and it left them behind. When the creature came to a sharp bend in the road where a dangerous cliff existed, without hesitation it leaped into the air, falling out of sight. With flashlights in hand, the men shone their beam into the rocks below, expecting to see a dead Sasquatch. To their amazement, there was nothing! No corpse or any sign of the creature was found. Did Bigfoot levitate itself to protect itself, or did it blip into the safety of another dimension to avoid smashing into the rocks below?

Several years ago, a Russian researcher sent me data about an expedition on which they were looking for the Almast, their Bigfoot. In the field report, it clearly stated that one night a member of the team observed a female creature that cautiously approached their campsite. When the Almast noticed it was being watched, it immediately walked to a large stream near the tents and effortlessly leaped over it with great ease, as if it "glided" or levitated to the other side.

Interdimensionality is yet another PSI phenomenon that repeatedly characterizes the psychic Sasquatch. Two percipients were told that the creatures have access to eight different dimensions. I am aware of only four of them: 1) our three-dimensional planet, 2) astral projection, 3) materialization/dematerialization, and 4) teleportation. Though I was never told this directly, I feel this ability is natural to them even though they must be taught, like a seven-foot tall man who never played basketball. He already has a natural stature for it, but would do poorly on the court if not properly trained.

Some witnesses distinctively heard a large "man" walking, but saw nothing, even though at times branches and bushes moved from an invisible Sasquatch. This was verified in Ohio, Indiana, Oregon, California, and Wisconsin. It happened to me many times. Eight witnesses, or 11%, experienced this phenomenon, which includes six people actually seeing physical materialization and dematerialization. When I was living in the field in major Bigfoot haunts, I observed interdimensionality with four separate races of ETs and 23 times with spaceships.

Teleportation, transporting the entire physical body from one dimension to a different geographic location, is rarely reported, but might happen frequently with some or all Sasquatch. Only two witnesses on record made this claim after I questioned them at length and they assured me they understood the definition and applied it accurately to their situation.

In "The Mount Hood Experiment," I mentioned finding two single tracks in two different places. And, similar to Medicine Mountain, there were daily sounds of elephantine footsteps by my campsite. There are numerous situations where I experienced sounds, tracks, and growls. After a while, it became boring for me; as important as struggling to get physical evidence is, it's the mental communication and what the creatures share that seems more critical. As far as acquiring the ultimate physical evidence as scientific proof—how can one talk to a corpse? There is absolutely nothing we have that they want, except respect. We have more to learn and gain from them as living beings than they do from us! They live in peace and harmony with nature; we do not.

Another sound I have heard twice is the eerie generator noise. Six other persons also reported this phenomenon in active Bigfoot and UFO areas. Investigators Alan Berry and Ann Slate state in their book on Bigfoot that they heard a generator noise as well. A researcher in Texas and another in rural New Jersey also reported a generator sound at a time when other anomalies were occurring, including Bigfoot sightings. And, of course, Mrs. Jones observed a spaceship just above the trees and later heard a generator noise at night. While I was investigating in the Mount Hood Wilderness, "something" or "someone" with technological ability was operating a subterranean machine, and it could hardly be attributed to the Sasquatch. It certainly was not the U.S. Forest Service on top of that mountain. A few years ago, I was told by a Sasquatch, as well as two other percipients, that subterranean openings are guarded by them, while the Starpeople did their work undisturbed in an underground laboratory. Again, these repeated patterns tell us the witnesses were not just "hearing things." After 8-1/2 hours of listening to the "generator," I still could not rationalize it away.

The Sasquatch have physically touched some people. The two teenage girls in "Terror in the Midwest" and "Speaking with Bigfoot" know what a creature feels like. In September 1984, a hunter in Fossil, Oregon, told me that just as he was about to shoot a deer in a low area below him, a seven-foot Sasquatch shoved him over the side. He tumbled down an embankment and was left shaken, but unscathed. His feeling was that he was trespassing into the creature's space, and he did not want anything killed. The hunter felt it was this Bigfoot's way of telling him to get out. He and his wife never went back to the area again.

A Sasquatch in the astral body touched me on three separate occasions. Also, in March 1984, in Roseburg, Oregon, I was visiting a friend when two female Sasquatches appeared in the room astrally. When I told my friend, she merely poked fun at me. But the laughter abruptly ended when one of them touched her on the leg to prove that they indeed were genuinely there interdimensionally. Shock and fear filled my friend's face. For the next two weeks, she was in a daze and often would stop and say, "I still can't believe what happened; it was so weird...yet I know it's true. No wonder it's so hard for people to believe you!"

From my research and others I interviewed, Bigfoot ate bread, trout, apples, grain, cucumbers, cabbage, mushrooms, deer, elk, used salt blocks, and even jumbo-sized Hershey bars with almonds—all signs of an omnivore.

In the last half century, there has been so much physical evidence for the existence of Sasquatch that it boggles the mind. Science is now looking to obtain a specimen by which to "compare" this evidence. Then there will be no nagging doubts as to its reality. In the meantime, we must learn to trust thousands of eye witnesses. Much of the physical evidence has been thoroughly covered by John Green and many other researchers in their books, listing an impressive number of footprints, hair samples, feces, blood, recorded bellows and howls, plus the controversial Patterson-Gimlin movie film. I found hair near a Sasquatch footprint near the Columbia Gorge in the northern Oregon Cascades in 1980 that was later analyzed at the Medical College of Wisconsin by Dr. Kenneth Siegesmund, a forensic scientist. When examined by a scanning electron microscope, the hair showed sign of both human and non-human primate qualities. The hair was more human than animal, yet it remained unidentifiable.

Today we have Bigfoot researchers recording data on encounters virtually all over the North American continent. There are 15 to 20 Bigfoot centers across Canada, in Oregon, Arizona, Ohio, Connecticut. Why? Because common citizens who could care less if Bigfoot exists or not suddenly have a stunning encounter and find it so unnerving that they need a place to report it to so that they can "get it off their chest." So, the centers are there because the Bigfoot are there and for no other reason. Some centers keep better records and conduct more thorough field work than others, yet, the accumulation of documented sightings suggests that something profound is occurring in that geographic area. Florida, for example, has the greatest number of Bigfoot reports on the East Coast. North Carolina and Pennsylvania also have had a good share of sightings.

The highly respected Cambridge scholar and noted primatologist, Dr. John Napier, who was once Director of Primate Biology at the Smithsonian Institution in Washington, D.C., emphatically stated:

...that such a creature should be alive and kicking in our midst, unrecognized and unclassifiable, is a profound blow to the credibility of modern anthropology.[1]

---

1. Napier, 1972, p. 199.

Why would a prominent scientist have to make such a strong statement to his colleagues concerning new research in primatology? Why should serious-minded researchers who make legitimate discoveries have to be fearful of sharing their excitement with fellow scientists, the government, or the general public? Would Dr. Jane Goodall be black-balled if she announced to the world that chimpanzees have been telepathically communicating with her? Interestingly, when I briefly met Dr. Goodall in 1980 in Seattle and told

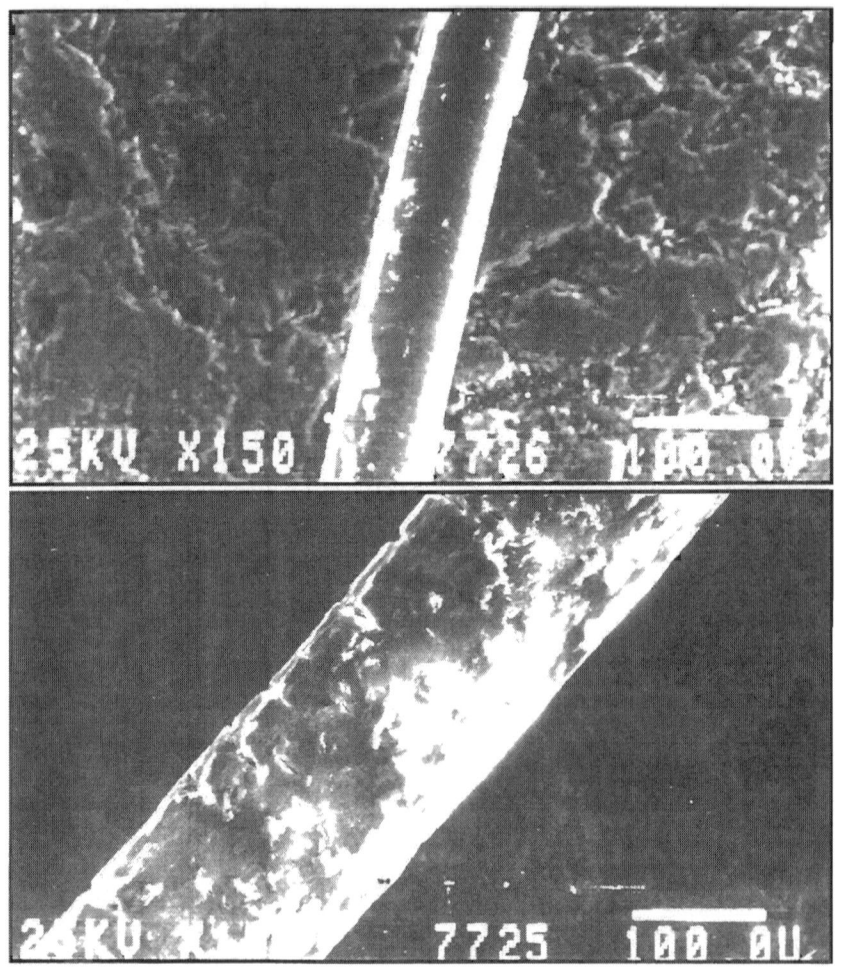

*Photomicrograph analyses of bear hair (top) and what is most probably a Sasquatch hair (bottom), which was picked up by the author at a location where a Sasquatch had recently been sited. The special characteristics of this hair match no recognized mammal species.*

her that the Sasquatch are a telepathic nature-people, her look was that of intense interest as she replied: "Jack, I hope what you're saying is true; I really hope it's true." It is nice to meet someone who is understandably cautious, yet apparently open-minded. But the challenge remains.

Some findings are not being reported because of researchers' fear of ridicule, ostracism, damaged reputation, reduced credibility, and, for some, a destroyed career. Are anomalous findings really *so* threatening that it is difficult to have a rational discussion with scientists in an academic setting? In a court of law, one witness's testimony can place a person in the electric chair! Yet, establishment scientists prefer to simply ignore people who witness anomalies, claiming that what witnesses tell researchers is largely unreliable. How can 76 percipients, who do not know each other and who were interviewed over the 40 year period that I have been studying the phenomenon, be unreliable when all reports are virtually the same and are supported by the anomalous PSI encounters, footprints, sightings, hair samples, and powerful roars?

But how "modern" is science? Has science discovered all known species on Earth yet? Most people believe that all the wilderness areas on this planet have been thoroughly explored and its fauna is thoroughly zoologically inventoried. But that is fallacious. A family of Sasquatch could be living in your back lot and you would never know it, even if you went looking for them. It might surprise the reader to know that about 5,000 new species of animals are discovered *each year*! About 4,000 of these are insects, over 100 are fish, around 20 are reptiles, ten are amphibians, less than half a dozen are birds, and approximately ten are mammals.[2]

In 1899, the massive Kodiac bear was discovered. In 1900, it was the white rhinoceros. The largest of the anthropoid apes, the mountain gorilla, was found in 1901. In 1912, the Komodo dragon, the world's largest lizard was captured. In Paraguay, in 1975, the largest member of the peccary family was discovered, which was only previously known in the fossil records. In 1976, an entirely new species of megamouth shark, 15 feet long, was caught and only then taxonomized by science. Also, the elk-sized Okapi in the Congo, and the Panda bear of China were new major animal species added to the list in this century. We must include the discovery of the largest herd of American Bison in the wilds of northern Canada.[3] In 1938, the once-

---

2. Cremo, 1993, p. 593.
3. Cremo, 1993, p. 593.

thought-extinct fish, the prehistoric coelacanth, was caught and resurrected as a living fossil. In 1992, in Vietnam, close to the Laotian border, the Vu Quang oryx was discovered by a team of international scientists. This ungulate is a large mammal of which the native people were already aware but whose existence they never saw a need to report.[4] In 1995, a team of British and French scientists discovered an ancient breed of horses completely unknown in the animal world, roaming the Tibetan Himalayas! The Riwoche horse is only four feet tall, with wedge-shaped heads, just exactly like the cave drawings of prehistoric man. Incredibly, these rare ungulates have survived undetected for 15,000 years![5]

Then we have Ishi, the last member the extinct Yahi Indian tribe in Northern California, who walked out of the wilderness into an urban world in 1911.[6] There are several tribes in the South American jungle that were only discovered in the 1960s. So, who says Bigfoot can't exist in the Twentieth Century? Who says the psychic Sasquatch can't have powers and anomalous abilities that help them survive? We have technology to help us to survive; these nature-people have their psychic powers! Arthur C. Clarke said: "Any sufficiently advanced technology is indistinguishable from magic." One might slightly alter that phrase and apply it to the Bigfoot people: "Any sufficiently advanced psychic abilities are indistinguishable from magic." This is important to understand.

The scientific paradigm is in dire need of revamping. It is clearly incomplete when trying to apply its limited measuring ability to elusive anomalies. I propose that the scientific establishment expand its variables of measurement in order to become comprehensive, holistic, and more complete in its efforts to define the world around us, so that all may better understand universal reality. At present, science is dysfunctional because it has divorced itself from nature.

We live in a dipoled universe. No white without black, no yin without yang. It is impossible to have one magnetic pole without the other. The universe can only exist within a specific movement of balance or "dance." This is the *natural* balance of the universe. Science, in its ineptness at measuring universal reality, is "out of balance," boxed inside the physical-material world it so proudly calls empirical science.

---

4. Bille, 1995.
5. Editor, *Atlantis Rising*, 1996, p. 13.
6. Kroeber, 1961.

I propose a paradigm that is empirical *and* experiential (to act as an adjunct when measuring parapsychology, metaphysics, spirituality, and other elusive phenomena). Since everything in universal nature is dipolar, so too our methodology must be dipolar. Science needs to be humble by "molding" itself to nature, not unnaturally construing a scientific model that superimposes itself on nature! I feel that the experiential sciences should be applied to elusive phenomena in nature that cannot be captured, controlled, or photographed, but can be "experienced" in mind, body, and spirit. The "subjective" human senses are definitely a part of science. If a researcher is conducting field work to gather empirical evidence, then he/she should patiently stay in the field until "experiential" evidence is obtained by personally encountering the phenomenon one-on-one. Also, in addition to first- hand experience and observations, a researcher should gather as many second-hand experiences as possible from percipients who witnessed what the scientist witnessed, thus objectifying his or her reality in relation to that specific phenomenon. Credit should be given to the researcher reporting the phenomenon, and more credibility should be given to people having eye-witness accounts, especially when multiple witnesses are reporting the same thing.

Physicist Fritjof Capra suggested a model for science that emphasizes the interactions of observer and participant for a more holistic study of consciousness in his book, *The Turning Point: Science and Society, and the Rising of Culture,*

> Science, in my view, need not be restricted to measurements and quantitative analyses. I am prepared to call any approach to knowledge scientific that satisfies two conditions: all knowledge must be based upon systematic observations and must be expressed in terms of self-consistent but limited and approximate models...true science of consciousness will deal with qualities rather than quantities, and will be based upon shared experiences....[7]

The new scientific paradigm will deal with the qualities of the shared experiences of human-Bigfoot interaction, whereas the old paradigm seeks to measure the quantity of Bigfoot corpses collected. Many, perhaps all, veteran Bigfoot researchers seek to kill a Sasquatch in order to obtain the once-and-for-all physical proof. Many Bigfooters with a camera or gun are more interested in fame and fortune than what sensitive research can provide. But we must avoid being barbaric at all costs if we are to gather more field data from

---

7. Capra, 1982, pp. 375-376.

the Sasquatch people. They distrust us enough. Murdering them in cold blood will not enhance our stature in their eyes.

Time and again, the behavioral pattern for an intelligent, benign, compassionate, and reasoning Sasquatch emerges from numerous reports, demonstrating an altruistic humanoid being living inside a giant animal-like body. Keep in mind, they are a cunning, psychic people, often peeping in on us from another dimension. Can you imagine what we must look like to the Sasquatch people and Space beings? There are at this writing, 52 active wars and 112 human conflicts on this planet—humans butchering humans in a so-called "modern" world—not to mention the senseless carnage of our wildlife and irresponsible pollution of our precious environment. We must look so primitive to the Sasquatch and Starpeople. Just who are the real role models here? Perhaps their view of us will change only if we can stop acting like Neanderthals and start treating the planet and its inhabitants with greater respect. Then all races of people will see only the positive and the good in each other, providing the very *proof* needed by these sentient beings that it is finally safe to come out. But, can society change its negative attitudes? Do we really want to change?

The Fourteenth Dalai Lama's book, *A Human Approach to World Peace*, speaks eloquently, yet with compassion and respect, while discussing the modern world in relation to nature. Here, he could easily be describing the Sasquatch. His Holiness says:

> Whether they belong to more evolved species like humans or to simpler ones such as animals, all beings primarily seek peace, comfort, and security. Life is as dear to the mute animals as it is to any human being; even the simplest insect strives for protection from dangers that threaten its life. Just as each one of us wants to live and does not wish to die, so it is with all other creatures in the universe, though their power to affect this is a different matter.[8]

Science will truly come of age when it decides to examine its own lack of spirituality in viewing and investigating living nature. Spirituality is seeing God in all living things and unconditionally respecting the Godliness in every creature, for each one, like us, has a purpose in this world that it instinctively seeks to fulfill. It is vital to remember that each living thing is an extension of ourselves, whether it be an insect, fish, or Siberian tiger. For, when a species becomes extinct, a part of us dies too, and when it does, we

---

8. Fourteenth Dalai Lama, 1984.

can never again interact with, observe, or enjoy its creatureness again. Extinction is forever! When the majority of the population on this planet gets in touch with their God selves, the Sasquatch and Starpeople will not have to worry about being shot at. Our vibrations will then be as high as theirs. Our spirituality will have caught up with our technology. If we do not change, there will be an ecological disaster and/or a nuclear holocaust that will affect all facets of cosmic reality.

We presume that these man-creatures are nomadic and spend time alone, away from their own kind. Scientific evidence for this hypothesis must come from evaluating patterns of behavior, but one can hardly come to any conclusions based on occasional brief sightings of Bigfoot passing through a region. Brief encounters cannot establish any hypothesis as fact. We must take into account the ability of the Sasquatch to become invisible as well as their access to interdimensional portals. They are masters at remaining hidden and being elusive.

Patient, prolonged field work is the answer. I have spent up to five months in the field in one place living alone in a tent. Another time I stayed in the field for twenty-two months changing locations some nine times. How can researchers gain any understanding of the problem or maintain their credibility if they do not conduct long-range field work to experience and observe what is really going on out there? Can you imagine what would happen to Jane Goodall's reputation if she went out to study a rare primate, spent two weeks in the field, never observed or interacted with the creatures in the wild, read up on the native folklore, and then proclaimed herself an "expert" after writing a book on the subject? Anyone who would do such a thing would be promptly booed out of the scientific community.

Since most Bigfoot researchers have jobs they need for income, and they have families and other responsibilities, they are not in a position to conduct vital, lengthy field work. Many vital patterns may be missed because the researcher was not there to observe or experience them. In an address to the American Association for the Advancement of Science, anthropologist Margaret Mead boldly stated: "The whole history of scientific advancement is full of scientists investigating phenomena the Establishment did not believe were there."

What is needed is a meeting of minds. We need to have psychically sensitive people who are being contacted by the Bigfoot people act as primary informants for the scientist in order to bring empiricists closer to universal reality. This is standard procedure when an anthropologist conducts field work closely with an informant, only with Bigfoot research, the informant would be a proven psychic and gifted telepath.

This book is meant to educate and expand the reader's perspective of previously unexplored and ignored natural phenomena going on around us. I and many other percipients would eagerly share and work with open-minded researchers as psychic informants or "middle men" in an effort to telepathically connect with a receptive Sasquatch. This would be a unique project indeed—using gifted psychic lay persons as research "tools" to conduct scientific field work in anthropology as an extension of the empirical method. In this way, science lets the phenomenon objectively guide them to its natural source. Who knows what cosmic secrets these sentient beings may share? However, they can't share anything with us if we keep telling ourselves that Bigfoot is merely an animal, or that it really doesn't exist at all!

Western civilization is convinced that high technology indicates an evolved society, thus we reward ourselves by labeling America "modern." In many ways, the term "modern" breeds arrogance and anthropocentrism, falsely allowing us to believe that we have the right to dominate and exploit all forms of life on this planet that we designate as "lower." But obviously, had Sasquatch been a lower life form, we would have obtained a corpse long ago, neatly taxonomized, stuffed, and proudly displayed in the Museum of Natural History. Based on this perspective, we must begin to act our age and become truly modern by giving all the respect and consideration to the Sasquatch by trying to see the world through its eyes before we irresponsibly act as judge, jury, and hangman.

If we are to progress scientifically, we must first become eclectic—more interdisciplinary while being ethical. Even cultural anthropology may carry more weight in learning about the secretive Sasquatch than physical anthropology. I say this because, since the Sasquatch are already telepathically communicating with certain persons of all levels of social status, their human intelligence becomes immediately obvious even to the most untrained, uneducated percipient. It is clear what is occurring. I feel I am correct to assume that contact by psychic Sasquatch and ETs will only continue to increase. The physical proof is sure to come last, since Sasquatch are not likely to give up one of their own at any cost. We are not to be trusted. Western man is not evolved enough to meet them on their terms, spiritually—meaning respecting other living things.

In a well-presented monograph written collectively by a group of world academicians, titled *The Sasquatch and Other Unknown Hominoids*, Dr. James

R. Butler, one of the contributing scientists, is exploring the possibility of "higher sensory perception" (his label for ESP) as a factor in Sasquatch avoidance in human contact. Butler emphasizes:

> There is much to be learned and applied from the accumulated data base of a diverse range of disciplines. This should function as the underlying framework for our inquiry and assist us in developing our categorizations. The Sasquatch phenomenon, along with its behavioral implications, may not be closely associated with or similar to any existing group of organisms. It is not enough to simply rewrite the Mountain Gorilla story with a change in the principal protagonist. We must develop our categories not on preconceptions but instead upon independently acquired hypothesis derived from analysis of the information at hand. The more generalized the available data, the wider and more diverse should be the constructs of our categories. We must not mask new possibilities from our theoretical framework.[9]

It is this new categorization of data that I have applied and am presenting here. Otherwise, how does a person prove the existence of a paraphysical being with innate psychic functioning used as a survival-defense mechanism to avoid its prime enemy—exploitative man? Because of this psychic element at work, it is the Sasquatch who is in control, not the scientist!

We must keep an open mind that clandestine research related to Sasquatch may already have been conducted by a government agency. For example, in September 1994, I was lecturing and doing healing work in Atlanta, Georgia, for a week. I had the privilege of having lunch with a well known, respected UFO investigator who told me of a close and trusting friend who had to install a utility for the prestigious Yerkes Primate Institute in Atlanta. Clearances were granted and the fix-it man was asked to work on the problem at night when virtually no one would be there. Though he was working off the floor plan, the technician needed to study the situation by checking out the walls and ceiling of the adjacent rooms. Upon entering an isolated room, he was shocked to observe a gigantic plexiglass-like pyramid with a ten- to twelve-foot-tall Sasquatch sitting inside of it! The technician described a manlike face in an apelike body. If this is true, then what was the institute doing with such a creature and where did they get it? From some branch of our secret government? Was it captured using highly advanced combat-type technology by the military? There must have been several captures of a Sasquatch using trained

---

9. Butler, 1984, p. 204.

psychics and the government's new high-tech inventions over the last ten or twenty years.

Recently a percipient I interviewed told me he had a beautiful two-and-a-half hour telepathic conversation with a Sasquatch. He was afraid I might belittle him for talking about psychic phenomena in relation to the creature. I also had to promise not to reveal his name or where he lived. He said he was quietly working directly with the Sasquatch people in Washington State and wanted no interference from anyone, particularly those affiliated with the federal government. In passing, when I brought up a name of a well-publicized anthropologist who was hunting for Sasquatch, he became upset. The man explained that after he first had the encounter, he felt that it was his duty to report it to a bonafide scientist so the truth of the matter would be publicly known. His earnestness was met with rudeness, scoffing, and rejection by the scientist, as if the anthropologist's disapproval would make these anomalies go away. This totally disillusioned the witness, and a distrust of researchers followed. The silence was broken after he read my psychic Sasquatch account in a newspaper and contacted me.

So, scientific observation and physical evidence is important in Sasquatch research, but communication is the key. Empiricists can become "experientialists" and still maintain academic integrity. To experience is to existentially know. Though we may be educated in one reality, we should never be afraid of a newly discovered reality, because objectively we truly do not know which reality is more real than another. Based on my research, it is clear that both the physical and non-physical aspects of Sasquatch are indeed valid and real. Thus, a revamping of the scientific paradigm is essential if we are to get better in touch with universal reality. Remember:

> There seemed to be no process of nature which could not be described in terms of ordinary experience, illustrated by a concrete model or predicted by Newton's amazingly accurate laws of mechanics. But before the turn of the past century certain deviations from these laws became apparent; and though these deviations were slight, they were of such a fundamental nature that the whole edifice of Newton's machine-like universe began to topple. The certainty that science can explain how things happen began to dim about twenty years ago. And right now it is a question whether scientific man is in touch with 'reality' at all—or can ever hope to be.
>
> —Lincoln Barnett in 1948, from
> *The Universe and Dr. Einstein*

# PART THREE

©1998 White Song Eagle

# SUPPORTING MATERIALS

# Afterword

# Wisdom from Sasquatch

by Standing Elk, Lakota Spiritual Leader

Bigfoot has played a major role in our spiritual system. The Medicine Men, Spiritual men and women, and many other members from different tribes have all experienced its presence. It is always an important event around the communities. The stories are always shared around the campfires. The Red Man's smoke signals travel with the Law of Light and Thought when the subject of Bigfoot is in the air.

Dreaming was my first experience with Bigfoot. He was there, but I could not see him. The second experience was also a dream in which he materialized. The third experience was visual near Durango, Colorado. The fourth experience was a spiritual vision during a vision quest. The fifth was one in which he appeared as a pure white being with a message for all:

"Hau Relatives. Sasquatchitan. I am a Chief of Sasquatchi Peoples. I am One called Bigfoot, Yeti, Abominable Snowman. I am known to the Indigenous Peoples of Mother Earth as Siha Tanka. I live within the fourth and fifth dimensional frequencies, and I sit with Star Nations in Higher Realms with the Council of 22.

"I have been a part of your existence beyond your Light and beyond the beginnings of what you know as Time. I honor all Universal and Spiritual Laws of this Universe and many that are seen and unseen, within and without. I am one with Unci Iktomi and Gautama Buddha. We are the Guardians of the Universal Law of Innocence, Truth and Family.

"Innocence is the True Mind of all that is created. Truth is the Path of Silence and All That IS. Family is the Purified Spark of Love that has allowed Mother Earth to protect all that live within her Sacred Realms.

"We have lived with the Two-leggeds for millennia until they separated themselves from Creation. We are one of many Two-legged Nations that did not agree with their separation at that time. The Universal Law of Symmetry was broken. The Four-leggeds, the Wingeds, the Ones that Swim, the Ones that Crawl, the Plants and the Elementals were separated only in the minds' eye of the Two-leggeds.

"Sasquatchi loves Two-leggeds because they are Spiritual Brothers and Sisters, and we are committed to help them to return to Sacred Responsibility.

"Your three-dimensional realities are very primitive to us. We respect your Mother Earth frequencies and we haven't forgotten those realties that you have struggled to survive in. We cannot and will not allow ourselves to descend down to your realities. It would upset the Natural Order of Balance that is within. We have shown ourselves briefly to many brothers and sisters when they have been pure in Heart and Mind. This was designed to help them in awakening their DNA to their Sacred Relationship.

"We will come to teach you Innocence, Truth and Purity when you call upon us. We ask first that you Purify yourself Spiritually, Physically, Mentally, and Emotionally. The Indigenous Brothers and Sisters of this Turtle Island know ceremonies that will help you balance yourself for this contact. The Indigenous Peoples of Mother Earth have held onto Sacred Thoughts produced by the Elements of Earth, Fire, Water and Air. These elements are sacred essences of their Spiritual, Physical, Emotional and Mental existence.

"The Indigenous Peoples were given the Sacred Gifts and instructions to help you in this effort. The first Rite is that of Thought Purification. We ask you first to be sincere in your thoughts and in your action. Four days are required to prepare you for Earth, Water, Fire and Wind Purification.

*"Bury yourself in Earth for one day. Pray and you will be cleansed.*

*"Stand with the Water of Life for one day. Pray and you will be cleansed.*

*"Sit with Grandfather Sun for one day. Pray and you will be cleansed*

*"Stand with the Grandfather Wind for one day. Pray and you will be cleansed*

"When you have purified your thought, then we will join with you, through the Sacred Law, the Law of True Heart. Go to the Sweat lodge to attain Purity and utilize the Sacred Waters and Sacred Breath of your Grandfathers. Remember your youth and you will remember your Innocence. Learn the Truth by controlling your tongue.

*"Learn from the Soil and Stone*

*"Learn from the River and Ocean*

*"Learn from the Fire and Lightning*

*"Learn from the Wind and Breath.*

"These are my instructions for your balance with Mother Earth. If you follow these disciplines that have been gifted you through the Universal and Spiritual Laws of Creator, then your lifeline will be unbroken as ours has been from the beginning.

"I am Sasquatchitan. *Mitakuye oyasin.*"

# How to Contact a Sasquatch

There is a specific criterion that I have found to be helpful, that if practiced, will statistically increase a researcher's percentage of being contacted by a psychic Sasquatch. Hunting and stalking with a gun is a primitive method used by the uneducated and foolhardy, and they have no place here. Most Sasquatch simply want to be left alone and prefer no contact of any kind. There are some individual families who desire contact with humans, but they remain selective because 99.9% of the human population react with fear, hostility, and violence, which drives the creatures away.

The characteristics in a man's or woman's personality that attract the interest of Sasquatch are as follows: open-mindedness, love of nature, a deep and genuine love toward animals, respect for both wildlife and plant life, lack of fear of the unknown, the propensity to treat others as they would want to be treated, patience and inner calmness, inclination toward being a giver not a taker, willingness to reach out to help someone else, a friendly attitude toward everyone, and a lack of deep-seated emotional problems that would harbor and thus project anger or hostility and other negativity.

The characteristics in a person that repel the Bigfoot people are: a strong desire to capture or kill the creature; an intense desire to obtain a photograph; "ego-oriented" and self-centeredness; greed with a desire to exploit the encounter for financial gain; also an aggressive, macho personality that shows having little respect for others. These observations about what attracts or repels these creatures are based on my success, plus having evaluated the personalities of hundreds of interviewees and contactees.

I advocate a "modified" field methodology in the Jane Goodall tradition of peaceful coexistence, while learning and employing telepathic communication. Remember the sentient Sasquatch are in control, not the researcher. A researcher needs to "surrender" himself or herself to nature and the universe on a childlike level while avoiding projection of inner fear, anger, hostility, or other negative emotions. Learning and practicing meditation two to three times daily is a most valuable "research tool" in this kind of ultrasensitive research.

Researchers who want to learn and practice meditation in the field will find themselves at peace while "projecting" that acquired inner peace. Mental telepathy takes practice and goes hand-in-hand with serious meditation. To start, simply visualize what one feels a Sasquatch looks like and hold onto that image. Next, say to the Bigfoot "image" in your mind: "Please come and visit. You are welcome." In order to make telepathy work, send them your feelings as well as your intellectual words while focusing on positive emotions, such as love, friendship, compassion, genuine caring, and respect. All of this can be done two or three times daily at base camp. This is the best way to conduct Sasquatch field research.

Ironically, if you continue to be preoccupied in your mind with Bigfoot for the rest of the day, he will not come! It is true what the Indians told me, that one's anticipation keeps them at bay. It's like what the poet John Keats said about how one can chase a butterfly all day, but as soon as you put your mind on other things, the butterfly comes and gently lights on your shoulder. This is how the Sasquatch people usually behave. While conducting field work, non-threatening things to do are: reading, writing, meditating, art sketching, studying the identification of edible herbs, as well as picking wild foods to eat—all peaceful endeavors, while living somewhat like a traditional Indian. Often I would branch out and go on a day hike, systematically exploring each section of the forest in a relaxed, non-intense manner. Sometimes I would exercise to stay fit or jog for miles on wilderness trails—always doing so with a genuine love of nature radiating from my heart. This is not airy-fairy stuff; it's really a giant step in human evolution and *is* the cure for the disease created by a spiritually deficient science.

I view this field model as scientific because whenever I go into the field for a good length of time and practice all this "hokey," stuff, the "experiential" *proof* is having squirrels jump in my lap, hawks and owls landing beside me, gawking. Often rabbits would come into camp, touch me, and hang out (sometimes every evening for weeks at a time). Once a whippoorwill landed on my head. Another time a pair of woodcocks repeatedly visited me every evening for two months by landing at my feet, wanting to be near me. Two other times a bear and a cougar walked up to my foodless tent unafraid. (My food was always sealed and hung high between two trees, well away from my campsite.)

These are the secrets of connecting with the psychic Sasquatch. To a degree, depending on other factors, it can be modified and used to connect with the benevolent Starpeople as well. They will know if one's intentions are sincere. You cannot deceive them no matter how much man-made technology you carry in the field.

Keep in mind, even though a Sasquatch is making physical impressions with their telltale spoor (footprints, feces, hair, etc.), they are actually more physical-"etheric" in their molecular structure than a physical-dense *Homo sapiens sapiens* or member of our three-dimensional animal kingdom. An ET told a reliable percipient, a woman in Oregon who was having ongoing contact with the Bigfoot people, that these man-creatures "are more like what you call 'spirits' in astral form. They are workers when alive. They are not in the physical body on your planet no matter how they appear to you!"

I wish you success with your communications with nature, and may the Great Spirit bless you as you begin your ambassadorship to this ancient, loving, and sensitive race of humanoid beings as they patiently wait for us to become more spiritually modern.

# Bibliography

- Alford, Alan. *Gods of the New Millennium.* Walsall, England: Eridu Books. 1996.
- Andrews, George C. *Extra-Terrestrials Among Us.* St. Paul, MN: Llewellyn Publications. 1986.
- *Atlantis Rising.* Livingston, MT. 1996.
- Barnett, Lincoln K. *The Universe and Dr. Einstein.* New York: W. Sloane Associates. 1948.
- Bear, Sun. *The Path of Power.* Spokane, WA: Bear Tribe Publishing. 1983.
- Begich, Nick Ph.D. and Jeane Manning. *Angels Don't Play This HAARP: Advances in Tesla Technology.* Homer, AK: Earthpulse Press. 1995.
- Benton-Banai, Edward. *The Mishomis Book.* Mayward, WI: Indian Country Communications. 1979.
- Beston, Henry. *The Outermost House.* New York, Toronto: Rinehart. 1949.
- Bille, Matthew A. *Rumors of Existence: New Discovered, Supposedly Extinct, and Unconfirmed Inhabitants of the Animal Kingdom.* Canada: Hancock House Publishing Ltd. 1995.
- Boatman, John. *My Elders Taught Me.* Milwaukee, Wisconsin: University Press. 1991.
- Bord, Janet and Colin. *Alien Animals.* Harrisburg, PA: Stackpole Books. 1981.
- Bowden, M. *Ape-Men: Fact or Fallacy?* Bromley, England: Sovereign Publications. 1977.
- Bramley, William. *The Gods of Eden: A New Look at Human History.* San Jose, CA: Daklin Family Press. 1989.
- Butler, James R. *"The Theoretical Importance of Higher Sensory Perception in the Sasquatch Phenomenon."* Editors: Vladimir Markotic, and Grover Krantz, *The Sasquatch and Other Unknown Hominoids.* Calgary, Alberta: Western Publishers. 1984.
- Byrne, Peter. *The Search for Bigfoot.* Washington, D.C.: Acropolis Books. 1975.
- Cameron, Constance. *Bigfoot Coop, Vol. 7.* CA: December 1986.

## Bibliography

- Capra, Fritjof. *The Turning Point: Science, Society, and the Rising Culture.* New York: Bantam. 1983.
- Chambers, John. "The New Paradigm: Mind Over Matter, Free Energy and Contacts with ETs." *UFO Universe Vol.6, No.1.* New York: GCR Publishing Group, Inc. Spring 1996.
- Chatelain, Maurice. *Our Ancestors Came From Outer Space.* New York: Dell. 1975.
- Clarke, Arthur C. *Childhood's End.* New York: Ballantine. 1953.
- Cohane, John Philip. *Paradox: The Case for the Extraterrestrial Origin of Man.* New York: Crown Publishers, Inc. 1977.
- Corrales, Scott. *Chupacabras and Other Mysteries.* Murfreesboro, TN: Greenleaf Publications. 1997.
- Cowan, Eliot. *Plant Spirit Medicine: The Healing Power of Plants.* Mill Spring, NC: Swan-Raven & Co. 1995.
- Cremo, Michael A., and Thompson, Richard L. *Forbidden Archaeology: The Hidden History of the Human Race.* Alachua, FA: Govardhan Hill Publishing. 1993.
- Dalai Lama. *A Human Approach to World Peace.* Newburyport, MA: Wisdom Publications. 1984.
- Deardorff, James W. *Celestial Teachings.* Tigard, OR: Wild Flower Press, 1991.
- Deloria, Jr., Vine. *God is Red.* New York: Grosset & Dunlap. 1973.
- Dennett, Preston. *UFO Healings.* Newberg, OR: Wild Flower Press. 1996.
- Feldman, D. H. and L. Goldsmith. *Nature's Gambit.* New York: Basic Book Publishers. 1986.
- Fell, Barry. *America B.C.: Ancient Settlers in the New World.* New York: Quadrangle/New York Times Book Co. 1976.
- Gilroy, Rex. *Mysterious Australia.* Mapleton, Queensland: NEXUS Publishing. 1996.
- Goodman, Jeffery. *The Genesis Mystery.* New York: Times Books. 1983.
- Green, John. *Sasquatch: The Apes Among Us.* Saanichton, British Columbia: Cheam Publishing Ltd.
- Grumley, Michael. *There Are Giants in the Earth.* Garden City, NY: Doubleday. 1974.
- Harner, Michael J. *The Way of the Shaman.* San Francisco: Harper & Row. 1980.

- Hillary, Sir Edmund and Desmond Doig. *High in the Thin Cold Air.* New York: Doubleday & Company, Inc. 1962.
- Horn, Arthur. *Humanity's Extraterrestrial Origins: ET Influences on Humankind's Biological and Cultural Evolution.* Lake Montezuma, AZ: A. & L. Horn. 1994.
- Jacobs, David Michael. *The UFO Controversy in America.* Bloomington, IN: Indiana University Press. 1975.
- Kannenberg, Ida M. *Project Earth: From the ET Perspective.* Mill Spring NC: Wild Flower Press. 1995.
- Kenyon, J. Douglas. "Exposing A Scientific Cover-up." *Atlantic Rising.* Livingston, MT. 1996.
- Krantz, Grover S. *Big Footprints: A Scientific Inquiry Into the Reality Of Sasquatch.* Boulder, CO: Johnson Books. 1992.
- —. and Roderick Sprague, Editors. *The Scientist Looks at the Sasquatch.* Moscow, ID: University of Idaho Publication. 1979.
- —. Lecture at Bigfoot Conference. University of British Columbia. 1978.
- Kroeber, Theodora. *Ishi in Two Worlds.* Berkeley: University of California Press. 1961.
- Lethbridge, T.C. *The Legend of the Sons of God.* Bury St. Edmunds, Suffolk: St. Edmundsbury Press. 1972.
- Lewels, Joe Ph.D. *The God Hypothesis: Extraterrestrial Life and its Implications for Science and Religion.* Mill Spring, NC: Wild Flower Press. 1997.
- Lilly, John Cunningham. *The Mind of the Dolphin: A Nonhuman Intelligence.* New York: Doubleday & Company, Inc. 1967.
- Lovelock, James. *Gaia: A New Look at Life on Earth.* Oxford, England: Oxford Univ. Press. 1987.
- Macer-Story, Eugenia. "Coming Back Into the Circle: An Interview with Australian Aboriginal Medicine Woman Lorraine Maffi Williams." *Magical Blend Issue 21.* San Francisco, California: January 1989.
- Matthiessen, Peter. *The Snow Leopard.* New York: Viking Penguin. 1978.
- Monroe, Robert A. *Journeys Out of the Body.* Garden City, New York: Anchor Press. 1977.

- Morris, John David. *Tracking Those Incredible Dinosaurs—And the People Who Knew Them.* San Diego, CA: Creation-Life Pub. 1981.
- Napier, John. *Bigfoot: The Yeti and Sasquatch in Myth and Reality.* Berkeley, CA: Berkeley Publishing Corporation. 1972.
- O'Leary, Brian. *The Second Coming of Science.* Berkeley, California: North Atlantic Books. 1993.
- Pye, Lloyd. *Everything You Know is Wrong; Book One: Human Evolution.* Madeira Beach, FL: Adamu Press. 1997.
- Sanderson, Ivan T. *Abominable Snowmen: Legend Come to Life,* New York: Chilton Book Company. 1961.
- Sitchin, Zecharia. *Divine Encounters.* New York: Avon Books. 1995.
- —. *Genesis Revisited.* New York: Avon Books. 1990.
- —. *The 12th Planet.* New York: Stein & Day Publishers. 1976.
- Slate, Ann and Berry, Alan. *Bigfoot.* New York: Bantam Books. 1976.
- Strieber, Whitley. *Communion.* New York: Beech Tree Books. 1987.
- Suttles, Wayne. "On the Cultural Track of the Sasquatch." Editors: Sprague, Roderick and Krantz, Grover. *The Scientist Looks at the Sasquatch.* Moscow, ID: University of Idaho Publications. 1979.
- Tart, Charles T. *Psi: Scientific Studies of the Psychic Realm.* New York: Dutton. 1977.
- Thompson, Richard L. *Alien Identities.* Alachua, FA: Govardhan Hill Publishing. 1993.
- Vallee, Jacques. *Dimensions.* Chicago: Contemporary Books. 1988.
- Watson, Byall. *Super Nature.* New York: Doubleday & Company, Inc. 1973.
- Watt, Roberta Frye. *Four Wagons West.* Portland OR: Binsford & Mort. 1934.
- Wiedemann, C. Louis. "Mysteries Breaking Out All Over," *FATE Vol. 30, No. 9.* Highland Park, IL: Clark Publishing Company. 1977.

# Jack "Kewaunee" Lapseritis

Jack "Kewaunee" Lapseritis, B.A., M.S., is a Holistic Health Practitioner and Master Herbalist with a background in anthropology, psychology, conservation, and holistic health. As a world authority on the Bigfoot/Sasquatch phenomenon, he has meticulously researched the subject for the last 40 years. Mr. Lapseritis is also a social scientist, a Master Dowser, and both a Bigfoot and ET "contactee."

As a world traveler, an amateur naturalist, and backpacker, Mr. Lapseritis spent five years out of the country living in England, East Africa, Japan, and later immigrated to Australia. He was in the Himalayas in 1968 investigating the yeti, or abominable snowman. In 1973, he conducted an ethnographic study in conjunction with the Colombian Institute of Anthropology in Bogota, living amongst the Tukuna Indians of Upper Amazonia.

In 1979, scientist Jack Lapseritis was first telepathically contacted by a Sasquatch and ET simultaneously, which was the shock of his life! To further complicate matters, the contact changed him and he developed psychic ability overnight, which triggered a spiritual transformation. At the time, he was Assistant Director of an urban Indian agency, worked as a hypnotherapist part-time, and had been lecturing at the Medical

College of Wisconsin - a background that left him ill-prepared for such a happening.

"Kewaunee" has been a guest on over one hundred radio and television talk shows. To date, he has been featured in three books and is often featured in the international press, including various newspapers. Some of the publications are: Australia's *People* and *Post* magazines, *OMNI* magazine, *Magical Blend*, *Cryptozoology Journal*, *Wildfire*, *Fate*, *Argosy*, *UFO* magazine, *Health Consciousness*, and many others. In 1991, he was on a panel of scientists on a two-hour Bigfoot documentary on national television. Also, he has lectured and presented papers throughout the United States.

There are people all over the globe encountering Bigfoot and UFOs simultaneously while the beings share information about themselves, human history, and the future of our planet. If anyone wishes to share in confidence their telepathic conversation(s) and experiences which they have encountered with the Bigfoot-people, please feel free to contact this author, and I will answer all correspondence personally.

No matter what the reader encountered, new realities are never too bizarre to share. Please remember:

"The most beautiful thing we can experience is the mysterious: it is the source of all true art and science. He to whom this emotion is a stranger, who can no longer pause to wonder and stand rapt in awe, is as good as dead, his eyes are closed."

—*Dr. Albert Einstein*

WRITE TO:

Jack "Kewaunee" Lapseritis, M.S.
c/o Wild Flower Press
P.O. Box 190
Mill Spring, NC  28756

# Acknowledgments

My deepest appreciation to Dr. R. Leo Sprinkle and Betty Hill for their significant contributions in my book. I cannot thank you enough.

I am grateful to Dr. J. Allen Hynek for his interest and encouragement during our lengthy meetings and discussions in 1980-81, while I struggled to make sense of my unusual contacts and PSI experiences. He is very much missed.

Many thanks to Dr. Kenneth Siegesmund, forensic scientist at the Medical College of Wisconsin—Milwaukee, for his time and expertise using the electron microscope in analyzing apparent Sasquatch hairs.

I want to dearly thank Ed Hertzberg, physical anthropologist, Harvard University graduate, and retired government scientist, for his help and kindness in editing my manuscript and offering so much of himself to the project. God bless you, Ed. I will never forget you.

My great appreciation goes out to Professor John Boatman, M.A., for his invaluable contribution.

Also, thank you kindly to Lee and Marlys Trippett for their endless support and love.

My many thanks to Corey Wolfe, illustrator for Walt Disney Productions, for his exceptional artwork on the book cover and for being such a wonderful friend.

Much appreciation to Isabel McDowell, a loving friend who is always there for me, giving sage advice.

My warmest appreciation to Terry Pezzi and Jean Hogan for all their help and support in making this book possible.

I am most grateful to my family, Bob and Janet Penfield, for being so supportive.

My sincere thanks to Joe, Lisa, and Sophia in Montana, for generously sharing your research.

Finally, many thanks to Julie Kuever; may God bless you a thousand fold.

# Index

**A**
abductions 97
Africa 183, 186
Alford, Alan F. 185
Allegheny National Forest 84
Almast 195
Alps 17
America 183
Andes 17
Andrews, George C. 171
animals
  unusual 95–96, 119
anomalous activity 54, 56
anthropology 1
Anunnaki 187, 190
Appalachian Mountains 65
appearance
  Sasquatch 46, 112
Arizona 169
  Sedona 157
  Tucson 155, 158
Armageddon 189
Asia 186
astral 133, 134, 155, 162–163, 166
  apparition 38, 138
  projection 154
Atlantis 182
Australia 179, 183
*Australopithecines* 176, 179, 187

**B**
baby 49
  Sasquatch 94
Babylon 181
Bahamas 119
Barnett, Lincoln 206
Benton-Banai, Edward 124
Bermuda Triangle 121
Berry, Alan 23, 196
Beston, Henry 189
Bible 180, 181, 191
Bimini 119
birth
  Sasquatch 93
black helicopter 105
Blue Mountains 78
Bowden, M. 179
Bramley, William 184
Brehm, Patty and Kim 56
Bug-way'-jinini 125–127
Buscaglia, Dr. Leo 123
Butler, James 205

**C**
California 169, 200
  San Diego 98
  Sierra Nevada 23
Callahan Mountains 166
Cambridge Antissarian Society 181
Canada 199
cancer 157
Capra, Fritjof 201
Carter, Jimmy 91
cattle, reactions of 90
cave 18, 20, 21, 22–24, 67, 69, 71
Chief Seattle 128–129
children, Sasquatch 49
China 199
chupacabras 84
church counsel 55
CIA 31, 34, 35
clairvoyants 16
Clarke, Arthur C. 200
clones 72
Coast Guard 121
coelacanth 200
Colorado
  Durango 209
Congo 199
Connecticut River 109–110
cosmic evolution 70
cosmic law 123
Cowan, Eliot 188
Creator 50, 158
Cremo, Michael 186
*Cro-Magnon* 176, 179
Crookes, Sir William 172
cucumbers 60–62

**D**
Dalai Lama 202
Darwinism 179, 183, 190
Davidson, Dan A. 169–171
Deardorff, James W. 184
Deloria, Vine 6
dematerialization 31, 58, 74, 171, 194
Department of Natural Resources 52
depression 55
devil 55
dimension 40, 157, 180
dinosaurs 178, 178–179
Dogon tribe 176
dogs
  reactions of 68, 90
dowsers 16

**E**
Easter Island 182
ecology
  Sasquatch 5
Egyptians 185
Elohim 181
elusiveness 53

**221**

environment
  concerns about 116, 117
Epigraphic Society 98
Eskimos 185
Eurasia 183
Europe 186
extraterrestrials 92
  and mining 58
  and telepathy 167
  as creators 191
  dimensional travel 95
  doctor 150
  environmental concerns of 188–190
  healing by 148–153
  in tribal history 177
  memory alteration 42
  rescue by 156–157
  Teluke & White Song Eagle 42
  theory about 180
  transporting Sasquatch 50
eyes 112

**F**
farm animals
  reaction to Sasquatch 53
fear 53, 55
feces 81
Fell, Dr. Barry 98–99
field research 203
Florida 160
  Miami 119
flying saucers 34, 62, 89, 141
food, Sasquatch 197
footprints 18, 66, 180, 199
  ancient 180
  and invisibility 50
  casts of 61
  dinosaur 178
  in campgrounds 58, 139
  in grass 64
  in residential areas 106–108
  in sand 103, 105
  size of 81, 115
footsteps 18, 20, 21, 167, 195
Friedman, Norman 172
Fuller, John 101

**G**
Gaia 188
garden
  Sasquatch using 61
Geller, Uri 163
gemstones 159
generator noise 1, 22–23, 67, 72, 76, 196
Genesis 182, 190

genitalia 118
Georgia
  vortex 96
*Gigantopithecus* 3, 176
Gilroy, Rex 179
Gitchi Manito 126
God 4, 45, 75, 177
  as creator 175, 179, 183
  of all races 129
  sons of 182
Goodall, Jane 198
Goodman, Jeffrey 183
government legislation 82
Great Lakes 73
Great Oneness 128
Great Purification 157, 189
Greece 182
Green, John 15, 197
growling 52, 57, 108, 169
Grumley, Michael 190
Guyana Highlands 17

**H**
hair 114, 118, 199
  analysis of 197
  photo of 198
hands 112
Harvard University 98
hate 55
Hebrew Midrash 190
hieroglyphics 98
Himalayas 17, 165
holographic 74
*Homo erectus* 176, 179, 183, 187
*Homo neanderthalis* 176, 179
*Homo sapiens sapiens* 179, 183
hostility 51
humor 45
Hynek, Dr. J. Allen 193
hypnosis 170
  telepathic 94

**I**
Ice Age 178
India 186
Indiana 37–50
Indians
  See Native Americans 6
Indonesia 177
interdimensional 133, 155, 163, 168
  explanations 169
  footprints 74
  levels 195
  other animals 84
  Sasquatch as 33, 40, 75
  space travel 70

222

# Index

Starpeople as 97
travel 161
invisible manifestation
  choice of 83
  dimensional 42
  footprints 49, 80
  footsteps 29
  in communication 29
  in physical environment 80
  odor 49
invisible manifestations
  footfalls 33

## J
Jacobs, David Michael 34
Japanese 185
Java 183
Jesus 184

## K
Kachina 157
Kannenberg, Ida 180
Kaplan, Deloris 74, 79–83
Klamath Falls 141
Krantz, Grover 2

## L
laughter 45
Lethbridge, T.C. 181–182
levitation 9, 156, 194
light, balls of 91
Lilly, John C. 7
Lodge, Sir Oliver 172
logging 116–117
love 123
Lovelock, James E. 188

## M
machinery noises 67, 71
manifestation 92
map dowsing 96, 167
Massachusetts 104
Matthiessen, Peter 20
Mead, Margaret 203
Medicine Mountain 67–78
megaliths 182
Meistor, William 180
Mesopotamia 184
Michigan 51, 56
Milky Way Galaxy 70
mining, Sasquatch and 58
missing links 176
Montana 57
Morris, John 178
Mount Hood Wilderness Area 16, 69
Mu 182
music 87

Mutual UFO Network 97

## N
Napier, John 197
NASA 186
Native Americans
  Cherokee 177
  Chippewa 169
  folklore 99
  Great Lake Woodland 124, 177
  Great Lakes 29
  Hopi 6, 157
  Klamath 141
  Lummi 94
  Northwest Coast 6
  Yahi 200
Neanderthal 136
Nefilim 181
negative aspects 51
Neo-Giants 185
Nepal 179
Nevada 186
New 103
New England 101
New Hampshire 101
  Hudson 103
  White Mountains 101
New South Wales 179
newspaper reports 53
Nibiru 187
nightmares 56
nocturnal 48
noises 19, 28
  breaking of sticks 29
  generator 23
  laugh 24
  mechanical 22
  walking 24
  whistles 24
North Carolina
  Charlotte 65
North Umpqua River 147
nose 112
nuclear fallout 72

## O
odor 111, 140, 194
Ohio 79–84
  Jefferson Lake 84
  Leesville Lake 84
  Wellington 84
Oppenheimer, Robert 171
Oregon 75, 85–97, 98, 111, 116, 156
  Cascades 15, 17, 25, 67
  Eugene 111

Roseburg 167, 196
Oregon State University 184
Ossipee Mountains 103
out-of-body travel 134, 169

**P**
Pacific Northwest 67
palm print 86
Paluxy River 178
Paraguay 199
paralysis, induced 88
Patterson, Roger 23
Patterson-Gimlin film 16
Pei, Wen-Chung 3
Pennsylvania 84
photograph 34
plants, edible 117
playfulness 57
Pleiades
 and origins 177
Pleistocene 186
Polanski family 59, 60–63
Polynesia 182
Precambrian 186
precognition 91
priest 55
Proto-Pygmies 185
psychic 8, 22, 40
 assistants 15, 16–23, 203
 healings 147–158
 interdimensional travel 172
 phenomena 2, 5
 Sasquatch abilities 33, 57
 survival mechanism 167
 vision 38, 40
public reaction
 to Sasquatch reports 54
pyramid 32, 205

**R**
reality, non-ordinary 42
Reines, Fred 171
religious beliefs 55
reporters 53
ridge, sagittal 119
Rocky Mountains 27, 165
Rogue-Umpqua Divide 25
Roman empire 100
Rube, Calvin 169
running 46

**S**
sagittal crest 82
Sanderson, Ivan T. 185
Satan 55
science, new view of 200

screams 65
sea-being 119
shape-shifting 39, 46
Siegesmund, Dr. Kenneth 197
Sirius 176
Sitchin, Zecharia 181–188
skeptics 53
sky-beings 39
Slate, Ann 23, 196
sleeping, Sasquatch habits of 48
Smart brothers 59
smell 49, 81, 111, 140
Smithsonian Air and Space Museum 70
snakes 95
snorting 19
snowmobiler 75
South Africa 187
South America 185, 186
spaceship 72, 76, 97, 150
Spanish-Iberic 99, 100
speaking, verbal 49
spheres, intelligence controlled 54
spherical object 54
spirituality 202
Sprinkle, R. Leo 93
Standing Elk 209
Starpeople 5, 39, 91, 172, 194, 196
 and Sasquatch 42, 176
 appearance 71, 148
 beliefs of 191
 communication with 97
 environmental concerns of 188
 evolution of 70
 healing 147, 154, 156–157
 human connection with 180
 in campground 77
 library 72
 machinery 23, 67
 mining 25
 races of 70
 soil sampling 30
 travel methods of 181
stench 56
stress 53
Sub-Hominids 185
Sub-Humans 185
subterranean
 openings 196
subterranean city 70
Sumeria 184, 186, 187
 archeological finds in 181
 writings of 190
Sun Bear 169
supernatural entity 56
Swaziland 187

## Index

swimming 49

### T
Tart, Charles T. 134
Teleel 48
telepathy 68, 164, 194
  "feeling" 88
  animal use of 25
  communication by 42
  emotional 136
  healing by 147–150, 157
  in children 49
  projecting images 43
  shaman use of 7
  UFO connection with 85, 137
  warnings by 90
teleportation 94, 195
television, appearances of Sasquatch 96
Teluke 37, 39, 41
Temple, Robert 176
Tennessee
  Nashville 151
Texas 121
  Paluxy River 178
Thompson, Richard 186
Torah 181
Torojas tribe 177
touched by a Sasquatch 50, 88, 196
tracks 178
transparent 75
Triassic 186
tunnels 107

### U
UFOs 1–2, 5, 12, 173
  abductees 42
  Bible and 182
  CIA interest in 31
  cigar-shaped 68
  Connecticut River sightings of 109
  garden landing 62
  investigators 40
  invisible 69
  landed 72
  lights on 66
  Michigan sightings 51
  mother ship 89
  multiple witnesses of 79, 147
  musical 87
  Native Americans and 39, 139–141
  New Hampshire 101
  Sasquatch association with 38, 63, 83, 137–138
  visibility of 42
  vortices and 181
underground city 71
universal reality 4–5, 193
University Museum of Archeology and Ethnology 182
University of California at Davis 134
University of Southern California 123
University of Wyoming 93
urine 81
Utah 180

### V
vandalize 52
Vermont 165
Vietnam 200
violence, advocating 56
vortices 84, 94, 95–96, 168, 181
Voyager 186

### W
war 72
Washington 78
  Spokane 25
  State University 2
'Way of Knowing' 127
Waynaboozhoo 124–127
weather control 93
weight 56
Wen-Chung, Pei 3
West Africa
  Mali 176
wheezing 62
White Song Eagle 37–50
Wichipek 169
wild woman 97
Willamette River 111
Williams, Lorraine Maffi 177
Wilson, Irene 85–98
Wisconsin 1, 9, 56, 59, 137
  Milwaukee 9, 16
  Shawano 143
worry 53
Wyoming 57

### Y
Yerkes Primate Institute 205
Yeti 112, 165, 167, 179
Ywahoo, Dhyani 164

### Z
Zimbabwe
  Monotapa 187
zoology 1, 3
Zululand 187

**225**

Made in the USA
San Bernardino, CA
08 February 2014